McGraw-Hill's

SAT 2400!

A Sneak Preview
of the New SAT I
Verbal Section

How To Use This Book

No matter how you decide to study, be systematic in your approach. Set up a routine and stick with it. I recommend that you study for a set amount of time every single day, at the same time. Aim for about half an hour a day, but be sure to start early enough in the year to get through this entire book. Cramming the last week may help you pick up some useful test-taking techniques, but it won't help you raise your scores as much as a sustained course of study will.

The following method has proven successful for many students:

1. Work through the book from start to finish.

2. As you work, analyze your test scores to figure out which aspects of the test proved the easiest for you and which the most difficult. For example, did you find sentence completions easier than critical reading? Did you have a difficult time writing the essay?

3. Isolate the areas where you need more practice.

4. Concentrate on improving those skills. Go back to those sections of the book, review the material, and work through the test questions again.

5. Stick with it. Make a commitment to study and improve your skills.

McGraw-Hill's

SAT 2400!

A Sneak Preview of the New SAT I Verbal Section

1

Overview of the SAT

Overview of the SAT

What Is the SAT?

The Scholastic Assessment Test (SAT) is a standardized test used by many colleges and universities as part of the admissions process. It is the most widely used college entrance exam. About 75 million Americans have taken the SAT for college admission since the Scholastic Aptitude Test (as it was then known) was first administered in 1926. In 2000–2001 alone, more than 2 million students took the SAT, which is given several times a year at different locations worldwide.

What Is the New SAT?

Starting in March 2005, the SAT will undergo the most drastic changes in its history. The total point count zooms from 1600 to 2400, analogies and quantitative comparisons will be dropped, and the math section will be expanded to include topics from Algebra II. Most radical of all, a new Writing section will be added. This section will require students to write an essay as well as answer multiple-choice questions about grammar, usage, and style. The new SAT will test three key areas of academic preparation—reading, writing, and math.

The Critical Reading Test

The old SAT Verbal section will become the new SAT Critical Reading section. It will now include a greater emphasis on analytical reading with passages from natural sciences, humanities, and social studies. Shorter reading passages are being added in place of the analogies. The sentence completion questions remain.

The New Writing Test

As the scoring scale indicates, the greatest change is the addition of the new writing component. Described by College Board officials as a way to "improve predictive validity" and "encourage writing in the schools," the new Writing section allows students another way to show they are prepared to do college-level work.

The new Writing test is 50 minutes long. During that time, you will have to write one essay (25 minutes) and answer multiple-choice questions (25 minutes) on improving sentences and paragraphs and identifying errors in diction, subject-verb agreement, proper word usage, and precision in writing.

How Does the New SAT Differ from the Old SAT?

The following box summarizes the changes you can expect on the Critical Reading test.

CRITICAL READING TEST

	Old SAT Length	New SAT Length
Time	75 minutes	70 minutes
Form	Two 30-minute sections One 15-minute section	Two 25-minute sections One 15-minute section
Content	Analogies Sentence completions Long critical reading passages	Sentence completions Short critical reading passages Long critical reading passages
Score	200–800	200–800

The following box summarizes the new Writing test. This part does not appear on the current SAT.

WRITING TEST

Component	Time	Content
Essay	25 minutes	Organize your ideas, express your ideas clearly, support the main idea, use standard written English
Multiple-choice questions	25 minutes	Identify errors in grammar, mechanics, usage, and style; improve sentences and paragraphs

Note: The College Board has not yet announced the number of multiple-choice questions on this part and how much each question will be worth.

The following box summarizes the overall changes to the SAT.

OVERALL CHANGES

Old SAT Scoring Scale	New SAT Scoring Scale
Verbal: 200–800	Verbal: 200–800
Math: 200–800	Math: 200–800
	New Writing section: 200–800
Total score: 400–1600	Total score: 600–2400

Why Do I Need to Take the SAT?

The move to revise the SAT was prompted by a number of college presidents and other academic officials who argued that the test assesses intelligence rather than achievement. Some of these leaders have argued that the SAT should be abolished; as a result, a handful of colleges have announced that the SAT will no longer be required for admission to their institutions.

So how much does the SAT *really* count when it comes to getting into the college of your choice? The best answer seems to be that despite the drive for reform, your score on the SAT still counts—a lot.

According to an article in *U.S. News and World Report,* most state colleges and universities admit most of their students based on the students' grades and percent SAT scores. At the University of Georgia, for example, about 33 percent of the admissions decisions are based on SAT scores (11/11/02, p. 56). According to the Educational Testing Service's website, nearly 80 percent of four-year colleges and universities use test scores in admissions decisions.

Many officials at small, select liberal arts colleges claim that their admissions decisions are based on many factors other than SAT scores. Nonetheless, despite all the talk about the importance of extracurricular activities, letters of recommendation, and being well-rounded, don't fool yourself for a moment: SAT scores often count far more than officials admit. Most colleges go with SAT scores because they offer one of the few objective measurements for comparing students from widely different academic backgrounds. As the director of undergraduate admissions at Duke University put it: "We find it [your SAT score] useful . . . because it does what it says it does. It adds to our ability to predict grades." (*U.S. News and World Report,* 11/11/02, p. 56.)

Your score on the SAT doesn't determine how well you will do in life. However, your score on the SAT *does* sharply correlate with your success during your freshman year in college, at least. It also provides a rough but accurate measure of how well you will do overall in your college work. That's because the SAT tests the skills you need to succeed in college: critical reading, clear writing, and computational abilities.

So don't fool yourself: your score on the SAT counts—a great deal.

What Do I Need to Take the SAT?

In addition to paying the registration fee (currently $26, but likely to go up by $10–$12), you will need the following items to take the test:

- Your admissions ticket
- A photo ID
- Sharpened number 2 pencils and an eraser
- An approved calculator
- A watch

When Do I Take the SAT?

The Educational Testing Service (ETS) administers the SAT. The test is given on Saturday mornings seven times a year: October, November, December, January, April, May, and June. The test is offered at different test centers, usually schools. The test is also offered on Sunday for those whose religion prohibits activity on Saturday.

Most students take the Preliminary Scholastic Assessment Test (PSAT) in tenth grade. The PSAT is a practice test for the SAT. However, the score may determine whether or not you are eligible for a National Merit Scholarship, so this test has ramifications as well.

Before you sign up for a specific test date, choose a number of colleges that offer your major, are within your price range, and match your abilities. Contact these colleges to find out their deadlines for receiving scores. This is especially critical if you are contemplating applying to a college through the Early Decision or Early Action programs. These programs have earlier deadlines for receipt of scores than do traditional application processes.

- If you plan to apply for Early Decision, take the SAT at the end of your junior year.
- If you plan to apply for regular consideration, you may take the SAT in October of your senior year.

Most students take the SAT more than once to help them improve their scores.

How Do I Register for the SAT?

You can obtain registration forms in several ways.

1. **Contact the Educational Testing Service online at etsinfo@ets.org. You cannot register online if**

   - You need services for students with disabilities
   - You are younger than 13
   - You are registering the first time for Sunday testing
   - You are testing in certain countries (including Taiwan, Nigeria, Benin, Togo, Ghana, and Kenya)

2. **Write to the Educational Testing Service.**

   Corporate Headquarters:
   Educational Testing Service
   Rosedale Road
   Princeton, NJ 08541
   Phone: 609-921-9000

   California Office:
   Educational Testing Service
   Western Field Office
   2731 Systron Drive
   Concord, CA 94518
   Phone: 925-808-2000

   Florida Office:
   Region XIV Comprehensive Center at ETS
   1000 N. Ashley Dr.
   Suite 312
   Tampa, FL 33602
   Phone: 813-275-0122

   Puerto Rico Office:
   Educational Testing Service
   Suite 315
   American International Plaza
   250 Munoz Rivera Avenue
   Hato Rey, PR 00918
   Phone: 787-753-7426

Washington, D.C., Office:
Educational Testing Service
Office of State and Federal Relations
Suite 900
1800 K Street, N.W.
Washington, DC 20006
Phone: 202-659-8075

3. Obtain an application from your school's guidance office.

The College Board will reduce fees for students who can demonstrate financial need. Do not send money to the College Board. Your school's guidance coordinator will have this information.

How Do I Get My Score?

About six weeks after you take the SAT, your scores will automatically be sent to you and to the colleges you listed on your registration form. Your score will include percentile ranks so you can see how you did compared to others taking the test. You will also receive information about planning for college.

Five Great Ways to Prepare for the SAT

The following five suggestions can go a long way to improving your score.

1. *Study.* **Contrary to what the people at ETS say, you *can* study for the SAT—and you *should*. To make the most of your study time, get into a study routine.**

   - Study every day.
   - Study for at least 30 minutes.
   - Turn off the television, radio, or CD player when you study. You will *always* study better without distractions.
   - Study at the same time and in the same place every day.
   - Study the part of the test you find most difficult first, when you are least tired.
   - As you study, give yourself a break. Stretch every 15 minutes or so.

   Practice on the SAT sample tests in this book to find out your strengths and weaknesses. For example, if you have trouble writing an essay in the time allocated, concentrate on learning this skill. Completing similar tests will also help you learn how to make the best use of your time.

Don't take the SAT "just for practice," because your scores go on your permanent record. Instead, practice on the tests in this book.

2. *Analyze the test.* To make the most of your study time, understand the SAT completely. Since you have only a minute or so to complete each SAT question, you must know what you are going to encounter.

   - *Understand question order.* Most SAT questions are arranged from easiest to more difficult. For example, in the Sentence Completion section, the first few questions may seem very easy, but then you'll notice that the questions get more and more difficult. The last questions are likely to be very hard. Critical Reading is the only section in which the order of difficulty does not build from question to question.
   - *Learn the directions.* Familiarize yourself with the directions ahead of time. This way you won't waste valuable time reading the directions on the day of the actual test. You'll get plenty of practice with the test directions as you take the practice tests in this book.
   - *Use process of elimination.* Always look for ways to eliminate incorrect answers. Remember, every time you eliminate an answer choice, your chance of picking the correct answer improves. You'll find more on the process of elimination in the next section, The Multiple-Choice Questions: Should You Guess?
   - *Work quickly and steadily.* Understand that you are not going to be able to answer every question; that's the way the test is designed. When you realize that you're not making any progress on a question, leave it and move on. You're just losing valuable time if you obsess over a few questions.
   - *Keep track of your place on the answer sheet.* If you skip a question, be very careful to skip the corresponding space on your answer sheet. You don't want to get a low score because you filled out the answer sheet incorrectly.

3. *Don't cram.* You might be tempted to compress all your study time into a week or two before the SAT. While some study is better than no study at all, you're deluding yourself if you think you can master the SAT in a few nights. You can't. The SAT measures years of study, so cramming the night before will probably get you nothing more than a headache.

4. *Learn to pace yourself.* As you study on your own every night, keep careful watch of the time. Timing is especially critical when it comes to the Writing test. On this part of the SAT, you will be graded on what you turn in: not what you *intended* to turn in but didn't get to finish. As you will learn later,

scorers are looking for well-crafted responses with a clear introduction, body, and conclusion. Learning to write a good essay in 20 minutes isn't hard if you practice—it can be close to impossible if you don't.

5. *Prepare.*

- *Prepare the night before.* Lay out your clothing, pens or pencils, watch, and other test supplies. You don't want to be rushing around in the morning.
- *Choose comfortable clothing.* Avoid itchy sweaters or starchy pants. Make sure your clothes are loose and you're comfortable so you can concentrate on the test.
- *Get a good night's sleep.* Believe it or not, a solid 8 hours of sleep can recharge your batteries and give you the winning edge on *any* test.
- *Be sure to eat breakfast.* Eat a nourishing breakfast of cereal, fruit, and toast. You might want to have eggs, French toast, or pancakes. Don't make do with a toaster pastry or donut.
- *Wake up!* If you're a morning sleepyhead, wake yourself up with a shower, a brief workout, or a short jog.
- *Leave yourself enough time in the morning.* Figure out how much time you will need in the morning to get ready for the test—and then add an extra 15 minutes. If an emergency arises, you'll have time to deal with it. If everything goes smoothly, you can relax for a few minutes at the test center.

The Multiple-Choice Questions: Should You Guess?

Should you guess wildly? No. Your score on the multiple-choice questions is based on the number of questions you answer right minus a percentage for incorrect answers. Here's the math:

What You Do	What You Get
A correct answer	1 point
A blank	0 points
An incorrect answer	Minus 0.25 point

Therefore, just running down the page and filling in answers will probably not help you earn a better grade. However, you do stand a good chance of improving your score if you make educated guesses. What's an *educated guess?* That's a guess you make after you have eliminated one or more answer choices as definitely incorrect. Each time you eliminate an answer choice, your chances of guessing correctly from the remaining choices go up.

Frequently Asked Questions

Before the Test

Q: **When should I use this book?**

A: If possible, look at the book early in the year to familiarize yourself with the test's content and format. Then, as you learn specifics about writing and rhetorical strategies, you can apply that knowledge to the test. If you have just purchased the book and the test is around the corner, you can still see marked benefits from reviewing the instructions and taking the practice tests.

Q: **How should I use this book?**

A: First, use the book to become completely familiar with the SAT content and format. Know what kinds of questions you'll be asked, how the exam is graded, how much time you'll have for each section, and so on. Knowing what to expect can help greatly to reduce the fear factor.

As you work your way through this book, concentrate on the parts of the test that present the greatest challenge for you. For example, if you're having trouble writing essays, spend most of your time reviewing the essay section.

Q: **How do you get a high score on the SAT?**

A: The same way you get to Carnegie Hall: practice, practice, practice! Do all the practice tests in this book. Go over the answer explanations. You're far better off spending half an hour every day preparing for the test than trying to cram it all in one week. Practice writing the essay. Studies show that the best writers (like the best brain surgeons, auto mechanics, and tightrope walkers) are the ones who practice the most.

Q: **Does my seat at the test matter?**

A: Yes! Choose your seat carefully because sitting near friends during a test can be disrupting. If you see your friends handing in their papers early, you may feel pressured to do the same, even if you're not yet finished with the test.

During the Test

Q: **Does listening to the proctor matter, or can I zone out for a minute?**

A: Pay close attention to *all* directions. Even though you'll be completely familiar with the test format, the proctor may say something very important, such as about safety procedures in the event of a fire drill or an actual fire.

Q: **How should I budget my time?**

A: If you don't complete a multiple-choice question in the time you have allotted, leave it and move on. You can return to the question if you have extra time at the end of the test.

Q: **Are there any special words I should watch for?**

A: On the multiple-choice questions, look for absolute words. These include *all, none, not, except.* Misreading one of these little—but crucial—words can trip you up, so be very careful with absolutes.

Q: **How should I mark my answers?**

A: Even the best students can tank if they mismark their answer sheets. Be especially careful if you skip a question. If you don't skip that answer space, then every answer that comes after will be wrong. To avoid this problem, check frequently to make certain that the number of the question on your answer sheet corresponds to the number of the question in your exam booklet.

Q: **Should I plan my essay or just start writing?**

A: Plan your answer carefully before you start to write. Think about the major points that you want to make and the evidence you plan to include to back up your assertions. Before you start writing your essay, be sure that you understand the passage that you have to analyze.

Q: **How much should I write?**

A: Write enough to make your point clearly and completely. Quantity doesn't always equal quality, but brief essays rarely get top scores. Figure that the essay should be at least three paragraphs, preferably four, and 350 to

500 words long. Cite examples from published works, your own experience, and current events, as relevant. Use a clear and logical method of organization.

Q: **What should I do if I have time left over?**

A: Stay focused and use your time to advantage.

- Return to questions you couldn't answer the first time and work on them now.
- Double-check your answers.
- Make sure you have marked all test bubbles correctly. You surely don't want to lose credit because you mismarked answers!
- Proofread your essay for errors in grammar, usage, and punctuation.
- Recopy messy parts of your essays.

Q: **What can I do about panic?**

A: Few test situations are as high-pressured as taking the SAT. If you find yourself with a case of the jitters, close your eyes and focus on a pleasant scene. When you open your eyes, you should be a little more relaxed.

Q: **What should I do if some questions seem harder than others?**

A: Don't panic if some questions seem much harder than others. They probably are. That's the way the test is designed.

Q: **What should I do if other students are writing and I'm not?**

A: Relax. They may be working on another part of the test or not have thought enough. By thinking a bit longer before you answer, you might do better than someone who plunges right in.

Q: **What if other students finish before I do?**

A: Finishing early doesn't guarantee the best grade. Usually the better papers are handed in by students who have spent more time thinking about their answers and checking their papers over.

Q: **What if I can't get an answer?**

A: Just skip the question and move on. If you have enough time, you can return to the question later. If you run out of time before you can return to it, you are still better off answering more questions correctly than wasting time on a question you can't answer.

Q: What should I do if I freeze and just can't go on?

A: If this happens, there are many different things that you can do. First, remind yourself that you have studied and so are well-prepared. Then remember that every question you have answered is worth points. Finally, stop working and close your eyes. Take two or three deep breaths. Breathe in and out to the count of 5. Then go on with the test.

Diagnostic Verbal SAT and Answer Key

Diagnostic Verbal SAT and Answer Key

General Directions for the Diagnostic Verbal SAT

This test was constructed to represent what you will encounter on the Verbal part of the SAT. Since the new SAT has yet to be given, this diagnostic test is based on the press releases issued by the College Board. There is always the chance that the College Board will adjust the format as it develops the test.

To get the most benefit from this test, try to get as close as possible to actual test conditions. Take the test in a quiet room without distractions. Tear out the answer sheets on pages 19 and 21 and use them to record the answers to all test questions. Follow all directions carefully, observe the time limits, and take the test in one sitting. The more closely you match test conditions, the more accurate your results will be and the better able you will be to evaluate your strengths and weaknesses. This will help you a lot as you study.

Answer Sheet—Diagnostic Verbal SAT

Remove answer sheet by cutting on dotted line

Section 1

1 Ⓐ Ⓑ Ⓒ Ⓓ Ⓔ   8 Ⓐ Ⓑ Ⓒ Ⓓ Ⓔ   15 Ⓐ Ⓑ Ⓒ Ⓓ Ⓔ   22 Ⓐ Ⓑ Ⓒ Ⓓ Ⓔ
2 Ⓐ Ⓑ Ⓒ Ⓓ Ⓔ   9 Ⓐ Ⓑ Ⓒ Ⓓ Ⓔ   16 Ⓐ Ⓑ Ⓒ Ⓓ Ⓔ   23 Ⓐ Ⓑ Ⓒ Ⓓ Ⓔ
3 Ⓐ Ⓑ Ⓒ Ⓓ Ⓔ   10 Ⓐ Ⓑ Ⓒ Ⓓ Ⓔ   17 Ⓐ Ⓑ Ⓒ Ⓓ Ⓔ   24 Ⓐ Ⓑ Ⓒ Ⓓ Ⓔ
4 Ⓐ Ⓑ Ⓒ Ⓓ Ⓔ   11 Ⓐ Ⓑ Ⓒ Ⓓ Ⓔ   18 Ⓐ Ⓑ Ⓒ Ⓓ Ⓔ   25 Ⓐ Ⓑ Ⓒ Ⓓ Ⓔ
5 Ⓐ Ⓑ Ⓒ Ⓓ Ⓔ   12 Ⓐ Ⓑ Ⓒ Ⓓ Ⓔ   19 Ⓐ Ⓑ Ⓒ Ⓓ Ⓔ
6 Ⓐ Ⓑ Ⓒ Ⓓ Ⓔ   13 Ⓐ Ⓑ Ⓒ Ⓓ Ⓔ   20 Ⓐ Ⓑ Ⓒ Ⓓ Ⓔ
7 Ⓐ Ⓑ Ⓒ Ⓓ Ⓔ   14 Ⓐ Ⓑ Ⓒ Ⓓ Ⓔ   21 Ⓐ Ⓑ Ⓒ Ⓓ Ⓔ

Section 2

1 Ⓐ Ⓑ Ⓒ Ⓓ Ⓔ   8 Ⓐ Ⓑ Ⓒ Ⓓ Ⓔ   15 Ⓐ Ⓑ Ⓒ Ⓓ Ⓔ   22 Ⓐ Ⓑ Ⓒ Ⓓ Ⓔ
2 Ⓐ Ⓑ Ⓒ Ⓓ Ⓔ   9 Ⓐ Ⓑ Ⓒ Ⓓ Ⓔ   16 Ⓐ Ⓑ Ⓒ Ⓓ Ⓔ   23 Ⓐ Ⓑ Ⓒ Ⓓ Ⓔ
3 Ⓐ Ⓑ Ⓒ Ⓓ Ⓔ   10 Ⓐ Ⓑ Ⓒ Ⓓ Ⓔ   17 Ⓐ Ⓑ Ⓒ Ⓓ Ⓔ   24 Ⓐ Ⓑ Ⓒ Ⓓ Ⓔ
4 Ⓐ Ⓑ Ⓒ Ⓓ Ⓔ   11 Ⓐ Ⓑ Ⓒ Ⓓ Ⓔ   18 Ⓐ Ⓑ Ⓒ Ⓓ Ⓔ   25 Ⓐ Ⓑ Ⓒ Ⓓ Ⓔ
5 Ⓐ Ⓑ Ⓒ Ⓓ Ⓔ   12 Ⓐ Ⓑ Ⓒ Ⓓ Ⓔ   19 Ⓐ Ⓑ Ⓒ Ⓓ Ⓔ   26 Ⓐ Ⓑ Ⓒ Ⓓ Ⓔ
6 Ⓐ Ⓑ Ⓒ Ⓓ Ⓔ   13 Ⓐ Ⓑ Ⓒ Ⓓ Ⓔ   20 Ⓐ Ⓑ Ⓒ Ⓓ Ⓔ   27 Ⓐ Ⓑ Ⓒ Ⓓ Ⓔ
7 Ⓐ Ⓑ Ⓒ Ⓓ Ⓔ   14 Ⓐ Ⓑ Ⓒ Ⓓ Ⓔ   21 Ⓐ Ⓑ Ⓒ Ⓓ Ⓔ   28 Ⓐ Ⓑ Ⓒ Ⓓ Ⓔ

Section 3

1 Ⓐ Ⓑ Ⓒ Ⓓ Ⓔ   4 Ⓐ Ⓑ Ⓒ Ⓓ Ⓔ   7 Ⓐ Ⓑ Ⓒ Ⓓ Ⓔ   10 Ⓐ Ⓑ Ⓒ Ⓓ Ⓔ
2 Ⓐ Ⓑ Ⓒ Ⓓ Ⓔ   5 Ⓐ Ⓑ Ⓒ Ⓓ Ⓔ   8 Ⓐ Ⓑ Ⓒ Ⓓ Ⓔ   11 Ⓐ Ⓑ Ⓒ Ⓓ Ⓔ
3 Ⓐ Ⓑ Ⓒ Ⓓ Ⓔ   6 Ⓐ Ⓑ Ⓒ Ⓓ Ⓔ   9 Ⓐ Ⓑ Ⓒ Ⓓ Ⓔ   12 Ⓐ Ⓑ Ⓒ Ⓓ Ⓔ

Section 5

1 Ⓐ Ⓑ Ⓒ Ⓓ Ⓔ 8 Ⓐ Ⓑ Ⓒ Ⓓ Ⓔ 15 Ⓐ Ⓑ Ⓒ Ⓓ Ⓔ 22 Ⓐ Ⓑ Ⓒ Ⓓ Ⓔ
2 Ⓐ Ⓑ Ⓒ Ⓓ Ⓔ 9 Ⓐ Ⓑ Ⓒ Ⓓ Ⓔ 16 Ⓐ Ⓑ Ⓒ Ⓓ Ⓔ 23 Ⓐ Ⓑ Ⓒ Ⓓ Ⓔ
3 Ⓐ Ⓑ Ⓒ Ⓓ Ⓔ 10 Ⓐ Ⓑ Ⓒ Ⓓ Ⓔ 17 Ⓐ Ⓑ Ⓒ Ⓓ Ⓔ 24 Ⓐ Ⓑ Ⓒ Ⓓ Ⓔ
4 Ⓐ Ⓑ Ⓒ Ⓓ Ⓔ 11 Ⓐ Ⓑ Ⓒ Ⓓ Ⓔ 18 Ⓐ Ⓑ Ⓒ Ⓓ Ⓔ 25 Ⓐ Ⓑ Ⓒ Ⓓ Ⓔ
5 Ⓐ Ⓑ Ⓒ Ⓓ Ⓔ 12 Ⓐ Ⓑ Ⓒ Ⓓ Ⓔ 19 Ⓐ Ⓑ Ⓒ Ⓓ Ⓔ
6 Ⓐ Ⓑ Ⓒ Ⓓ Ⓔ 13 Ⓐ Ⓑ Ⓒ Ⓓ Ⓔ 20 Ⓐ Ⓑ Ⓒ Ⓓ Ⓔ
7 Ⓐ Ⓑ Ⓒ Ⓓ Ⓔ 14 Ⓐ Ⓑ Ⓒ Ⓓ Ⓔ 21 Ⓐ Ⓑ Ⓒ Ⓓ Ⓔ

SECTION 1 TIME—25 MINUTES; 25 Questions

DIRECTIONS: The following sentences have one or two blanks, each of which indicates a missing word. Beneath each sentence are five words or pairs of words. Choose the word or pair of words which, when inserted in the sentence, best fits the meaning of the sentence as a whole. Indicate your answer by filling in the corresponding circle on your answer sheet.

1. The party boss shrewdly shifted party lines; hence, he was able to _____ any voting bloc out of _____.

   (A) sanction, hand
   (B) disavow, actuality
   (C) validate, district
   (D) countenance, reluctance
   (E) gerrymander, existence

2. The restaurant itself was beautiful and the service was excellent, but the food was _____.

   (A) superb
   (B) shabby
   (C) inedible
   (D) delicious
   (E) palatable

3. He was the chief _____ of his uncle's will; in short, he was left with a(n) _____ of $200,000.

   (A) beneficiary, inheritance
   (B) heir, invoice
   (C) adjudicator, reckoning
   (D) plethora, estate
   (E) reader, legacy

4. When his temperature _____ above 104°F, then he became agitated and _____.

   (A) descended, demented
   (B) rose, mobile
   (C) stayed, ambulatory
   (D) soared, robust
   (E) climbed, delirious

5. Although he was never at the scene of the crime, his complicity was uncovered; he had _____ and _____ the robbery by disposing of the stolen property.

   (A) aided, abetted
   (B) assisted, foiled
   (C) hindered, eschewed
   (D) impeded, shunned
   (E) thwarted, warned

6. The offenders then prostrated themselves and _____ for mercy.

   (A) conceded
   (B) petitioned
   (C) reiterated
   (D) submitted
   (E) approached

7. If you find peeling potatoes to be _____, then perhaps you would _____ scrubbing the floors.

(A) burdensome, despise
(B) galling, detest
(C) onerous, prefer
(D) tiresome, encourage
(E) genial, fancy

8. The film was completely devoid of any plot or character development; it was merely a _____ of striking images.

(A) proximity
(B) duration
(C) dilettante
(D) montage
(E) dearth

DIRECTIONS: Each of the following passages is followed by questions. Answer each question based on what is directly stated or suggested in the related passage. Indicate your answer by filling in the corresponding circle on your answer sheet. Questions 9 and 10 are based on the following passage.

Global warming is a serious issue that affects all countries around the globe. The following passage discusses one aspect of this problem.

1   According to the National Academy of Sciences, Earth's surface temperature has risen by about 1 degree Fahrenheit in the past century, with accelerated warming during the past two decades. There is new and stronger evidence that most of the warming over the last 50 years is attributable to human activities. Human activities have altered the chemical composition of the atmosphere
5   through the buildup of greenhouse gases—primarily carbon dioxide, methane, and nitrous oxide. The heat-trapping property of these gases is undisputed although uncertainties exist about exactly how Earth's climate responds to them.

---

9. The writer repeats the phrase "human activities" for all the following reasons *except* to

(A) ensure clarity
(B) create emphasis
(C) provide specific details and description
(D) help readers follow the flow of ideas
(E) lead from one idea to the next

10. The next paragraph of this essay will most likely

(A) explain what people can do to stop global warming
(B) trace how the National Academy of Sciences began and elucidate its role today
(C) list other greenhouse gases
(D) suggest ways that the world's meteorological conditions respond to greenhouse gases
(E) illustrate the heat-trapping properties of greenhouse gases

Questions 11 and 12 are based on the following passage.

New techniques have boosted cattle production and resulted in more meat at lower prices.

1   To raise meat output, livestock producers have adopted new, intensive rearing techniques relying on grains and legumes to feed their animals. For example, farmers have moved nearly all of the pigs and poultry in industrial countries into giant indoor feeding facilities. There, they eat carefully measured rations of energy-rich grain and protein-rich soybean meal. Cattle everywhere still spend

5   most of their time dining outdoors, although beef producers—particularly in the United States, but also in Russia, South Africa, and Japan—supplement that roughage with grain in the months before slaughter. By contrast, Australian and South American cattle graze their entire lives, while European beef comes mostly from dairy herds, which eat less grain than American beef herds.

11. In line 2, *legumes* most likely means

(A) vegetables
(B) meats
(C) solid food
(D) oats and barley
(E) rice

12. This passage is developed primarily through

(A) time order
(B) comparison and contrast
(C) most to least important details
(D) least to most important details
(E) advantages and disadvantages

Questions 13 to 19 are based on the following passage.

Chief Joseph, leader of the Nez Perce Indians, delivered the following surrender speech in 1877. The speech has come to be called "I Will Fight No More Forever."

1   Tell General Howard I know his heart. What he told me before, I have in my heart. I am tired of fighting. Our chiefs are killed. Looking Glass is dead. Toohoolhoolzote is dead. The old men are all dead. It is the young men who say yes and no. He who led on the young men is dead. It is cold and we have no blankets. The little children are freezing to death. My people, some of them, have run

5   away to the hills and have no blankets, no food: no one knows where they are—perhaps freezing to death. I want to have time to look for my children and see how many I can find. Maybe I shall find them among the dead. Hear me, my chiefs. I am tired; my heart is sick and sad. From where the sun now stands I will fight no more forever.

13. Chief Joseph's reasons for deciding to "fight no more forever" include all the following *except*

(A) the chiefs have been killed
(B) he is dying

(C) it is cold and his people have no shelter
(D) his people are starving
(E) the leader of the young warriors has died

14. Rather than fighting, Chief Joseph wants time to

    (A) negotiate honorable surrender terms with the federal government
    (B) escape to Canada from the tribe's home in Oregon
    (C) fight one last battle and then never fight again
    (D) meet with General Howard, with whom he has an understanding
    (E) look for his scattered children

15. Who are Looking Glass and Toohoolhoolzote?

    (A) young men in the tribe
    (B) other Native Americans who are helping the tribe negotiate with the federal government
    (C) Chief Joseph's favorite children
    (D) great chiefs of his tribe
    (E) historical leaders, long dead before the time of this speech

16. As used in line 3, the sentence "It is the young men who say yes and no" is best understood to mean

    (A) even the young men cannot save them now
    (B) Chief Joseph laments the necessity of having the tribe led by inexperienced men
    (C) young men are better leaders than older men
    (D) Chief Joseph has been forced from power by the young men
    (E) young men cannot be trusted as older men can

17. Chief Joseph's writing style contributes to the impact of his speech by

    (A) decreasing the emotional appeal of his words
    (B) downplaying his main points with arrogance
    (C) emphasizing his main points with dignity
    (D) revealing his reliance on literary allusions
    (E) emphasizing the difference between appearance and reality

18. Chief Joseph's language reinforces the effect of his rhetoric by

    (A) making the speech easy to read
    (B) allowing the facts to tell the story without any literary contrivances
    (C) masking his true sorrow
    (D) relying on symbolism to convey his emotion
    (E) excoriating the federal government for betraying his people

19. The *tone* of this speech is best described as

    (A) ironic
    (B) somber and despairing
    (C) resigned and thoughtful
    (D) hopeful
    (E) combative

Questions 20 to 25 are based on the following passage.

Few creatures capture our imagination like the shark. The following passage describes some facts you may not know about sharks.

1   Described as a "swimming and eating machine without peer," the shark is considered an evolutionary success story, having changed little over 60 million years. Sharks are models of efficiency with
their boneless skeletons, simple brains, generalized nervous systems, and simple internal structures.
Their hydrodynamically designed shapes, razor-sharp replaceable teeth, powerful jaws, and vora-
5   cious appetites make them excellent marauders. Through scavenging and predation, the 250 species
of sharks perform a valuable service in maintaining the ecological balance of the oceans. Their well-
developed sensory systems enable them to detect extreme dilutions of blood in water, low frequency
sounds of splashing made by a fish in distress, and movements and contrasts in water.

While many sharks are caught by fishermen for sport, sharks can and do sustain small commercial
10   ventures. Their skins provide a hide tougher than leather, out of which boots and wallets are fabri-
cated, and their enormous livers contain a valuable source of vitamin A. Shark meat is processed for
fertilizer and livestock feed as well as for human consumption. The British "fish-and-chips" industry
depends on shark meat; the Italians annually consume about 10 million pounds of smooth dogfish
shark; the Chinese use shark fins for soup. Generally, shark meat is consumed unknowingly under
15   other, more appetizing names.

Sharks are also contributing to medical research through studies of their immunological systems. While
this research may result in saving human lives, sharks do, at times, take lives. Each year about 25 to
30 shark attacks on people are reported worldwide with the victims either maimed or killed. The vast
majority of these attacks occur off the coast of Australia—only a few occur off the coast of the United
20   States. Research on shark attacks may eventually lead to the development of an effective shark repellent.

20. As used in line 1, *peer* most nearly means

(A) friend
(B) better
(C) equal
(D) dock
(E) improvement

21. According to the first paragraph, all the following contribute to the shark's success as a hunter *except*

(A) hydrodynamically designed shape
(B) razor-sharp replaceable teeth

(C) powerful jaws
(D) voracious appetite
(E) great age

22. Which conclusion is best supported by the first paragraph?

(A) The author is very afraid of sharks.
(B) The author admires sharks.
(C) People should learn more about sharks.
(D) Sharks are not very intelligent.
(E) Sharks are very dangerous because they attack humans.

23. It can be inferred from the information in the second paragraph that shark meat is sold under different names because

    (A) people don't want to know that they are eating shark
    (B) shark meat is an excellent source of vitamin A
    (C) shark meat is used for fertilizer
    (D) shark meat used to be called something else
    (E) shark meat is not very appetizing

24. As used in line 18, *maimed* most nearly means

    (A) traumatized
    (B) terrified
    (C) assassinated
    (D) injured
    (E) butchered

25. Which of the following best states the main idea of the third paragraph?

    (A) Most shark attacks occur off the coast of Australia.
    (B) On average, sharks kill fewer than 50 people a year.
    (C) Sharks are found in waters throughout the world.
    (D) Although sharks occasionally attack people, some medical treatments may come from research with sharks.
    (E) Sharks that live in southern waters are more dangerous than those that inhabit northern waters.

If you finish before time is up, go over your work in this section only.

SECTION 2   TIME—25 MINUTES; 28 Questions

DIRECTIONS: The following sentences have one or two blanks, each of which indicates a missing word. Beneath each sentence are five words or pairs of words. Choose the word or pair of words which, when inserted in the sentence, best fits the meaning of the sentence as a whole. Indicate your answer by filling in the corresponding circle on your answer sheet.

1. During the Revolutionary War, Hessian troops fought on the British side, not as _____, but as _____. They were paid in money, not glory.

    (A) confederates, partners
    (B) antagonists, nonpartisans
    (C) rebels, insurgents
    (D) allies, mercenaries
    (E) traitors, novices

2. Professor Martin spent his entire career as a teacher trying to _____ his students to appreciate the _____ of poetry.

   (A) encourage, beauty
   (B) invite, difficulty
   (C) dissuade, benefit
   (D) deter, marvel
   (E) encourage, confusion

3. Although the movie was panned by all the major critics, audiences around the country seemed to find it _____.

   (A) appalling
   (B) reprehensible
   (C) intolerable
   (D) genial
   (E) mediocre

4. Peter was _____ by the repeated rejections of his novel; as a result, he _____ to submit his manuscript to other publishers.

   (A) devastated, proceeded
   (B) undaunted, continued
   (C) shattered, wanted
   (D) undiscouraged, suspended
   (E) unaffected, refused

5. Since there is a stigma attached to this job, it is _____, even at a(n) _____ salary.

   (A) unappealing, lucrative
   (B) repulsive, menial
   (C) enticing, fabulous
   (D) alluring, profitable
   (E) attractive, mean

6. A week of sun and exercise had a _____ effect; due to this, the dark circles under her eyes were _____ and her skin took on a rosy glow.

   (A) peremptory, reinstated
   (B) healthful, restored
   (C) salubrious, erased
   (D) curative, deepened
   (E) harsh, expunged

7. A system of education should be _____ by the _____ of students it turns out; in summary, quality is preferable to quantity.

   (A) evaluated, abundance
   (B) judged, caliber
   (C) reckoned, generosity
   (D) disregarded, essence
   (E) considered, maturity

8. Avoid becoming involved with _____ politicians lest you get caught in a(n) _____ from which you have difficulty extricating yourself.

   (A) venal, anathema
   (B) virtuous, entanglement
   (C) poised, muddle
   (D) corrupt, lawsuit
   (E) loquacious, discourse

9. You should have _____ trouble ahead when the speeding traffic suddenly _____ to a crawl.

   (A) anticipated, slowed
   (B) interrogated, started
   (C) expected, grew
   (D) enjoyed, transformed
   (E) seen, collected

10. If he hasn't yet _____ the importance of speaking well of others, he must be quite _____.

    (A) rejected, arcane
    (B) mastered, astute
    (C) rationalized, shrewd
    (D) learned, simple
    (E) understood, profound

DIRECTIONS: Each of the following passages is followed by one or more questions. Answer each question based on what is directly stated or suggested in the related passage. Indicate your answers by filling in the corresponding circle on your answer sheet. Question 11 is based on the following passage.

The following passage describes how ranchers compensate for poor land quality.

1   Eradicating tree cover sets the wheels of land degradation in motion. Shallow, acidic, and nutrient-poor, tropical soils rapidly lose critical phosphorus and other nutrients when the forest is converted to pasture. To compensate for the fertility decline, ranchers often stock newly cleared land at four times the standard rate of one cow per hectare, which accelerates erosion and the vegetative shift to
5   annual weeds and shrubs. Stocking rates fall precipitously thereafter, and most pasture is abandoned for land newly carved from the forest.

11. As used in line 5, *precipitously* most nearly means

(A) prematurely
(B) early
(C) abruptly
(D) sadly
(E) tragically

Question 12 is based on the following passage.

The key deer was hunted to near extinction, but the creature was protected by compassionate and hard-working conservationists.

1   One of the rarest and most prized animals in the United States is the key deer. This tiny creature was once hunted without mercy. It was not uncommon for a single hunter to kill more than a dozen key deer in one day. Often, hunters set grass fires to drive the creatures out of hiding; other times, they were attacked with harpoons while they were swimming. In the 1950s, conservationists—led by the
5   Boone and Crockett Club—saved the key deer from extinction. Today, the surviving key deer are protected by the United States government in the Key Deer National Wildlife Refuge, created in 1957.

12. Which of the following is implied in the passage?

(A) Species become at risk of dying out when they are hunted too extensively.
(B) The government is still the most effective way to safeguard the environment because it has the resources to establish effective programs.
(C) Endangered species will only be saved if they become a priority.
(D) Government officials and private citizens must work together to help the environment.
(E) The key deer is valuable for its beautiful coat.

Question 13 is based on the following passage.

"Tsunami," the Japanese word for seismic sea-waves, is also used as the scientific term for this phenomenon. Most tsunamis originate around the so-called Ring of Fire, a zone of volcanoes and seismic activity that encircles the Pacific Ocean.

1 Tsunamis, or seismic sea-waves, are gravity waves set in motion by underwater disturbances associated with earthquakes. These waves are frequently called "tidal waves" although they have nothing to do with the tides. Tsunamis consist of a decaying train of waves and may be detectable on tide gauges for as long as a week. Near its origin, the first wave of a tsunami may be the largest; at greater
5 distances, the largest is normally between the second and seventh wave. Since 1819, more than forty tsunamis have struck the Hawaiian Islands.

13. It can be inferred from this passage that

(A) tsunamis are rare occurrences, so few people have experienced them

(B) scientists know a great deal about tsunamis, especially their cause and prevention

(C) tsunamis are short-lived phenomena

(D) tsunamis have been studied extensively and are well-understood by scientists

(E) tsunamis can be very dangerous

Questions 14 to 20 are based on the following passage.

Studying has many uses, as the following passage argues.

1 Studies serve for delight, for ornament, and for ability. Their chief use for delight is in privateness and retiring; for ornament, is in discourse; and for ability, is in the judgment and disposition of business. For expert men can execute, and perhaps judge the particulars, one by one; but the general counsels, and the plots and marshaling of affairs, come best from those that are learned. To spend
5 too much time in studies is sloth; to use them too much for ornament is affectation; to make judgment wholly by their rules is the humor of a scholar. They perfect nature and are perfected by experience: for natural abilities are like natural plants that need proyning by study; and studies themselves do give forth directions too much at large, except they be bounded in by experience.

Crafty men contemn [condemn] studies, simple men admire them, and wise men use them; for they
10 teach not their own use; but that is a wisdom without them and above them, won by observation. Read not to contradict and confute; nor to believe and take for granted; nor to find talk and discourse; but to weigh and consider. Some books are to be tasted, others to be swallowed, and a few to be chewed and digested; that is, some books are to be read only in parts; others to be read, but not curiously, and some few to be read wholly, and with diligence and attention. Some books also may
15 be read by deputy, and extracts made of them by others; but that would be only in the less important arguments, and the meaner sorts of books, else distilled books are like common distilled waters, flashy things. Reading maketh a full man; conference a ready man; and writing an exact man. And therefore, if a man write little, he had need have a great memory; if he confer little, he need have a great wit; and if he read little, he need have much cunning, to seem to know that he doth not.

14. By using the word *delight* in the first sentence and repeating it in the second sentence, the author specifically emphasizes

    (A) how studying serves only for pleasure
    (B) his personal resolve to master as much information as possible
    (C) his own devotion to study
    (D) the rewards that the attainment of knowledge brings
    (E) the sacrifices necessary to become learned

15. According to the author, what are the three primary benefits of study?

    (A) privateness, discourse, humor
    (B) enjoyment, adornment, competence
    (C) secrecy, character, self-respect
    (D) pleasure, advancement, reputation
    (E) self-respect, proficiency, direction

16. All the following dangers can result from excessive study *except*

    (A) accomplishment
    (B) laziness
    (C) simplified judgments
    (D) an attitude of superiority
    (E) inactivity

17. As used in line 5, *affectation* most nearly means

    (A) fondness
    (B) respect
    (C) pretense
    (D) gratification
    (E) decoration

18. According to the author, you should read to

    (A) challenge what you read
    (B) believe the writer's main points
    (C) think about the writer's ideas
    (D) find things to talk about
    (E) take the writer's ideas for granted

19. As used in the line 16, *meaner* most nearly means

    (A) cruel
    (B) inferior
    (C) fierce
    (D) unnatural
    (E) cheaper

20. The speaker's tone is best described as

    (A) diffident and modest
    (B) precarious
    (C) ironic
    (D) authoritative and confident
    (E) arrogant and overbearing

Questions 21 to 28 are based on the following passage.

The American Revolution (1776–1783) resulted in America's independence from Great Britain. The first armed encounter of the Revolution took place in Concord, Massachusetts, where the British force in Boston numbered about 3500 men. The following is a contemporary account of the landmark battle.

1   On the 18th of April at eleven at night, about eight hundred Grenadiers and light infantry were ferried across the Bay to Cambridge, from whence they marched to Concord, about twenty miles. The Congress had been lately assembled at that place, and it was imagined that the General had intelligence of a magazine being formed there and that they were going to destroy it.

5   The people in the country (who are all furnished with arms and have what they call Minute Companies in every town ready to march on any alarm) had a signal, it is supposed, by a light from one of the steeples in town. Upon the troops' embarking, the alarm spread through the country, so that before daybreak the people in general were in arms and on their march to Concord.

    About daybreak a number of people appeared before the troops on Lexington Common. When they
10 [the American colonists] were told to disperse, they fired on the troops and ran off, upon which the Light Infantry pursued them and brought down about fifteen of them. The troops went on to Concord and executed the business they were sent on, and on their return found two or three of their people lying in the agonies of death, scalped, with their noses and ears cut off and eyes bored out—which exasperated the soldiers exceedingly. A prodigious number of people now occupied the
15 hills, woods, and stone walls along the road. The Light Troops drove some parties from the hills, but all the road being enclosed with store walls served as a cover to the rebels, from whence they fired on the troops. . . . In this manner were the troops harassed in their return for seven or eight miles.

---

21. What story does the writer tell of the confrontation on Lexington Common?

(A) When the British told the colonists to disperse, the British fired first and the colonists pursued them. The Native Americans joined the battle on the American side.

(B) The British attacked the colonists, who fought back with great bravery and zeal.

(C) When the British told the colonists to disperse, the colonists fired first but the British pursued them.

(D) An unknown person fired, and then a British solider fired on an unarmed American. Finally, all the British soldiers started firing.

(E) The Americans gathered to fight off the invading British, who greatly outnumbered the rebels.

22. As used in line 4, a *magazine* is most likely

(A) a periodical publication featuring nonfiction articles, commentary, and light fiction

(B) a building in which ammunition and explosives are stored for military use

(C) an ammunition gunbelt

(D) a preacher advocating rebellion

(E) a mutinous newspaper determined to bring down the government

23. The writer's tone in the second paragraph is best described as

    (A) carefully impartial
    (B) horrified and dismayed
    (C) astonished and amazed
    (D) disdainful and condescending
    (E) admiring and worshipful

24. The writer refers to the American colonists as "rebels" to

    (A) show her sympathy for the British
    (B) reveal her secret support for the colonists
    (C) further the cause of American independence
    (D) address her audience with respect
    (E) indicate that the colonists were justified in their actions in this instance

25. The writer is most likely

    (A) a British soldier
    (B) an American colonist loyal to England
    (C) an American rebel
    (D) a visitor to America from Europe
    (E) someone considering moving to America to join the colonists

26. As used in line 14, *prodigious* most nearly means

    (A) accomplished
    (B) unusual
    (C) huge
    (D) meager
    (E) few

27. The author includes the description "lying in the agonies of death, scalped, with their noses and ears cut off and eyes bored out" to

    (A) convince readers that the difficulties between the British and Americans must be settled as soon as possible, and without any further violence
    (B) make her narrative more compelling reading
    (C) elicit pity for the rebel soldiers, oppressed by the British
    (D) evoke sympathy for the British troops
    (E) portray the Native Americans as brutal savages and justify their mass relocation and slaughter

28. This document is most likely a(n)

    (A) letter to the editor of a Massachusetts newspaper
    (B) plea for peace and moderation
    (C) editorial for a colonial newspaper
    (D) diary entry
    (E) letter to a friend

If you finish before time is up, go over your work in this section only.

SECTION 3   TIME—15 MINUTES; 12 Questions

> **DIRECTIONS:** The two passages presented are followed by questions about their content and the relationship between the passages. Answer each question based on what is directly stated or suggested in the passages. Indicate your answer by filling in the corresponding circle on your answer sheet.

Passage 1

The following passage is from a speech that Sojourner Truth delivered at the women's rights convention in Akron, Ohio, in 1851.

1   Well, children, where there is so much racket there must be something out of kilter. I think that 'twixt the Negroes of the South and the women at the North, all talking about rights, the white men will be in a fix pretty soon. But what's all this here talking about?

That man over there says that women need to be helped into carriages, and lifted over ditches, and
5   to have the best place everywhere. Nobody ever helps me into carriages, or over mud-puddles, or gives me any best place! And ain't I a woman? Look at me! Look at my arm! I have ploughed and planted, and gathered into barns, and no man could head me! And ain't I a woman? I could work as much and eat as much as a man—when I could get it—and bear the lash as well! And ain't I a woman? I have borne thirteen children, and seen them all sold off to slavery, and when I cried out
10   with my mother's grief, none but Jesus heard me! And ain't I a woman?

Then they talk about this thing in the head; what's that they call it? ["Intellect" someone whispers.] That's it, honey. What's that got to do with women's rights or Negro's rights? If my cup won't hold but a pint, and yours holds a quart, wouldn't you be mean not to let me have my little half-measure full? . . .

15   If the first woman God ever made was strong enough to turn the world upside down all alone, these women together ought to be able to turn it back, and get it right side up again! And now they is asking to do it, the men better let them.

Obliged to you for hearing me, and now old Sojourner ain't got nothing more to say.

Passage 2

The following is an excerpt from Harriet Beecher Stowe's essay, "Sojourner Truth, the Libyan Sibyl."

Many years ago, the few readers of radical Abolitionist papers must often have seen the singular
20   name of Sojourner Truth, announced as a frequent speaker at Anti-Slavery meetings, and as travel- ing on a sort of self-appointed agency through the country. I had myself often remarked the name, but never met the individual. On one occasion, when our house was filled with company, several eminent clergymen being our guests, notice was brought up to me that Sojourner Truth was below, and requested an interview. Knowing nothing of her but her singular name, I went down, prepared
25   to make the interview short, as the pressure of many other engagements demanded. When I went into the room, a tall, spare form arose to meet me. She was evidently a full-blooded African, and though now aged and worn with many hardships, still gave the impression of a physical develop- ment which in early youth must have been as fine a specimen of the torrid zone as Cumberworth's celebrated statuette of the Negro Woman at the Fountain. Indeed, she so strongly reminded me of

30 that figure, that, when I recall the events of her life, as she narrated them to me, I imagine her as a living, breathing impersonation of that work of art. I do not recollect ever to have been conversant with any one who had more of that silent and subtle power which we call personal presence than this woman. In the modern Spiritualistic phraseology, she would be described as having a strong sphere. Her tall form, as she rose up before me, is still vivid to my mind. She was dressed in some
35 stout, grayish stuff, neat and clean, though dusty from travel. On her head, she wore a bright Madras handkerchief, arranged as a turban. She seemed perfectly self-possessed and at her ease,—in fact, there was almost an unconscious superiority, not unmixed with a solemn twinkle of humor, in the odd, composed manner in which she looked down on me. Her whole air had at times a gloomy sort of drollery which impressed one strangely.

1. In passage 1, by directly addressing the members of the audience as "children," Sojourner Truth suggests that

   (A) they are acting very immaturely
   (B) we are all equal in God's eyes
   (C) she is morally and intellectually superior to the members of her audience
   (D) the members of the audience should be ashamed of the way they are acting
   (E) the delegates at the assembly are young but she is elderly and thus wiser

2. As used in line 1, the idiom "something out of kilter" means that

   (A) something is evil
   (B) something is dangerous
   (C) people are foolish
   (D) something is mysterious
   (E) something is wrong

3. The idea that "women need to be helped into carriages and lifted over ditches" (line 4) in passage 1 can be understood

   (A) in both a literal and metaphorical way
   (B) as an insult to women who do not work

   (C) as an acknowledgment of the wide social gulf between Sojourner Truth and wealthy white women
   (D) as an awareness of the social mores of the time
   (E) as Sojourner Truth's rage at the maltreatment she has received as a slave and as a woman

4. The phrase "Look at my arm" in line 7 suggests

   (A) a threat
   (B) Sojourner Truth has been injured and bears the scars
   (C) Sojourner Truth is as strong as any man
   (D) the speaker's physical strength represents her psychological strength
   (E) Sojourner Truth is physically superior to most men

5. The repeated refrain "And ain't I a woman?" in passage 1 serves to

   (A) convey Sojourner Truth's ironic stance
   (B) stress the equality of *all* women while pointing out inequalities
   (C) alert the reader to the specific details to follow

(D) intimidate the reader with the harsh question

(E) provide evidence that the speaker is bitter at the treatment she has received

6. In passage 1, the speaker is critical of

(A) upper-class women of leisure
(B) men
(C) the possibility that real social change can ever be effected
(D) religion
(E) male claims that women are the "weaker sex"

7. The statement "That's it, honey" in line 12 serves most directly to

(A) provide an ironic counterpoint to Sojourner Truth's previous comments
(B) signal the hopeless mood
(C) remind the audience that the speaker is a woman
(D) distance the audience from the speaker
(E) draw the audience closer to the speaker

8. From her speech, you can infer that Sojourner Truth wants to prove that

(A) some women, but not all, can take up the mantle of autonomy
(B) women are vastly superior to men
(C) slavery must be abolished throughout the union
(D) women will get the vote, regardless of what men say or do
(E) women are as capable as men and deserve equal rights

9. What does passage 2 suggest about Sojourner Truth's reputation?

(A) She was well-known only among a small, select group of religious leaders.
(B) She was so famous that she had posed for a famous work of art, Cumberworth's celebrated statuette of the Negro Woman at the Fountain.
(C) In the past, she had been a familiar name among people who worked to make slavery illegal.
(D) She had been well-known in the past, and her fame had only grown in the present.
(E) She was well-known, but rejected fame because she accomplished more by traveling incognito.

10. In passage 2, Harriet Beecher Stowe compares Sojourner Truth to a statue chiefly to

(A) show her admiration for the abolitionist's dignity and carriage
(B) suggest that Sojourner Truth was stiff and ill at ease in company
(C) indicate that Sojourner Truth looks strangely familiar to her
(D) imply that Sojourner Truth is a disappointment in person, because Stowe expected her to be larger than life
(E) hint that Sojourner Truth deserves a statue erected in her honor

11. The two passages differ in tone in that passage 1 is

    (A) neutral
    (B) whiny
    (C) resentful
    (D) calm
    (E) incendiary

12. From both passages, you can infer that

    (A) everyone worked to abolish slavery
    (B) slavery was an evil institution
    (C) Harriet Beecher Stowe worked hard for the abolition of slavery
    (D) Sojourner Truth was an admirable, extraordinary person
    (E) Harriet Beecher Stowe and Sojourner Truth were close personal friends

---

If you finish before time is up, go over your work in this section only.

SECTION 4 — Time—25 Minutes; Essay

DIRECTIONS: Read the excerpt presented and the assignment that follows it. Then plan and write an essay that explains your ideas about the topic. Remember to support your position with both reasons and examples to make your ideas convincing to the reader.

> Whenever you are asked if you can do a job, tell 'em, "Certainly I can!" Then get busy and find out how to do it.

Assignment: In this statement, former President Theodore Roosevelt advocates taking chances. On the other hand, you can fall flat on your face if you go into a new school, job, or any challenge without sufficient experience or learning. On your own paper, discuss the extent to which you agree or disagree with Roosevelt's statement. Support your position by providing reasons and examples from your own experience, observations, or reading.

SECTION 5 TIME 25—MINUTES; 25 Questions

> **DIRECTIONS:** The following sentences require you to identify errors in grammar, usage, style, and mechanics. Not every sentence has an error, and no sentence will have more than one error. Each sentence error, if there is one, is underlined and lettered. If there is an error, select the one underlined part that must be changed to make the sentence correct and blacken the corresponding circle on your answer sheet. If there is no error, blacken circle E. Elements of the sentence that are not underlined are not to be changed.

1. After Louis <u>fractured</u> his leg in <u>a skiing accident</u>, he <u>is absent</u> from school
            A   B   C

   <u>for a full</u> semester. <u>No error</u>.
        D   E

2. If <u>you</u> are upset over an <u>insult or affront</u>—even if it <u>occurred intentionally</u>
        A   B   C

   and maliciously—<u>one</u> should try not to hold grudges. <u>No error</u>.
                  D   E

3. Masses of white clouds <u>hanging</u> low above the <u>flat marshy plain</u> and
                       A   B

   <u>seemed to be</u> tangled in the tops of <u>distant palm</u> and cypress trees. <u>No error</u>.
        C   D   E

4. <u>Not only</u> does lightning often <u>strike</u> twice in the same place, <u>but it is</u> more
        A   B   C

   likely <u>than not</u> to do so. <u>No error</u>.
           D   E

5. Hector has <u>scarcely no</u> money because he <u>is saving</u> all his <u>spare cash</u> to buy
              A   B   C

   a car; in addition, he <u>is contributing</u> to the family budget. <u>No error.</u>
                              D   E

6. One reason <u>for the abundance</u> of fresh produce <u>in our grocery</u> stores <u>is</u>
              A   B   C

   speeding trucks that carry food <u>great distances.</u> <u>No error.</u>
                                  D   E

7. Two bond traders, <u>Alice and her,</u> <u>were given</u> very large bonuses because
                    A   B

   <u>their accounts</u> had performed <u>unusually well.</u> <u>No error.</u>
        C   D   E

8. You are <u>welcome to visit</u> the cemetery where <u>famous French composers,</u>
               A   B

   artists, and writers <u>are buried daily</u> <u>except Sunday.</u> <u>No error.</u>
                     C   D   E

9. The resolution that <u>has just been</u> <u>agreed with</u> by the school board members
                      A   B

   will <u>result in</u> a five percent tax increase <u>in the upcoming</u> year. <u>No error.</u>
       C   D   E

10. Computerized grammar checkers <u>are software programs</u> that flag
                                     A

   errors or doubtful usage <u>in a passage</u> so that <u>you can correct</u> these
                            B   C

   <u>writing problems.</u> <u>No error.</u>
        D   E

DIRECTIONS: In each sentence below, part or all of the sentence is underlined. Each sentence is followed by five ways of phrasing the underlined part. Choose the best version of the underlined portion of each sentence and blacken the corresponding circle on your answer sheet. Choice A is always the same as the underlined portion of the original sentence. Choose answer A if you think the original sentence needs no revision.

11. Each year it seems to get harder to pay for a college education because a college education costs so much and <u>it has been difficult to get scholarships</u>.

   (A) it has been difficult to get scholarships
   (B) scholarships are difficult to get
   (C) and it is being difficult to get scholarships
   (D) it be difficult to get scholarship money
   (E) getting scholarships is difficult to do

12. <u>Although it</u> has been estimated that many people are deprived of much-needed medical care in this country, especially follow-up visits and preventative medication.

   (A) Although it
   (B) Since it
   (C) In spite of the fact that it
   (D) It
   (E) If it

13. According to some <u>sources nearly</u> one-third of all American children go to bed hungry each night, despite social welfare programs designed to combat hunger.

   (A) sources nearly
   (B) sources: nearly
   (C) sources, nearly
   (D) sources—nearly
   (E) sources; nearly

14. College financial aid officers claim the money would all be used if applicants looked <u>more thorough</u> for funds.

   (A) more thorough
   (B) thorough
   (C) more, thorough
   (D) more thorougher
   (E) more thoroughly

15. A new industry has sprung up that <u>used computers to locate</u> parents who fail to pay child support for their children.

   (A) used computers to locate
   (B) would be using computers to locate
   (C) had been using computers to locate
   (D) uses computers to locate
   (E) use computers to locate

16. <u>A turkey instead of an eagle was first wanted by Ben Franklin as our national symbol.</u>

    (A) A turkey instead of an eagle was first wanted by Ben Franklin as our national symbol.
    (B) First, a turkey instead of an eagle was wanted by Ben Franklin as our national symbol.
    (C) As our national symbol, a turkey instead of an eagle was first wanted by Ben Franklin.
    (D) Ben Franklin first wanted a turkey instead of an eagle as our national symbol.
    (E) By Ben Franklin, a turkey instead of an eagle was first wanted as our national symbol.

17. <u>Confirming our conversation of March 17,</u> the shipment of books and magazines that you ordered will be delivered first thing Friday morning.

    (A) Confirming our conversation of March 17,
    (B) Confirming the March 17 conversation,
    (C) On March 17, confirming our conversation,
    (D) Confirming our conversation of March 17 by me,
    (E) As I stated in our conversation of March 17,

18. During a thunderstorm, people who are inside should not talk on the telephone, stand near any open windows, or <u>using large appliances.</u>

    (A) using large appliances
    (B) use large appliances
    (C) have been using large appliances
    (D) used large appliances
    (E) were using large appliances

19. Of all the movies ever made, *The Godfather* has been recognized as one of America's <u>greater movies</u>.

    (A) greater movies
    (B) more great movies
    (C) greatest movies
    (D) more greater movies
    (E) most greater movies

20. Most people who drink coffee do not know where it comes <u>from it is</u> actually the fruit of an evergreen tree.

    (A) from it is
    (B) from, it is
    (C) from it is,
    (D) from; it is
    (E) from it; is

DIRECTIONS: The following passage is an early draft of an essay. Some parts of the passage need to be rewritten. Read the passage and select the best answers to the questions that follow. Some questions are about particular sentences or parts of sentences and ask you to improve sentence structure and word choice. Other questions refer to parts of the essay or the entire essay and ask you to consider organization and development. In making your decisions, follow the conventions of standard written English. After you have chosen your answer, fill in the corresponding circle on your answer sheet.

Questions 21 to 25 are based on the following first draft of an essay.

1   *(1) Samuel Morse patented the telegraph in 1842 on March 3, 1843, Morse was granted $30,000 from Congress to build a trial line between Baltimore and Washington. (2) From a social aspect, it is important to note that the telegraph played a major part in connecting the continent. (3) Together, the telegraph and the railroads reduced isolation and increased mobility, and speeded up life in the United*
5   *States. (4) The telegraph made it possible to synchronize clocks at distant train stations and make accurate schedules. (5) It also allowed stations to tell each other where each train was, and prevent accidents.*

(6) Morse code can be considered the first modern information system. (7) It is a simple means of communicating messages with as few errors as possible, and even when errors occur, the message is still
10   *understandable. (8) In fact, almost any sort of signal in patterns of three is considered a call for help. (9) Even though it's rarely used, Morse code still resonates symbolically in today's society. (10) Almost everyone knows the three-dot, three-dash, three-dot code for S.O.S., which is still widely used as a distress call.*

21. In context, which is the best way to revise and combine the underlined portion of sentence 1 (reproduced here)?

> *Samuel Morse patented the telegraph in 1842, on March 3, 1843, Morse was granted $30,000 from Congress to build a trial line between Baltimore and Washington.*

   (A) As it is now.
   (B) Samuel Morse patented the telegraph in 1842, on March 3, 1843,
   (C) Samuel Morse patented the telegraph in 1842, yet on March 3, 1843,
   (D) Samuel Morse patented the telegraph in 1842, because on March 3, 1843,
   (E) Samuel Morse patented the telegraph in 1842, and on March 3, 1843,

22. Which sentence would be most appropriate to follow sentence 2?

    (A) As it is now.
    (B) Morse himself, as a historical figure, has made a mark on the art world as well.
    (C) Not only did the telegraph allow fast communication over large distances for the first time, but it also made train travel safer and more efficient.
    (D) Morse appears in a central, prominent position in Christian Schussele's *Men of Progress,* clearly indicating him as a driving force in progress.
    (E) Samuel Morse was an innovator, and he took the ideas of many people and gathered them into a workable network that helped connect the continent.

23. Which of the following best replaces the word *It* in sentence 7?

    (A) They
    (B) Morse's dot-dash system
    (C) The first modern information system
    (D) Communication
    (E) Morse

24. What is the best order of sentences in the last paragraph to create logic and unity?

    (A) As it is now.
    (B) 9, 10, 8
    (C) 8, 10, 9
    (D) 10, 8, 9
    (E) 9, 8, 10

25. Including a paragraph on which of the following would most strengthen the writer's argument?

    (A) Morse's effect on modern art
    (B) Morse's childhood and training as a scientist
    (C) Other methods of communication
    (D) Samuel Morse's legacy
    (E) The disadvantages of Morse code

Diagnostic Verbal SAT Answer Key

Section 1

1. **E.** The correct sentence reads: "The party boss shrewdly shifted party lines; hence, he was able to gerrymander any voting bloc out of existence." *Gerrymander* means "to divide a state, county, and so on into election districts to give one political party a majority in many districts while concentrating the voting strength of the other party into as few districts as possible." The word was coined from the last name of Elbridge Gerry, a former governor of Massachusetts, whose party redistricted the state in 1812, and the word *salamander,* from the resemblance of the redistricting to this creature. By "shifting party lines," the party boss reformed (*gerrymandered*) any "voting bloc out of *existence.*"

2. **C.** The correct sentence reads: "The restaurant itself was beautiful and the service was excellent, but the food was inedible." If a restaurant is beautiful and the service is excellent, you would expect the food to be delicious. The transition *but* indicates that just the opposite is true. Hence, the food must not be up to the same high standards; it must be *inedible,* or not able to be eaten.

3. **A.** The correct sentence reads: "He was the chief beneficiary of his uncle's will; in short, he was left with an inheritance of $200,000." The chief *beneficiary* is the main inheritor, the person who gets the bulk of an estate when the will is read. Someone who gets the money receives an inheritance. *Inheritance* is the word used to mean "any property passing at the owner's death to the heirs."

4. **E.** The correct sentence reads: "When his temperature climbed above 104°F, then he became agitated and delirious." Since a person's normal temperature is 98.6°F, it must rise to reach 104°F. This automatically eliminates choice A. When a person's temperature rises that high, he or she would become *delirious,* or "wild with excitement." The clue word is *agitated.*

5. **A.** The correct sentence reads: "Although he was never at the scene of the crime, his complicity was uncovered; he had aided and abetted the robbery by disposing of the stolen property." *Complicity* means "complying, obeying, or yielding." Only choices A and B fit. Someone who complies would *abet,* meaning "help or aid," so choice A fits best.

6. **B.** The correct sentence reads: "The offenders then prostrated themselves and petitioned for mercy." If people *prostrate* themselves, they "lie down in helplessness."

People who assume this posture are asking for mercy. Only choice B ("petitioned") fits. Choice E ("approached") is close, but assumes that the people crawled forward on their stomachs, which is unlikely.

7. **C.** The correct sentence reads: "If you find peeling potatoes to be onerous, then perhaps you would prefer scrubbing the floors." The transition *if* tells you that the second clause will be the opposite of the first. Thus, if the person finds peeling potatoes to be *onerous* (burdensome or demanding), he or she would want something different. The person would *prefer* scrubbing the floors. Of course, the entire sentence is ironic and lightly humorous.

8. **D.** The correct sentence reads: "The film was completely devoid of any plot or character development; it was merely a montage of striking images." Since the film is devoid of (lacks) "any plot or character development," the images do not hold together. Rather, they are a series of disjoined images, a *montage.*

9. **C.** The writer repeats the phrase "human activities" primarily to ensure clarity (choice A). The previous sentence reads: "There is new and stronger evidence that most of the warming over the last 50 years is attributable to human activities." If the writer had followed with the pronoun *It,* readers would not know if the writer was referring to "human activities" or "new and stronger evidence." The writer also repeats the phrase "human activities" to create emphasis (choice B). Choices D (to help readers follow the flow of ideas) and E (to lead from one idea to the next) are variations on these two writing strategies, so they are correct. Since there are no "specific details and description" in the phrase "human activities," choice C is incorrect. That makes it the answer that fits the question.

10. **D.** The last sentence provides a clear transition into ways the world's climate will respond to greenhouse gases. This is stated in choice D—suggest ways that the world's meteorological conditions respond to greenhouse gases. Thus, the second paragraph is most likely to suggest ways the world's meteorological conditions respond to greenhouse gases.

11. **A.** The farmers are using "grains and legumes to feed their animals." Using the process of elimination, you can knock out choices D (oats and barley) and E (rice) because they are both grains. Choice C—solid food—doesn't make sense, because grains are solid foods. That leaves Choices A—vegetables—and B—meats. It makes sense that farmers would feed vegetables to their animals rather than meat, since vegetables cost less than meat. Thus, *legumes* most likely are "vegetables." Thus choice A is correct.

12. **B.** This passage is developed primarily through comparison and contrast. The clue is the phrase "By contrast" in the last sentence of the passage.

13. **B.** Chief Joseph's reasons for deciding to "fight no more forever" include all the following *except* he is dying. Chief Joseph says: "I am tired; my heart is sick and sad." You cannot infer from this that he is dying, however. All the other choices are directly stated in the speech.

14. **E.** Rather than fighting, Chief Joseph wants time to look for his scattered children. This is directly stated in the line: "I want time to look for my children and see how many of them I can find." Choice B is partly correct—his Nez Perce tribe did try to escape to Canada from their home in Oregon—but this cannot be inferred from Chief Joseph's words. Choice A is again historically correct, since the tribe had negotiated honorable surrender terms with the federal government, but these terms were ignored. This question illustrates the importance of reading a text closely and not bringing in outside information, which may be factually or historically correct, but neither correct nor relevant in context.

15. **D.** Looking Glass and Toohoolhoolzote are great chiefs of his tribe. This comes from the line: "Our chiefs are killed. Looking Glass is dead. Toohoolhoolzote is dead."

16. **B.** As used in context, the sentence "It is the young men who say yes and no" is best understood to mean that Chief Joseph laments the necessity of having the tribe led by inexperienced men. You cannot assume that he does not trust these leaders (choice E) or that Chief Joseph has been forced from power by the young men (choice D). In fact, just the opposite must be true if he has been charged with surrendering to the federal government. Since you can infer from the passage that older leaders are more valued than younger ones, choice A— even the young men cannot save them now—is not valid.

17. **C.** The writer's style contributes to the impact of his speech by emphasizing his main points. Chief Joseph's simple style focuses the reader's attention on the meaning of his words. This is the direct opposite of choices A—decreasing the emotional appeal of his words—and B—downplaying his main points with arrogance. The speech does not have any literary allusions, so you can eliminate choice D. He stresses his people's plight in specific, concrete language, so choice E—emphasizing the difference between appearance and reality— is illogical.

18. **B.** The simplicity of his language reinforces the effect of Chief Joseph's rhetoric by allowing the facts to tell the story without any literary contrivances. Therefore, choice D—relying on symbolism to convey his emotion—cannot be true. That the speech is easy to read (choice A) has nothing to do with the effect of his rhetoric. Rather than masking his true sorrow (choice C), the speech reveals it. The tone is sorrowful, not violent, so choice E—excoriating the federal government for betraying his people—is false.

19. **B.** The tone of this speech is best described as somber and despairing. The next closest choice—resigned and thoughtful—(choice C) is not quite as accurate a description. The other choices are far off the mark.

20. **C.** The word *peer* in the first sentence "described as a 'swimming and eating machine without peer,' " most nearly means "equal." No other creature in the sea can match the shark, as the second part of the first sentence suggests: "the shark is considered an evolutionary success story."

21. **E.** This is an easy question to solve through the process of elimination and logic. Every detail but the last one is mentioned in the paragraph as a reason why sharks are successful hunters.

22. **B.** From the details "the shark is considered an evolutionary success story" and "through scavenging and predation, the 250 species of sharks perform a valuable service in maintaining the ecological balance of the oceans," you can infer that the author admires sharks. There is no support in the first paragraph for any of the other answer choices.

23. **A.** You can infer from the information in the second paragraph that shark meat is sold under different names because people don't want to know that they are eating shark. Use the sentence "Generally, shark meat is consumed unknowingly under other, more appetizing names." From the phrase "more appetizing names," you can infer that people find the notion of eating shark unappealing.

24. **D.** *Maimed* in line 18 most nearly means "injured." You can eliminate *butchered* (choice E) and *assassinated* (choice C) because both essentially mean the same as *killed*. The writer would not say either "killed or killed." Choices A (*traumatized*) and B (*terrified*) mean the same thing, so they are not valid.

25. **D.** The main idea in the third paragraph is best stated as "Although sharks occasionally attack people, some medical treatments may come from research with sharks." Choices A, B, and C are details; choice E is an invalid conclusion because there is not sufficient information in the essay to support it.

Section 2

1. **D.** The correct sentence reads: "During the Revolutionary War, Hessian troops fought on the British side, not as allies, but as mercenaries. They were paid in money, not glory." The sentence, "They were paid in money, not glory," tells you that the Hessian troops were *mercenaries*—paid soldiers.

2. **A.** The correct sentence reads: "Professor Martin spent his entire career as a teacher trying to encourage his students to appreciate the beauty of poetry." You can eliminate choices C and D because they do not make sense. Choices A, B, and E

each offer a possible choice for the first blank, but only choice A provides a word that also makes sense in the second blank.

3. **D.** The correct sentence reads: "Although the movie was panned by all the major critics, audiences around the country seemed to find it genial." The critics had a negative reaction to the film. The transition "although" tells you that you are looking for a positive result.

4. **B.** The correct sentence reads: "Peter was undaunted by the repeated rejections of his novel; as a result, he continued to submit his manuscript to other publishers." The transition "as a result" shows a cause-and-effect relationship: the second half of the sentence explains the first half. Since Peter was *undaunted* (not discouraged) by the repeated rejections of his novel, he *continued* to submit his manuscript to other publishers.

5. **A.** The correct sentence reads: "Since there is a stigma attached to this job, it is unappealing, even at a lucrative salary." The word *since* shows a cause-and-effect relationship: Because of the *stigma* (shame) attached to the job, it is not a good deal, even at a good salary. Only choice A fits this context.

6. **C.** The correct sentence reads: "A week of sun and exercise had a salubrious effect; due to this, the dark circles under her eyes were erased and her skin took on a rosy glow." Logic dictates that a week of sun and exercise would have a beneficial effect, so you can eliminate choices A and E, since they have the opposite meaning. We can expect the dark circles under her eyes to vanish as her skin takes on a rosy glow. Choice C has both meanings required by context.

7. **B.** The correct sentence reads: "A system of education should be judged by the caliber of students it turns out; in summary, quality is preferable to quantity." The phrase "in summary, quality is preferable to quantity" tells you that you need two words that show value over amount. Choice B best fits the context.

8. **E.** The correct sentence reads: "Avoid becoming involved with loquacious politicians lest you get caught in a discourse from which you have difficulty extricating yourself." *Loquacious* people are very talkative, so you are likely to get involved in a long *discourse* or conversation with them.

9. **A.** The correct sentence reads: "You should have anticipated trouble ahead when the speeding traffic suddenly slowed to a crawl." Trouble is not something you enjoy or interrogate, so you can eliminate choices B and D. Now look at the second blank. Traffic cannot grow (choice C) or collect (choice E) to a crawl. Only choice A provides words that logically fit both the first and second blanks.

10. **D.** The correct sentence reads: "If he hasn't yet learned the importance of speaking well of others, he must be quite simple." Look for a cause-and-effect relationship, as shown by the word *If*. The best choice is D, where *simple* means "unintelligent."

11. **C.** As used in this passage, *precipitously* most nearly means "abruptly." You can infer this from context: since erosion is accelerated and weeds take over the land. With greater erosion and weeds, there would be fewer animals, so stocking rates would decline quickly.

12. **C.** The passage implies that endangered species will be saved only if they become a priority. The key deer escaped extinction only when conservationists, led by the Boone and Crockett Club, took measures to protect the animal. Choice A—species become at risk of dying out when they are hunted too extensively—clearly applies to the key deer, but a species can also become endangered when its habitat disappears or when members fall prey to disease. Thus, choice A is too general. Choice B—the government is still the most effective way to safeguard the environment because it has the resources to establish effective programs—is another gross generalization. Choice D—government officials and private citizens must work together to help the environment—is wrong because either group can accomplish much on its own. Further, we do not know if the conservationists and Boone and Crockett Club members are government employees or private citizens. Finally, choice E—the key deer is valuable for its beautiful coat—is not supported by the evidence in the passage. The key deer may have been hunted for sport or for their meat.

13. **E.** It can be inferred from this passage that tsunamis can be very dangerous. Since they are coupled with earthquakes and affect tide gauges for as long as a week, you can deduce that tsunamis are significant occurrences. There is no support in the passage for the other choices.

14. **D.** By using the word *delight* in the first sentence and repeating it in the second sentence, the author specifically emphasizes the rewards that the attainment of knowledge brings. Choice A (how studying serves only for pleasure) cannot be correct because it directly contradicts the first sentence in which the author lists three purposes of study: "Studies serve for delight, for ornament, and for ability." Choices B (his personal resolve to master as much information as possible) and C (his own devotion to study) are too narrow to be correct. Choice E (the sacrifices necessary to become learned) has nothing to do with delight; rather, it implies just the opposite.

15. **B.** According to the author, the three primary benefits of study are enjoyment, adornment, and competence. This information is directly stated in the first sentence: "Studies serve for delight, for ornament, and for ability."

16. **A.** All the following dangers can result from excessive study *except* accomplishment. The information is contained in the following sentence: "To spend too much time in studies is sloth; to use them too much for ornament is affectation; to make judgment wholly by their rules is the humor of a scholar." Choice B

laziness, is the same as "sloth." So is Choice E, inactivity. Choice C, *simplified judgments,* means the same as "to make judgment wholly by their rules is the humor of a scholar." Choice D, *an attitude of superiority,* is the same as "affectation."

17. **C.** As used in this passage, *affectation* means "pretense." That is the only meaning the word can have. Do not confuse *affectation* with *affection.* This could result in incorrectly selecting choice A, *fondness,* in error.

18. **C.** According to the author, you should read to think about the writer's ideas. This is directly stated in the following sentence: "Read not to contradict and confute; nor to believe and take for granted; nor to find talk and discourse; but to weigh and consider." None of the other choices shows this relationship between reading and considering the writer's ideas.

19. **B.** As used in the second paragraph, *meaner* most nearly means "inferior." Choice A is wrong because "cruel" is the wrong meaning of *meaner* in this context. The same is true for choices C (fierce), D (unnatural), and E (cheaper).

20. **D.** The speaker's tone is best described as authoritative and confident. The author projects a tone of assurance, learning, and conviction. This is the direct opposite of choices A (diffident and modest) and B (precarious). Since he is being completely straightforward, choice C (ironic) cannot be correct. While he is self-assured, he is not "arrogant and overbearing" (choice E).

21. **C.** The writer says, "When they [the American colonists] were told to disperse, they fired on the troops and ran off, upon which the Light Infantry pursued them." There are no Native Americans in the account at all, so choice A cannot possibly be correct.

22. **B.** The soldiers would be gathering to eliminate a military depot, which only choice B explains. It would not be logical to gather 800 soldiers to destroy a publication, no matter how seditious, so choices A and E cannot be correct. The same is true for choices C and D.

23. **D.** The writer's tone in the second paragraph is best described as disdainful and condescending. This is shown especially in the phrases "and have what they call Minute Companies" and "it is supposed." This directly contradicts choice A, as the author is clearly biased toward the British. The writer is not "horrified and dismayed" or "astonished and amazed" until describing the brutality in the third paragraph, eliminating choices B and C. Overall the writer admires the British (choice E), but the tone of this passage is not worshipful toward them.

24. **A.** The writer clearly sets forth the events on that fateful day to convince readers that the colonial rebels are barbarians and the British soldiers were justified in their actions. This shows her sympathy for the British.

25. **B.** The writer's sympathetic account of the problems the British soldiers faced at the hands of American rebels and her familiarity with the situation suggests that she is a colonist loyal to the British. This directly contradicts choice C, an American rebel. A British soldier would most likely use the first-person point of view, so choice A cannot be correct. A visitor to America from Europe (choice D) would not be as familiar with the situation. The same is true of someone considering moving to America to join the colonists (choice E).

26. **C.** The answer can be derived from the context. Since the Light Troops were "harassed in their return for seven or eight miles," there must be many, many people gathered on the road. Otherwise, they would not be able to cover so much distance. This is the direct opposite of choice E, *few*, and choice D, *meager*. The other choices have nothing to do with the context.

27. **D.** Since the American rebels attacked the British and left them "lying in the agonies of death, scalped, with their noses and ears cut off and eyes bored out," this description serves to evoke sympathy for the British troops (choice D). This is the direct opposite of choice C, elicit pity for the rebel soldiers oppressed by the British. Therefore, choice C cannot be correct. The description does make the narrative more compelling reading (choice B), but it is more than mere gratuitous violence. There are no Native Americans mentioned in the article, so choice E—portray the Native Americans as brutal savages and justify their mass relocation and slaughter—cannot be correct. Finally, while the writer may indeed want the difficulties between the British and Americans settled as soon as possible, there is no indication that she wishes to convince her readers of this, nor that she believes that further violence must be avoided. Therefore, choice A cannot be correct.

28. **E.** The informal tone suggests the document is a letter to a friend (choice E). The next best choice is D, a diary entry, but the tone suggests the document was intended for a specific audience. The writer would not be foolish enough to publish these sentiments in an editorial for a colonial newspaper (choice C) or a letter to the editor of a Massachusetts newspaper (choice A) with emotions running so high and such bloodshed going on. Since the document has such a marked bias toward the British, it cannot be a plea for peace and moderation (choice B).

Section 3

1. **B.** By directly addressing the members of the audience as "children," Sojourner Truth suggests that we are all equal in God's eyes. Her tone is sincere, so choices A (they [the audience] are acting very immaturely) and D (the members of the audience should be ashamed of the way they are acting) cannot be correct.

Choice C (she is morally and intellectually superior to the members of her audience) misses her point. Sojourner Truth's strength lies in her experience and her common sense; she makes no claim to intellectual achievements. Choice E (the delegates at the assembly are young but she is elderly and thus more experienced) cannot be correct because we do not know Sojourner's age nor the ages of the people she is addressing. She may indeed be older than they are, but she could just as easily be younger. It is logical to assume that most of the people in the audience would be mature, given their leadership roles.

2. **E.** As used in the first sentence of passage 1, the idiom "something out of kilter" means that something is wrong. You can infer this from the "racket" (fuss) she notes. There is no suggestion that this is evil (choice A), dangerous (choice B), or mysterious (choice D)—it is simply amiss. While people are indeed foolish (choice C), that does not necessarily cause things to go wrong.

3. **A.** "Women being helped into carriages and lifted over ditches" can be understood in both a literal and metaphorical way. Literally, women were helped into high carriages and carried over ditches. But Sojourner Truth's comments can also be understood in a metaphorical way: upper-class and middle-class women were shielded from the harsh and unpleasant aspects of life. The cost? They were treated as children and denied a voice in their life. Truth is not insulting women who do not work (choice B), for she is not even addressing the issue of working women. While this comment does acknowledge the wide social gulf between Sojourner Truth and wealthy white women (choice C), that is not her point. She is clearly aware of the social mores of her time (choice D), but again that is not her point. Since her tone is level, you can eliminate choice E. Sojourner Truth's rage at the maltreatment she has received as a slave and as a woman.

4. **D.** "Look at my arm" suggests the speaker's physical strength represents her psychological strength. Not only can she toil as well as (or better than!) any man, but she has withstood the mental effects of brutal work. Eliminate choice A because she is not threatening anyone. You cannot assume from this comment that she has been injured and bears the scars (choice B), for there is no evidence in the text of any scars. While she is indeed as strong as any man (choice C), her point is wider. The same is true of choice E. She is physically superior to most men.

5. **B.** The repeated refrain "And ain't I a woman?" serves to stress the equality of *all* women while pointing out inequalities. The speaker is being serious, not ironic, so you can eliminate choice A (convey her ironic stance). The phrase is not a lead-in to specific details, so you can cross out choice C (alert the reader to the specific details to follow). She is not trying to frighten the reader, so choice D (intimidate the reader with the harsh question) is off. Finally, "bitter" is too strong a word for her feelings, so choice E is wrong.

6. **E.** The speaker is critical of male claims that women are the "weaker sex." This is shown through the examples she cites: "I have ploughed and planted, and gathered into barns, and no man could head me! . . . I could work as much and eat as much as a man—when I could get it—and bear the lash as well! . . . I have borne thirteen children, and seen them all sold off to slavery, and when I cried out with my mother's grief, none but Jesus heard me!"

7. **E.** The statement "That's it, honey" serves most directly to draw the audience closer to the speaker. This is accomplished by the familiar word *honey*, which forges an intimacy between the speaker and her audience. Therefore, choice D (distance the audience from the speaker) cannot be correct. The mood is not hopeless, so you can eliminate choice C as well. There is nothing ironic about her statement, as it matches what has come before. Therefore, choice A (provide an ironic counterpoint to her previous comments) is wrong.

8. **E.** Sojourner Truth uses rhetorical devices and persuasive techniques to prove that women are as capable as men and deserve equal rights. She does not discriminate among women, so choice A (some women, but not all, can take up the mantle of autonomy) is wrong. Neither is she trying to prove that women are vastly superior to men, simply that they are equal. Therefore, choice B is wrong. She is not talking about slavery, so you can cross out choice C, slavery must be abolished throughout the union. If choice D (women will get the vote, regardless of what men say or do) was true, there would not be any reason for her to speak at the assembly. Therefore, it cannot be correct.

9. **C.** Passage 2 suggests that Sojourner Truth was a familiar name from the past among people who worked to make slavery illegal. You can infer this from the first sentence (the key phrases are in italics): "*Many years ago*, the *few readers* of radical Abolitionist papers must often have seen the singular name of Sojourner Truth, announced as a frequent speaker at Anti-Slavery meetings, and as traveling on a sort of self-appointed agency through the country."

10. **A.** In passage 2, Harriet Beecher Stowe compares Sojourner Truth to a statue chiefly to show her admiration for the abolitionist's dignity and carriage (posture). You can infer this from the following description (key words are in italics): "still gave the impression of a physical development which in early youth must have been *as fine a specimen of the torrid zone* as Cumberworth's *celebrated statuette* of the Negro Woman at the Fountain."

11. **E.** Sojourner Truth uses a fiery, incendiary tone in passage 1 to convey her passionate opposition to slavery. You can deduce this from lines like this: "I could work as much and eat as much as a man—when I could get it—and bear the lash as well!"

12. **D.** From both passages, you can infer that Sojourner Truth was an admirable, extraordinary person. There is no support for choices A (everyone worked to

abolish slavery) or C (Harriet Beecher Stowe worked hard for the abolition of slavery). Since passage 2 describes how Stowe and Truth met late in Truth's life, choice E (Harriet Beecher Stowe and Sojourner Truth were close personal friends) is unlikely to be true. Choice B (slavery was an evil institution) is true, but is not addressed in passage 2.

Section 4

"Whenever you are asked if you can do a job, tell 'em, 'Certainly I can!' Then get busy and find out how to do it."   *Theodore Roosevelt*

Assignment: In this statement, former President Roosevelt advocates taking chances. On the other hand, you can fall flat on your face if you go into a new school, job, or any challenge without sufficient experience or learning. Discuss the extent to which you agree or disagree with Roosevelt's statement. Support your position by providing reasons and examples from your own experience, observations, or reading.

The following model essay would receive a 6, the highest score, for its specific details, organization, and style (appropriate word choice, sentence structure, and consistent facility in use of language). It is an especially intelligent and insightful response.

Theodore Roosevelt said: "Whenever you are asked if you can do a job, tell 'em, 'Certainly I can!' Then get busy and find out how to do it." I fully agree with Roosevelt's statement; in fact, I have found it to be a credo for being successful in life.

My junior year in high school, I started looking for a job to earn some extra money. I looked around at the various jobs available, but since I had never held a job before, I didn't have any useful skills. Eventually, I applied for a job in a supermarket as a cashier, where the manager asked me, "Can you work a cash register?" I responded truthfully, "I've never done it before, but I bet I could learn." For any business, hiring someone who needs training is always a risky venture. It costs the business money to train the new employee, and the employee could quit the next day or simply prove unwilling or unable to complete the tasks required by the job. I was able to complete the training quickly and was a very productive employee. I think the supermarket likely took the chance on me because I was eager and willing to learn new skills.

This past summer, I worked in an office, inputting data, making copies, sending faxes, and generally doing odd tasks that saved time for others. One day, my boss approached me with the address of a website and said, "There's a bunch of data on this site that I need sorted out and put into pie charts. Do you know how to do that?" I replied, "No, but I'm sure I can figure it out." She gave me a smile and as she walked off, said, "That's what makes you such a great employee—you're such a 'can-do' guy." After two calls to tech support and one to the site administrator, I was able to retrieve the data from the site and make it into exactly the charts my boss needed.

My own experience shows that, with determination, courage, and some hard work, you can get ahead on the job. Embracing challenges is the crucial factor in this equation, because it shows you have that "can-do" attitude. Theodore Roosevelt's bravery got him up San Juan Hill during the Spanish-American War. That same determination can help you climb every mountain, too!

Section 5

1. **C.**   Use consistent tenses in a sentence. The past tense *fractured* requires the past tense *was* rather than the present tense *is*.

2. **D.**   Use a consistent pronoun. Since the sentence starts with the pronoun *you*, do not switch to the pronoun *one*. Rather, stay with the pronoun *you*.

3. **A.**   This word group is a fragment because it is missing a complete verb. The sentence should read "were hanging."

4. **C.**   *Not only* and *but also* are correlative conjunctions that operate as a pair. Choice C should read "but it is also . . ."

5. **A.**   The error is a double negative. Use *scarcely* or *no,* but not both together in the same sentence.

6. **C.**   The plural subject *trucks* agrees with the plural verb *are,* not the singular verb *is.* Do not be mislead by the singular predicate nominative *reason.* (A predicate nominative is a noun or a pronoun used after some form of *to be.*)

7. **A.**   A pronoun used in apposition to a noun is in the same case as the noun. An *appositive* is a noun or pronoun placed after another noun or pronoun to identify or explain it. Here, the pronoun (*she*) must be in the nominate case because it is in apposition with the noun *bond traders,* which is also in the nominative case.

8. **D.**   This sentence has a *misplaced modifier,* a phrase, clause, or word placed too far from the noun or pronoun it describes. As a result, the sentence fails to convey its intended meaning. As written, this sentence implies that the famous French composers, artists, and writers come back to life on Sundays! The sentence should read: "Daily, except Sunday, you are welcome to visit the cemetery where famous French composers, artists, and writers lie buried." or "You are welcome to visit the cemetery daily except Sunday where famous French composers, artists, and writers lie buried."

9. **B.**   The correct idiom is *agreed to,* not *agreed with.* The correct sentence reads: "The resolution that has just been agreed to by the school board members will result in a five percent tax increase in the upcoming year."

10. **E.**   The sentence is correct as written.

11. **B.**   Only choice B maintains parallel structure (matching sentence parts).

12. **D.**   Every choice but D creates a fragment. The sentence should read: "It has been estimated that many people are deprived of much-needed medical care in this country, especially follow-up visits and preventative medication."

13. **C.**   Use a comma after an introductory subordinate clause.

14. **E.** Use an adverb (*thoroughly*) to modify or describe an adjective (*more*).

15. **D.** The other choices violate the tense (or time) in the passage.

16. **D.** As written, the sentence is in the *passive voice.* In this construction, the subject receives the action. In the *active voice,* the subject performs the action named by the verb. In general, the active voice is preferable to the passive voice because the active voice is less wordy. The sentence should read: "Ben Franklin first wanted a turkey instead of an eagle as our national symbol."

17. **E.** As written, the sentence states that the shipment—not the speaker—confirmed the conversation. This is called a *dangling modifier,* since the noun or pronoun is missing. Only choice E corrects the error by providing the missing pronoun (*I*). The correct sentence reads: "As I stated in our conversation of March 17, the shipment of books and magazines that you ordered will be delivered first thing Friday morning."

18. **B.** As written, the sentence lacks parallel structure (having ideas of the same rank in the same grammatical structure). The sentence should read: "During a thunderstorm, people who are inside should not talk on the telephone, stand near any open windows, or use large appliances." In the revised sentence, "*talk* on the telephone" and "*stand* near any open windows" parallel "*use* large appliances."

19. **C.** Use the superlative case (*-est* or *most*) to compare three or more things, as is the case here since more than three movies are being compared. Never use *-er* and *more* or *-est* and *most* together. The correct sentence reads: "Of all the movies ever made, *The Godfather* has been recognized as one of America's greatest movies."

20. **D.** As written, this is a *run-on sentence,* two independent clauses run together. Just adding a comma (choice B), creates a comma splice. You can correct the error by adding a semicolon or a coordinating conjunction (*and, for, but, yet, so, nor, or*). Choice D is the only correct version: "Most people who drink coffee do not know where it comes from; it is actually the fruit of an evergreen tree."

21. **E.** This question asks you to connect two related sentences. Only choice E correctly joins the two sentences in a logical way. The other conjunctions do not make sense in context. The correct sentence reads: "Samuel Morse patented the telegraph in 1842, and on March 3, 1843, Morse was granted $30,000 from Congress to build a trial line between Baltimore and Washington."

22. **C.** Choice C—Not only did it allow fast communication over large distances for the first time, but it also made train travel safer and more efficient—is the best choice because it shows how the telegraph connected the continent, an example that supports the previous sentence.

23. **B.** In sentence 7, the word or idea to which *It* refers is not clear. The sentence must be revised to specify Morse code. The revised sentence reads: "Morse's dot-dash system is a simple means of communicating messages with as few errors as possible, and even when errors occur, the message is still understandable."

24. **B.** The paragraph should read: "Even though it's rarely used, Morse code still resonates symbolically in today's society. Almost everyone knows the three-dot, three-dash, three-dot code for S.O.S., which is still widely used as a distress call. In fact, almost any sort of signal in patterns of three is considered a call for help."

25. **D.** Ending with a paragraph on Samuel Morse's legacy would bring the essay full circle, from the origin of Morse code to its contemporary uses.

PART **3**

Strategies for Success
on the Critical Reading Test

Strategies for Success on the Critical Reading Test

The critical reading questions on the new SAT assess your ability to read, understand, analyze, and evaluate material in a short passage, a long passage, or a pair of related passages. Traditionally, most of the passages concerned literature and the arts. On the new SAT, in contrast, the critical reading will include a greater emphasis on analytical reading with passages from natural sciences, humanities, and social studies. Despite the wide variety of subject matter, this part of the new SAT tests your ability to read and to understand what you read—not your knowledge of a particular subject.

Some passages may be paired. If that is the case, read the passages as one unit, comparing and contrasting the ideas, styles, and tone as you do so. Then follow the instructions for finding the correct answers provided here for the single passages.

Remember: Everything you need to answer the question will be contained in the passage.

What Strategy Should I Use?

Use the following five-step process to solve critical reading questions.

Step 1. If the passage has an introduction, always read it first. This preface helps you set the passage in context.

Step 2. Skim the question parts—not the answer choices. This helps you focus on the information you're seeking.

Step 3. Read the passage. To be sure you understand what you're reading, paraphrase and summarize the meaning. Make sure you can restate the author's main idea in your own words.

Step 4. After you have read the passage, read each question and the answer choices. Choose your answers. Return to the passage to confirm your choices.

Step 5. For difficult problems, use the process of elimination. Guess if you can eliminate even one choice.

The critical reading questions on the SAT are presented in chronological order. For example, you can find the information you need to answer question 10 between the information for questions 9 and 11. Taken together, the questions present a story map or chronological reading of the passage. Therefore, try to answer the questions in order rather than skipping around.

Try the Five-Step Strategy now with the following sample passage.

The following passage is an excerpt from a NASA article on Earth microbes on the moon. The article describes how a remarkable colony of lunar survivors was discovered 30 years after Apollo 1 landed on the moon.

1   For a human, unprotected space travel is a short trip measured in seconds.
    What could be worse for would-be space travelers than a catastrophic breach in their protective spacesuits, the hightech, multilayered fabric blanket that balloons under the pressure of a lifesaving flow of oxygen and insulates against the frozen
5   harshness of deep space vacuum?
    But for some kinds of microbes, the harshness of space travel is not unlike their everyday stressful existence, the successful execution of ingenious survival tricks learned over billions of years of Earthbound evolution.
    Space historians will recall that the journey to the stars has more than one life on its
10   passenger list: the names of a dozen Apollo astronauts who walked on the moon and one inadvertent stowaway, a common bacteria, *Streptococcus mitis*, the only known survivor of unprotected space travel. As astronomers and biologists met recently to discuss biological limits to life on Earth, the question of how an Earth bacteria could survive in a vacuum without nutrients, water and radiation protection was less speculative than
15   might first be imagined.
    In 1991, as Apollo 1 Commander Pete Conrad reviewed the transcripts of his conversations relayed from the moon back to Earth, the significance of the only known microbial survivor of harsh interplanetary travel struck him as profound: "I always thought the most significant thing that we ever found on the whole . . . Moon was that little bac-
20   teria who came back and lived and nobody ever said [anything] about it." As the lunar voyagers answered a similar question more than a century ago, in Jules Verne's classic, *From the Earth to the Moon:* "To those who maintain that the planets are not inhabited one may reply: 'You might be perfectly in the right, if you could only show that the earth is the best possible world.'" The remarkable lunar survivor from Apollo 1 thus
25   gives scientific pause.
    To a biologist, freeze-drying microbes for harsh space travel conjures up rather mundane kitchen science, a simple reenactment of how a yeast packet taken from the freezer can make bread dough rise prior to baking. But to a new breed of biologist exploring the harshest conditions on Earth, how a delicate microbe manages to counteract vacuum,

30 boiling temperatures, burning radiation, and crushing pressures deep in the frozen ice-
    caps is the study of life itself.
        For example, only now after many years of biological progress can scientists begin to
    scan down the genetic script underlying the causes of malaria, syphilis, cholera and
    tuberculosis. Within a few years, it is estimated that 50 to 100 complete genomes of
35 living organisms will be entirely deciphered, presenting the first opportunities for deep
    evolutionary comparisons and insights into exactly the remarkable means by which the
    common Strep. bacteria could revive itself after years on the moon.
        How this remarkable feat was accomplished only by Strep. bacteria remains specula-
    tive, but it does recall that even our present Earth does not always look as environmen-
40 tally friendly as it might have 4 billion years ago when bacteria first appeared on this
    planet.

1. In line 7, *ingenious* most nearly means

    (A) rocklike
    (B) youthful
    (C) resourceful
    (D) arduous
    (E) complex

2. In line 11, the phrase "inadvertent stowaway" used in reference to *Streptococcus mitis* means that

    (A) someone cleverly hid the bacteria to use later in an experiment
    (B) bacteria commonly hide on space missions but it is difficult to find them later
    (C) the bacteria have a will, like any living organism, and planned the ruse itself
    (D) none of the astronauts or mission specialists realized the bacteria were on the spacecraft
    (E) we must be very careful of all bacteria, because they are far more harmful than we suspect

3. You can infer that Apollo 1 Commander Pete Conrad found the survival of the bacteria "profound" because

    (A) he understands its implications for life on other worlds
    (B) he is terrified of bringing new germs to Earth
    (C) he believes the entire incident is make-believe, like something you would find in a science-fiction book
    (D) he does not understand what it means
    (E) he feels that the rest of the mission was disappointing and worries that funding will be cut for space travel

4. Which of the following is the best statement of the main idea of this passage?

   (A) There are more things in space and on Earth than we can ever understand.
   (B) Small objects can be far more dangerous than large ones.
   (C) Genetic research cannot be successful without the input from space missions.
   (D) *Streptococcus* bacteria are mighty and powerful and might even unlock the origins of life.
   (E) Bacteria are tremendously important to our understanding of life.

5. You can infer that the author of this passage

   (A) is not a scientist
   (B) admires bacteria
   (C) was an astronaut
   (D) is a well-respected microbiologist
   (E) believes in extraterrestrial life

Answers

1. **C.** The word *ingenious* (line 7) most nearly means "resourceful." You can infer this from the context clues "successful execution" and "survival tricks." These clues tell you that *ingenious* must be a positive response to the threat of extinction.

2. **D.** The phrase "inadvertent stowaway" used in reference to *Streptococcus mitis* means that none of the astronauts or mission specialists realized the bacteria were on the spacecraft. You can figure this out from the contrast between the passenger list that contained "the names of a dozen Apollo astronauts who walked on the moon" and the passenger not listed, the bacteria.

3. **A.** You can infer that Apollo 1 Commander Pete Conrad found the survival of the bacteria "profound" because he understands its implications for life on other worlds. This inference comes from the reference to Jules Verne's classic, *From the Earth to the Moon*. The key passage is: "To those who maintain that the planets are not inhabited one may reply: 'You might be perfectly in the right, if you could only show that the earth is the best possible world.'" The remarkable lunar survivor from Apollo 1 thus gives scientific pause. Here, the writer suggests that the bacteria raise the possibility of extraterrestrial life.

4. **E.** The main idea of this passage can best be stated as: "Bacteria are tremendously important to our understanding of life." Choice A (There are more things in space and on Earth than we can ever understand) is incorrect because the writer describes bacteria in great detail. From this detail, you

can conclude that we *do* know a lot about bacteria and we are learning more each day. Choice B (Small objects can be far more dangerous than large ones) is not proven in the passage because there is no suggestion that the bacteria are very dangerous. There is no proof for choice C (genetic research cannot be successful without the input from space missions). The same is true for choice D (*Streptococcus* bacteria are mighty and powerful and might even unlock the origins of life). It is too big a leap to these conclusions from the information presented in the passage.

5. **B.** You can infer that the author admires bacteria. There is no support for any of the other choices in the passage. Specifically, you cannot conclude that the author is not a scientist (choice A), an astronaut (choice B), or a well-respected microbiologist (choice D).

Look back at the passage and the questions. You'll notice that they fall into specific types. The first question, for example, asks about vocabulary. The second question requires you to define a phrase; the third question, to make an inference or figure out an unstated meaning. The fourth question asks you to find the main idea. The final question has you figure out something about the writer. Let's look at each question type—and more—in turn.

How Can I Figure Out What a Passage Means?

As you learned in step 3, *always* begin by figuring out what a passage means. You can do this by following these steps:

1. **Read the passage through once and see how much of the author's meaning you can immediately grasp.**

2. **Then go back through the passage a second time and define all the unfamiliar words, concepts, ideas, and references. Decode any images and symbols, too.**

3. **Paraphrase the passage by restating it in your own words. If you can do this, you likely have a clear understanding of the meaning.**

When writers don't directly state the main idea of a passage, you have to make *inferences* to find the main idea. You can figure out the implied main idea by asking yourself the following questions:

■ What is this passage about?

■ What does the passage describe?

■ What does the passage suggest?

■ What is the author trying to communicate about the subject?

■ What can be inferred from the information stated in the passage?

Read the following passages and answer the practice SAT questions that follow. Questions 1 to 3 are based on the following passage.

> 1   Ancient savage tribes played a primitive kind of football. About 2,500 years ago there was a ball-kicking game played by the Athenians, Spartans, and Corinthians, which the Greeks called *Episkuros*. The Romans had a somewhat similar game called *Harpastum*. According to several historical sources, the Romans brought the game
> 5   with them when they invaded the British Isles in the first century, AD. The game today known as "football" in the United States can be traced directly back to the English game of rugby, although there have been many changes to the game. Football was played informally on university fields more than a hundred years ago. In 1840, a yearly series of informal "scrimmages" started at Yale University. It took more than
> 10   twenty-five years, however, for the game to become part of college life. The first formal intercollegiate football game was held between Princeton and Rutgers teams on November 6, 1869 on Rutgers's home field at New Brunswick, New Jersey, and Rutgers won.

1. The subject of this passage is

    (A) ancient Greek sports
    (B) brutality in sports
    (C) rugby
    (D) sports in the United States
    (E) the history of football

2. The writer's main idea is best stated as:

    (A) The Romans, Athenians, Spartans, and Corinthians all played a game like football.
    (B) Football is a very old game; its history stretches back to ancient days.
    (C) American football comes from a British game called "rugby."
    (D) Football is a more popular game than baseball, even though baseball is called "America's pastime."
    (E) Football is a brutal sport with roots in barbarous cultures.

3. The best title for this passage would be

    (A) Play Ball!
    (B) Football in America
    (C) The Origins of Football
    (D) America's Pastime
    (E) Savage Games

Question 4 is based on the following passage.

> 1   It takes no calendar to tell root and stem that the calm days of mid-summer are here. Last spring's sprouted seed comes to fruit. None of these things depends on a calendar of the days and months. They are their own calendar, marks on a span of time that reaches far back into the shadows of time. The mark is there for all to see, in every
> 5   field and meadow and treetop, as it was last year and then years ago and when the centuries were young.
>
>   The time is here. This is the point in the great continuity when these things happen, and will continue to happen year after year. Any summer arrives at this point, only to lead on to the next and the next, and so to summer again. These things we can
> 10   count on; these will happen again and again, so long as the earth turns.

4. The passage indicates that the author experiences a feeling of

(A) frustration
(B) fear of the forces of nature
(C) pessimism
(D) serene confidence
(E) regret at the rapid passage of time

Answers

1. E. The subject of this passage is the history of football. You can figure this out from the very first sentence: Ancient savage tribes played a primitive kind of football. Now go through the passages and find other references to football. You will find that the author mentions football over and over to help the reader follow the subject.

2. B. This passage has an unstated main idea, so you have to infer it from details in the reading. Only choice B correctly gives the main idea of the passage: Football is a very old game; its history stretches back to ancient days. Eliminate choices A and C because they are too narrow to be the main idea. They give supporting details from the paragraph, not the main idea. Eliminate choices D and E because they contain information that is not included in the paragraph.

3. C. The best title for this passage would be *The Origins of Football*. The other choices are too narrow, describing only part of the passage, not its entirety.

4. D. The passage indicates that the author experiences a feeling of serene confidence, as the phrases "calm days," "great continuity," and "we can count on" reveal. The author has no fear of nature nor any regret at the passage of time; rather, we sense, through the phrases cited, a calm acceptance of the seasons.

How Do I Answer Vocabulary Questions?

Some SAT questions require you to define a word as it is used in the passage. The questions may be on difficult, unfamiliar words. Just as often, however, the vocabulary questions on the critical reading will test easier words that have uncommon meanings, as they are used in context. In either case, follow these four steps as you work through these test items:

1. **Go back to the passage and find the word.**

2. **Fill in your own word for the word you are asked to define.**

3. **Eliminate the answer choices that don't match your word.**

4. **Choose the best answer.**

As you look for the correct meaning, always use context clues.

- *Definition clues* may be provided right in the passage. The definition is a *synonym* (a word that means the same). It may come before or after the unfamiliar word. For example: "*Tsunamis,* or seismic sea-waves, are gravity waves set in motion by underwater disturbances associated with earthquakes." *Seismic sea-waves* is a synonym for the unfamiliar word *tsunamis.*
- *Contrast clues* tell you what something is not rather than what it is. Often, you'll find contrast clues set off with *unlike, not,* or *instead of,* for example, "Then arrange a handful of mulch, not fresh leaves, on the top." *Mulch* must be the opposite of fresh leaves. It must mean "decayed leaves."
- *Commonsense clues* encourage you to use what you already know to define the unfamiliar word, for example, "Airplanes make daily *ascents* to gather data." Since airplanes go into the air, *ascent* must mean "to rise."

Read the following passage and answer the practice SAT questions that follow. Questions 1 to 3 are based on the following passage.

---

1   The nation had few taxes in its early history. From 1791 to 1802, the United States government was supported by internal taxes on distilled spirits, carriages, refined sugar, tobacco, property sold at auction, corporate bonds, and slaves. The high costs of the War of 1812 brought about the nation's first sales tax on gold, silverware, jewelry,
5   and watches. In 1817, however, Congress expunged all internal taxes, relying on tariffs on imported goods to provide sufficient funds for running the government.
    In 1862, in order to support the Civil War effort, Congress enacted the nation's first income tax law. It was a forerunner of our modern income tax in that it was based on the principles of graduated taxation and of withholding income at the source. During
10   the Civil War, a person earning from $600 to $10,000 per year paid tax at the rate of 3%. Those with incomes of more than $10,000 paid taxes at a higher rate. Additional sales and excise taxes were added, and an "inheritance" tax also made its debut. In 1866, internal revenue collections reached their highest point in the nation's 90-year-history—more than $310 million, an amount not reached again until around 1911.

1. As used in line 5, *expunged* most nearly means

   (A) collected
   (B) retained
   (C) revamped
   (D) reconsidered
   (E) eliminated

2. In line 8, *forerunner* is used to mean

   (A) sequel
   (B) supplement
   (C) outcome
   (D) precursor
   (E) continuance

3. Which best captures the meaning of *graduated* in line 9?

   (A) equal
   (B) progressive
   (C) selective
   (D) mature
   (E) intelligent

Answers

1. **E.** As used in line 5, the best synonym for *expunged* is *eliminated.* You can infer this from the word *however*, which shows contrast—the opposite meaning of the clause that came before.

2. **D.** In line 8, *forerunner* is used to mean "precursor." Both *fore* and *pre* mean "before."

3. **B.** From its context, you can deduce that *graduated* most nearly means "progressive." You can infer this from the fact that the tax rate rises: "During the Civil War, a person earning from $600 to $10,000 per year paid tax at the rate of 3%. Those with incomes of more than $10,000 paid taxes at a higher rate."

How Do I Answer Questions on Style?

Rhetoric is the strategic use of language to accomplish the author's purpose. Writers create their distinctive *style,* their unique way of writing, by the rhetorical choices they make. Style is made up of elements such as diction, sentence length and structure, figures of speech, tone, and mood.

Some of the questions on the SAT concern an analysis of rhetorical language and techniques. These questions are designed not only to determine how well you know the elements of style but also to judge how well you can integrate these literary techniques with the writer's purpose and main idea.

Read the following passages and answer the practice SAT questions that follow. Questions 1 to 3 are based on the following passage.

---

1   Nature is by the art of man, as in many other things, so in this also imitated, that it can be made an artificial animal. For seeing life is but a motion of limbs, the beginning whereof is in some principal part within, why may we not say that all automata (engines that move themselves by springs and wheels as doth a watch) have an artifi-
5   cial life? For what is the heart but a spring; and the nerve but so many strings; and the joints but so many wheels, giving motion to the whole body such as it was intended by the artificer? Art goes yet further, imitating the rational and most excellent work of nature, man.

---

1. The phrase "artificial animal" in line 2 does which of the following in the opening sentence?

   (A) presents a judgment on the artificial man
   (B) introduces the writer's main idea
   (C) emphasizes the theoretical rather than the practical side of the argument
   (D) shifts the focus from generalities to individual cases
   (E) introduces the speaker

2. The writer uses the word *artificer* in line 7 to connote

   (A) a compassionate scientist
   (B) a monster who perverts nature for his own ends
   (C) a master builder
   (D) an inventor who has failed in the past but is likely to succeed in the future
   (E) a pompous and insolent bureaucrat

3. The passage is most likely part of

   (A) an argumentative speech
   (B) a historical essay
   (C) a general audience magazine article
   (D) a light-hearted novel
   (E) a book introduction

Questions 4 to 6 are based on the following passage.

> 1   Rather than love, than money, than fame, give me truth: I sat at a table where were
> rich food and wine in abundance, but sincerity and truth were not; and I went away
> hungry from the inhospitable board. The hospitality was as cold as the ices. I thought
> that there was no need of ice to freeze them. They talked to me of the age of the wine
> 5   and the fame of the vintage; but I thought of an older, newer, and purer wine, of a
> more glorious vintage, which they had not got, and could not buy. The style, the house
> and grounds and "entertainment" pass for nothing with me. I called on the king, but
> he made me wait in his hall, and conducted like a man incapacitated for hospitality.
> There was a man in my neighborhood who lived in a hollow tree. His manners were
> 10   truly regal. I should have done better had I called on him.

4. The word *ice* in line 4 is used symbolically to suggest

(A) people with spiritually empty lives
(B) rude and vulgar guests
(C) curt and tasteless hosts
(D) money wasted on frivolous social pretense
(E) the difficulty that rich people, especially monarchs, endure

5. Throughout the passage, the diction suggests

(A) the rewards of gainfully earned possessions
(B) the pleasures of fine food and drink
(C) the delight of being with close friends and warm hosts
(D) the hollowness of materialism and the fulfillment of simplicity
(E) the importance of showing consideration and good manners

6. The passage as a whole introduces contrasts between all the following *except*

(A) wealth and poverty
(B) integrity and pretense
(C) intelligence and misunderstanding
(D) graciousness and reserve
(E) royalty and commoners

Answers

1. B. The phrase "artificial animal" introduces the writer's main idea: "Art goes yet further, imitating the rational and most excellent work of nature, man."

2. C. The writer uses the word *artificer* to connote a master builder, for only a master builder could construct something as complex as a human.

3. **E.** The passage is most likely part of a book introduction. Use the process of elimination to solve this critical reading question. The passage is far too serious to be a light-hearted novel (choice D). It's far too specific to be a general audience magazine article (choice C). It's not based on history, so a historical essay (choice B) cannot be the best choice. Finally, an argumentative speech (choice A) isn't on target because the author is not arguing. Rather, the author is stating his or her viewpoint. In an argument, the author will refute the other side, which is not the case here.

4. **A.** The word *ice* is used symbolically to suggest people with spiritually empty lives. You can infer this from the comparison of their hospitality to the ices. "I thought that there was no need of ice to freeze them," the writer says.

5. **D.** Throughout the passage, the diction suggests the hollowness of materialism and the fulfillment of simplicity. Key words and phrases include: "but sincerity and truth were not," "I went away hungry," "the hospitality was as cold as the ices." Also focus on the following line: "They talked to me of the age of the wine and the fame of the vintage; but I thought of an older, newer, and purer wine, of a more glorious vintage, which they had not got, and could not buy."

6. **C.** The passage as a whole introduces contrasts between all the following *except* intelligence and misunderstanding. The hosts show no intelligence, and there is no misunderstanding their blatant materialism.

Practice Critical Reading Passages and Questions

Read the following passages and answer the practice SAT questions that follow. Questions 1 to 8 are based on the following passage.

---

1 How many are the solitary hours I spend, ruminating upon the past, and anticipating the future, whilst you, overwhelmed with the cares of state, have but a few moments you can devote to any individual. All domestic pleasures and enjoyments are absorbed in the great and important duty you owe your country, for our country is, as it were, a
5 secondary god, and the first and greatest parent. It is to be preferred to parents, wives, children, friends, and all things, the gods only excepted; for, if our country perishes, it is as impossible to save an individual, as to preserve one of the fingers of a mortified hand. Thus I do suppress every wish, and silence every murmur, acquiescing in a painful separation from the companion of my youth, and the friend of my heart.

 I believe't near ten days since I wrote you a line. I have not felt in any humor to
10 entertain you if I had taken up my pen. Perhaps some unbecoming invective might have fallen from it. The eyes of our rulers have been closed, and a lethargy has seized almost every member. I fear a fatal security has taken possession of them. Whilst the building is in flames, they tremble at the expense of water to quench it. In short, two
15 months have elapsed since the evacuation of Boston, and very little has been done in that time to secure it, or the harbor, from future invasion. The people are all in a flame, and no one among us, that I have heard of, even mentions expense. They think,

universally, that there has been an amazing neglect somewhere. Many have turned out as volunteers to work upon Noodle's Island, and many more would go upon Nantasket,
20 if the business was once set on foot. "'Tis a maxim of state that power and liberty are like heat and moisture. Where they are well mixed, everything prospers; where they are single, they are destructive."
A government of more stability is much wanted in this colony, and they are ready to receive it from the hands of Congress. And since I have begun with a maxim of state, I
25 will add another, namely, that a people may let a king fall, yet still remain a people; but if a king let his people slip from him, he is no longer a king. And as this is most certainly our case, why not proclaim to the world, in decisive terms, your own importance?
Shall we not be despised by foreign powers, for hesitating so long at a word?

1. Who is most likely the intended audience for this letter?

   (A) a stranger to the writer, someone highly placed in public office
   (B) a general newspaper audience
   (C) an ambassador with great political influence
   (D) someone with whom the writer is intimately associated
   (E) a friend from the writer's childhood from whom she had become estranged

2. How does the audience affect the tone and content of the passage?

   (A) The tone is more relaxed and the content more personal.
   (B) The tone is more formal and the content more ceremonial.
   (C) The tone is more ironic and the content more scathing.
   (D) The tone is more sarcastic and the content more personal.
   (E) The tone is more fiery and the content more specific.

3. The writer uses the comparison between the nation and a hand to suggest that

   (A) the hand that controls America controls the world
   (B) a country is only as great as its hired hands, its working men and women
   (C) individual parts work in unison; the part cannot survive apart from the whole
   (D) in the present situation, individual sacrifice is inevitable
   (E) America needs a helping hand from outsiders

4. As used in line 10, the word *humor* most nearly means

   (A) amusement
   (B) witticism
   (C) strain
   (D) tone
   (E) mood

5. In the context of the passage, the phrase "The eyes of our rulers have been closed, and a lethargy has seized almost every member" in lines 12 and 13 is used to convey the writer's

   (A) realization that the country is in a dire position
   (B) anger at defeat
   (C) relief at the leaders' ability to take a break from their hard work
   (D) preference for assertive leaders who are not afraid to be confrontational
   (E) frustration at the leaders' inaction in the face of a serious situation

6. In the phrase "Whilst the building is in flames," (lines 13–14) the building symbolizes

   (A) the writer's home
   (B) America
   (C) Great Britain
   (D) the state capitol
   (E) freedom

7. This symbol in question 6 is most effective because it

   (A) conveys the writer's feeling that the situation is desperate
   (B) communicates the writer's belief that time is on their side
   (C) shows the country's determination to survive
   (D) is a commonplace symbol used in many poems, essays, and novels
   (E) describes the country's terrible drought and its appalling results

8. The writer's goal in this passage is to

   (A) convince readers that she alone has the right solutions to the current problems
   (B) spark sympathy for America's beleaguered leaders
   (C) persuade the Congress to resign so new members can be elected
   (D) convince her reader to take action
   (E) stir up pity for the difficulties the writer has experienced living in Massachusetts

Answers

1. **D.** The last sentence in the first paragraph reveals that the audience for this letter is someone with whom the writer is intimately associated: "Thus I do suppress every wish, and silence every murmur, acquiescing in a painful separation from the companion of my youth, and the friend of my heart." The last phrase in the sentence, "friend of my heart," shows that the audience is a lover. It was, in fact, the writer's husband.

2. **A.** The intimate audience creates a more relaxed tone and more personal content. This is the direct opposite of choice B: The tone is more formal and the content more ceremonial. While choices C (The tone is more ironic and the content more scathing) and D (The tone is more sarcastic and the content more personal) could fit with a personal audience, the diction reveals that this is not the case here.

3. **C.** The writer uses the analogy between the nation and a hand to suggest that individual parts work in unison; the part cannot survive apart from the whole. This is revealed through a close reading of the relevant portion of the text: ". . . if our country perishes, it is as impossible to save an individual, as to preserve one of the fingers of a mortified hand."

4. **E.** As used in the first sentence of the second paragraph, the word *humor* most nearly means "mood." The writer has not been in the right frame of mind to write pleasantries, and so she has refrained from writing until now. As you answer vocabulary questions, remember to start by thinking of your own synonym for the word in question. Then look for the best match from among the choices.

5. **E.** In the context of the passage, the phrase "the eyes of our rulers have been closed, and a lethargy has seized almost every member" is used as a metaphor to convey the writer's frustration at the leaders' inaction in the face of a serious situation. The writer suggests that the leaders have abdicated their responsibility rather than taking action.

6. **B.** In the phrase "Whilst the building is in flames," the building symbolizes America. This is shown by her references throughout the passage to Boston and other locations in the colonies.

7. **A.** This symbol is most effective because it conveys the writer's feeling that the situation is desperate. The strong image of a building burning down conveys her sense of urgency.

8. **D.** The writer's goal is to convince her reader to take action. She states this outright in the last paragraph: "A government of more stability is much wanted in this colony, and they are ready to receive it from the hands of Congress. . . . And as this is most certainly our case, why not proclaim to the world, in decisive terms, your own importance?"

P A R T 4

Strategies for Success on Sentence Completions

Strategies for Success on Sentence Completions

What Are Sentence Completion Test Items?

Sentence completion questions test two areas of English language proficiency:

- A broad range of vocabulary, measured by your ability to understand the meaning of the sentences

- The ability to understand the logic of sentences, measured by your ability to insert the correct words

Sentence completion questions consist of a sentence with one or two blanks indicating a missing word or words within the sentences. With one blank, each answer choice will provide one word to fill in the blank. For sentences with two blanks, each answer choice will provide a pair of words, the first one to be inserted in the first blank and the second one in the second blank. Here is a typical one-blank sentence completion question:

Through his _____ he managed to cheat his partners out of their earnings.

(A) inefficiency
(B) ineptness
(C) machinations
(D) regime
(E) dealings

The Basic Five-Step Plan

Use the following five steps to solve sentence completion test items:

1. **Read the sentence through to get a general sense of its meaning. As you read, ask yourself the following questions:**
   - What does the sentence mean?
   - What word(s) will best fill in the blank(s)?
   - What part of speech is necessary to complete the sentence correctly? The part of speech may be a noun, verb, adjective, or adverb, for example.

2. **Anticipate the answer. Determine whether the missing word(s) must support or contrast with another idea in the sentence.**
   - Words such as *so, for, because, therefore,* and *as a result* signal support.
   - Words such as *although, not, but,* and *however* signal contrast.

3. **Read the five answer choices. Always check every one of the choices. Remember that the instructions for all the verbal questions ask you to choose the *best* answer. One choice may appear to fit, but it still might not be the best of the five choices. You have to try all the choices to find the best one.**

4. **If you have to guess, use these methods:**
   - First eliminate all choices that don't make sense.
   - As a last resort, select a difficult vocabulary word.

5. **Check your answer by reading the entire sentence with the word(s) you have selected in place. This will help you ensure that the sentence makes sense.**

Now reread the sample question. This time around, try approaching the question using the five-step approach you just learned. Then read the explanation in the answer that follows.

Through his _____ he managed to cheat his partners out of their earnings.

(A) inefficiency
(B) ineptness
(C) machinations
(D) regime
(E) dealings

Answer

C. After you have read the sentence through for sense, ask yourself, "Through *what* (blank) does one cheat?" The word *cheat* is a clue that the sentence is dealing with underhanded behavior, deception, or dishonesty. Further, the missing word must be a noun—a thing—to make sense in the sentence. In addition, the missing word must support the main idea of the sentence; there is no contrast here. Therefore, you might come up with answers such as this one: "Through *unfair means, evil planning,* or *conspiracy,* he managed to cheat his partners out of their earnings."

Now read the five answer choices, looking for the *best* answer. Try each choice, as follows:

(A) *Inefficiency* means "ineffectiveness or inability to produce the desired effect with minimum use of time or effort." Although inefficiency would fit the general meaning of the sentence, it does not imply a deliberate attempt to cheat.

(B) *Ineptness* means nearly the same as choice A, so neither word implies the deliberate attempt to defraud implicit in the word *cheat.* Since both choices are essentially the same, then why would (this choice) be better than choice A? It's not.

(C) *Machinations* are "a secret plot or scheme." This is the best choice so far, since it is the only word that implies an intentional effort to deceive.

(D) *Regime* means "a political system or manner of government or rule." It does not fit the meaning of the sentence as shown in the word *cheat.*

(E) *Dealings* means "business transactions." It is even more neutral than choices A and B, so it clearly doesn't fit with *cheat.*

> Even though you may feel sure of your answer, be sure to check it by rereading the entire sentence with the word(s) you have selected. This step helps you double-check that the sentence makes sense.

Strategies for Tackling Sentence Completion Questions

The strategies that follow apply to any sentence completion question. You will get a chance to revisit these tips as we look at more sample questions later in this chapter.

1. *Pace yourself.* Since sentence completion questions become more difficult as the section progresses, allocate your time carefully. If you spend too much time on the earlier, easier questions, you won't have enough time to complete the final, more difficult items.

2. *Know your vocabulary.* Define the answer choices and the most important words in the sentence. These key words will usually be nouns, verbs, adjectives, or adverbs. Look for roots, suffixes, and prefixes as you decode words.

3. *One letter can make all the difference, so read each answer choice carefully.* *Dessert* and *desert,* for instance, may appear the same on first glance, but *dessert* is a sweet served at the end of a meal, while *desert* is a dry, arid expanse of land.

4. *Always understand the sentence before you try the choices out.* You *must* understand the meaning of a sentence before you can start filling in the blanks. Otherwise, most of the words will seem to fit.

5. *Watch out for little words that can have a big effect on sentence meaning.* Little words like *not, but,* and *and* can make a big difference in what a sentence means. Be sure to pick the answer choice that makes sense in the context of the entire sentence.

6. *Look for words that have the same meaning.* If the words mean the same thing—as with *inefficiency* and *ineptness* in the sample question—then obviously neither word can be the correct choice. As a result, you can safely eliminate both words and concentrate on the other choices.

7. *Check part of speech and verb tenses.* Effective sentences are parallel: The grammatical elements are in the same form. For example, all the verbs in a sentence will end in *-ing* or *-ed.* When you are considering answer choices, look for ones that match with the rest of the sentence.

8. *With two-blank questions, test the first word in each pair to save time.* When the test item has two blanks, first read the sentence all the way through. Then try the first word of each answer pair in the first blank in the sentence. If it doesn't make sense, you can eliminate the pair of words without trying the second word at all.

9. *Don't be thrown by nonsensical answer choices.* Some answer choices will simply not make sense. Don't waste your time puzzling over a choice to determine exactly *why* it doesn't make sense. If you have better choices, just eliminate the choice that doesn't make sense.

10. *Look for the **best** choice, not the **perfect** choice.* Sometimes the best choice from among the five choices given is good but not necessarily the word that you would have chosen if you had written that sentence yourself. Nevertheless, if it is the *best* choice available, that's the one you want.

Using Contrast Clues to Answer Sentence Completion Questions with Two Missing Words

As you try to fill in the blanks by anticipating what word fits best, determine if the missing words *contrast* with another idea stated in the sentence. The following box lists the words and phrases used most often in standardized sentence completion questions to show contrast.

CONTRAST WORDS

although, though	not	but	rather than
yet	on the other hand	nevertheless	nonetheless
conversely	in contrast	on the contrary	however
despite	even though	in spite of	instead of

If you spot any these words or phrases in a sentence completion question, look for an answer that *contrasts* with an idea stated elsewhere in the sentence. Try it now.

Although the concert had been enjoyable, it was overly _____ and the three encores seemed _____.

(A) extensive, garrulous
(B) protracted, excessive
(C) inaudible, superfluous
(D) sublime, fortuitous
(E) contracted, lengthy

Answer

B. The contrast word *although* tells you that the second half of the sentence will state an idea that is the opposite of the idea stated in the first half. The first half of the sentence states that the concert had been enjoyable; therefore, you should look for words that suggest the opposite of enjoyable. The phrase "overly protracted" tells you the concert was drawn out and thus too long. This would clearly decrease the listener's enjoyment. *Excessive* encores are overdone and not necessary. This, too, is something the audience would not find enjoyable.

In choice A, *extensive* fits in the first blank, but *garrulous,* which means "very talkative," does not fit in the second blank. Eliminate choice B because *inaudible* does not make sense with *enjoyable;* the same is true with *sublime* (inspiring) in choice C and *contracted* in choice E.

Answer two-blank questions one blank at a time. Work on the first blank, and then on the second blank.

Using Support Clues to Answer Sentence Completion Questions with Two Missing Words

Support clues are words used to show supporting statements between main clauses. The following box lists the support clues used most often.

SUPPORT CLUES

so	for	because	therefore	moreover	besides
as a result	thus	consequently	accordingly	likewise	in addition
due to this	additionally	and	also	furthermore	

When you see one of these words or phrases in a sentence completion question, look for answer choices that support the other part of the sentence. The correct choice will most often be a synonym or near-synonym for a key word or words in the sentence. Try it now.

The team was _____ so it was _____ with cheers from its fans.

(A) undisciplined, regaled
(B) defeated, plagued
(C) famous, unhappy
(D) victorious, rewarded
(E) ecstatic, challenged

Answer

D. The team was *victorious* (it won). As a result, it was *rewarded* with cheers from its fans. If the fans cheered, the team must have done something good, so you can eliminate choices A and B. It makes no sense that a famous team would be unhappy with cheers, so choice C is wrong. Likewise, it makes no sense for an ecstatic team to be challenged with cheers, so choice E is wrong.

Using Summary Clues to Answer Sentence Completion Questions with Two Missing Words

Sometimes the blanks require a word that condenses an idea already mentioned in the sentence. In this case, you will be using summary clues to find the missing words. The transitions listed in the following box show that ideas are being summarized.

SUMMARY CLUES

as a result	hence	concluded	in conclusion	realized	decided
in short	in brief	in summary	finally	on the whole	

Look for a summary word as you work though the following test item.

After seeing shocking films of animals maimed and tortured by traps set by unscrupulous hunters, Leeza concluded that buying a fur coat would be ———, even ———.

(A) repulsive, immoral
(B) mandatory, immortal
(C) subliminal, sinful
(D) glamorous, priceless
(E) redundant, exorbitant

Answer

A. Summarizing the first part of the sentence, you know that the films of the creatures were *shocking* since they showed the "animals being maimed and tortured by traps." Therefore, the summary must show something highly offensive. Only choice A shows this: The speaker feels purchasing a coat would be not only *repulsive* but also *immoral* (not moral). Choice B is wrong because *mandatory* is the opposite of the meaning required by the sentence. The same is true with *glamorous* in choice D. *Subliminal* in choice C has nothing to do with the sentence; neither does *redundant* (superfluous) in choice E.

Using Cause-and-Effect Clues to Answer Sentence Completion Questions with Two Missing Words

The cause is *why* something happens. The effect is the *result,* what happens due to the cause. Writers use specific signal words to identify cause-and-effect relationships. The following box lists some of the most common ones you will encounter on the sentence completion items.

CAUSE-AND-EFFECT WORDS

accordingly	because	consequently		due to	thus
for	hence	if . . . then	as a result	so	when . . . then
in order to	so . . . that	therefore	since	so that	

Some signal words, such as *because, for,* and *thus,* can be used to show more than one type of relationship. As a result, you always have to analyze the sentence and the choices *completely* to make sure that you have found the correct relationship from among the ideas.

If you _____ your energy wisely, then you will never _____ for it.

(A) burn, cauterize
(B) use, want
(C) husband, economize
(D) expend, wish
(E) economize, alter

Answer

B. The *cause* is stated in the first part of the sentence; the *effect* or result, in the second part. If you *use* your energy wisely, then you will never *want* for it. It may be easier to see the cause-and-effect relationship if you replace the pronoun with the noun: "then you will never *want* for energy [it]."

You can eliminate choice A because it is illogical: *burn* and *cauterize* mean the same thing and so do not show cause and effect. The same is true of choice C. Choice D is wrong because *expending* your energy wisely does not mean that you will never *wish* for it again. Similarly, choice E does not make sense.

Practice SAT Exercises

DIRECTIONS: For each of the following sentences, choose the word or pair of words which, when inserted into the sentence, best fits the meaning of the sentence as a whole.

1. Louis XIV was the _____ of _____ elegance because he wore a different outfit for practically every hour of the day.

   (A) epitome, sartorial
   (B) paragon, tawdry
   (C) acme, gourmet
   (D) architect, gastronomic
   (E) root, European

2. Joan was abrasive and curt with her clients; as a result, her supervisor put a letter in her file citing her _____ and _____.

    (A) enthusiasm, impertinence
    (B) lethargy, stamina
    (C) diligence, acumen
    (D) rudeness, abrasiveness
    (E) discourtesy, incompetence

3. The ship was in a(n) _____ position, having lost its rudder; therefore, it was subject to the _____ of the prevailing winds.

    (A) inexcusable, direction
    (B) unintended, riptides
    (C) dangerous, breezes
    (D) untenable, vagaries
    (E) favored, weaknesses

4. A good trial lawyer will argue only what is central to an issue, eliminating _____ information or anything else that might _____ the client.

    (A) seminal, amuse
    (B) erratic, enhance
    (C) extraneous, jeopardize
    (D) prodigious, extol
    (E) reprehensible, initiate

5. We waited patiently for the storm to slacken, but it _____ refused to _____.

    (A) persistently, strengthen
    (B) stoutly, abate
    (C) consistently, perambulate
    (D) wanly, sublimate
    (E) sternly, mollify

6. Giving preference to his brother's son for that office smacks of _____ to me!

    (A) nihilism
    (B) chauvinism
    (C) sycophancy
    (D) pleonasm
    (E) nepotism

7. Favoring one child over another will only intensify _____ rivalry.

    (A) fraternal
    (B) sororal
    (C) parental

    (D) sibling
    (E) maternal

8. The general _____ his order; he had the traitor shot instead of _____.

    (A) countermanded, hanged
    (B) reinforced, hung
    (C) confirmed, roasted
    (D) rescinded, hung
    (E) reviewed, canonized

9. The _____ from the factory was _____; consequently, the thick, black smoke was evil-smelling and noxious.

    (A) effluvium, noisome
    (B) overflow, salubrious
    (C) outflow, aromatic
    (D) view, provoking
    (E) effluent, redolent

10. She was known for her _____; in short, no one was more _____ than she.

    (A) virtue, wanton
    (B) economy, profligate
    (C) altruism, selfless
    (D) conservatism, leftist
    (E) communism, conservative

Answers

1. **A.** The correct sentence reads: "Louis XIV was the epitome of sartorial elegance because he wore a different outfit for practically every hour of the day." Louis was the height (*epitome*) of fine dressing (*sartorial elegance*).

2. **D.** The correct sentence reads: "Joan was abrasive and curt with her clients; as a result, her supervisor put a letter in her file citing her rudeness and abrasiveness." The clues are "abrasive and curt." Since there is no contrast word, match all words in the second clause to the meaning of the words in the first clause.

3. **D.** The correct sentence reads: "The ship was in an untenable position, having lost its rudder; therefore, it was subject to the vagaries of the prevailing winds." An *untenable* position is one that cannot be defended. *Vagaries* means "erratic actions."

4. **C.** The correct sentence reads: "A good trial lawyer will argue only what is central to an issue, eliminating extraneous information or anything else that might jeopardize the client." When someone is *jeopardized,* he or she is placed in a position of danger or trouble.

5. **B.** The correct sentence reads: "We waited patiently for the storm to slacken, but it stoutly refused to abate." *Stoutly* is not used here to mean "heavy" or "overweight." Rather, it means "stubbornly." When something refuses to *abate,* it refuses to lessen.

6. **B.** The correct sentence reads: "Giving preference to his brother's son for that office smacks of nepotism to me!" *Nepotism* means "patronage or favoritism shown on the basis of family relationships."

7. **D.** The correct sentence reads: "Favoring one child over another will only intensify sibling rivalry." *Sibling* refers to brothers and sisters.

8. **A.** The correct sentence reads: "The general countermanded his order; he had the traitor shot instead of hanged." When an order is *countermanded,* it is reversed. Choice D is wrong because people are *hanged;* pictures are *hung.*

9. **E.** The correct sentence reads: "The effluent from the factory was redolent; consequently, the thick, black smoke was evil-smelling and noxious." The clue word *consequently* shows results. As a result of the *redolent* (smelly) *effluent* (material flowing forth), the black smoke was thick and odorous. You might have been able to define *effluent* from its root *fluent*—to flow.

10. **C.** The correct sentence reads: "She was known for her altruism; in short, no one was more selfless than she." *Altruistic* people are selfless; they give of themselves freely by doing good deeds for other people.

P A R T 5

Strategies for Success on the Multiple-Choice Writing Questions

Strategies for Success on the Multiple-Choice Writing Questions

What Are the Multiple-Choice Writing Items?

The new Writing test contains multiple-choice questions. Remember that the Writing test is 50 minutes long. During that time, you will have to write one essay (25 minutes) and answer multiple-choice questions (25 minutes).

The multiple-choice writing items fall into three different categories: *identifying sentence errors, improving sentences,* and *improving paragraphs.* Here are some of the topics you can expect to encounter on this part of the new SAT:

Shifts in verb tense	Pronoun usage
Parallel structure (matching sentence parts)	Subject and verb agreement
Subordination and coordination	Logical comparisons
Misplaced modifiers (describing words)	Dangling modifiers
Word order	Unclear pronouns
Wordiness	Sentence fragments and run-on sentences
Passive voice	Adjective and adverb use
Double negatives	Pronoun case
Idioms	Unity and cohesiveness

The Basic Five-Step Plan

Use the following five steps to solve multiple-choice Writing test items:

1. **Read the sentence or paragraph all the way through to get a general sense of its meaning.**

2. **Anticipate the answer. Determine how to best revise the sentence or passage.**

3. **Read the five answer choices. Always check each choice in context.**

4. **If you have to guess, use these methods:**

    -   First eliminate all choices that don't make sense.
    -   Keep it simple. Go for the answer that creates the most direct, least convoluted sentence.
    -   Make the effort to understand *why* you made the choice you did.
    -   If you can eliminate even one choice, it is to your advantage to guess.

5. **Check your answer by reading the entire sentence or passage with the revision you have selected in place.**

Identifying Sentence Errors

Using what you learned, choose the correct answers for these sample questions.

DIRECTIONS: The following sentences require you to identify errors in grammar, usage, style, and mechanics. Not every sentence has an error, and no sentence will have more than one error. In each sentence, the error, if there is one, is underlined and lettered. If there is an error, select the one underlined part that must be changed to make the sentence correct. If there is no error, select answer E. Elements of the sentence that are not underlined are not to be changed.

---

1. <u>Grasshoppers are</u> the <u>most commonly</u> consumed <u>insect, wasps</u> have the
       A   B   C

    highest protein content—<u>81 percent</u>—of all edible insects. <u>No error.</u>
                              D   E

2. <u>Her influence</u> over the next <u>40 years</u> was tremendous, <u>as she writes</u> essays,
       A   B   C

    lectured, and espoused the cause of fine <u>children's books</u> all over New York
                                              D

    and New England. <u>No error.</u>
                      E

Answers

1. **C.** This is a run-on sentence—two sentences incorrectly joined. The sentence can be corrected by adding a coordinating conjunction as follows: "Grasshoppers are the most commonly consumed insect, *but* wasps have the highest protein content—81 percent—of all edible insects."

2. **C.** This sentence has an error in verb tense. Every sentence must have a consistent use of verb tenses. Since the sentence begins in the past tense (*was*), the sentence must stay in the past tense (*wrote*). The correct sentence reads: "Her influence over the next 40 years was tremendous, as she wrote essays, lectured, and espoused the cause of fine children's books all over New York and New England."

Improving Sentences

DIRECTIONS: In each of the following sentences, part or all of the sentence is underlined. Each sentence is followed by five ways of phrasing the underlined part. Choose the best version of the underlined portion of each sentence. Choice A is always the same as the underlined portion of the original sentence. Choose answer A if you think the original sentence needs no revision.

3. Cultivating insects is far easier and requires much less space than <u>to raise</u> conventional Western protein sources such as cattle, pork, and chicken.

    (A) to raise
    (B) having raised
    (C) will be raising
    (D) raise
    (E) raising

4. Sam found a letter <u>in the mailbox that does not belong to her.</u>

    (A) in the mailbox that does not belong to her
    (B) in the mailbox to her that does not belong
    (C) in the mailbox which does not belong to her
    (D) that does not belong to her in the mailbox
    (E) in the mailbox who does not belong to her

Answers

3. **E.** The sentence can be improved by creating parallel structure: matching sentence parts. Here, the word *raising* parallels the word *cultivating* because both words end in *-ing*. The correct sentence reads: "Cultivating insects is far easier and requires much less space than raising conventional Western protein sources such as cattle, pork, and chicken."

4. D. The original sentence has a *misplaced modifier:* a word, phrase, or clause placed too far from the noun or pronoun it describes. This misplaced modifier creates a sentence that says the mailbox—not the letter—does not belong to Sam. Only choice D corrects the error. The correct sentence reads: "Sam found a letter that does not belong to her in the mailbox."

Improving Paragraphs

> **DIRECTIONS:** The following passage is an early draft of an essay. Some parts of the passage need to be rewritten. Read the passage and select the best answers to the questions that follow. Some questions are about particular sentences or parts of sentences and ask you to improve sentence structure and word choice. Other questions refer to parts of the essay or the entire essay and ask you to consider organization and development. In making your decisions, follow the conventions of standard written English.

> 1 (1) The leap into a "true" language is made when the pidgin speakers have children these children learn the pidgin as their native language. (2) Amazingly, though, the language they speak has much greater grammatical complexity. (3) Such children use a consistent word order, prefixes or suffixes, tenses to indicate past or future events,
> 5 complex sentence structures, and similar grammatical devices the pidgin lacked.

5. In context, which version of the underlined section of sentence 1 (reproduced here) is the best?

> *(1) The leap into a "true" language is made when the pidgin speakers <u>have children these children learn</u> the pidgin as their native language.*

(A) As it is now.
(B) have children, these children learn
(C) have children that learn
(D) have children, who learn
(E) learn

6. Which of the following sentences, if added immediately after sentence 3, would provide the best concluding sentence for the paragraph?

(A) Since 1979, in Nicaragua, children at schools for the deaf have essentially formed a pidgin.
(B) This newly formed, "true" language is called a creole.
(C) Like any spoken pidgin, LSN is a collection of jargon that has no consistent grammar; as a result, all speakers tend to use it differently.

(D) Many grammatical devices, such as tenses and complex sentence structures, don't exist in LSN.

(E) Children can create grammar—and the grammar created by different children is very similar.

Answers

5. **D.** As written, this is a run-on sentence, two sentences run together without the correct punctuation or conjunction. Choice B is a comma splice, a run-on sentence separated by a comma. Choice C is weak because we use *that* to refer to things, not people. Choice E changes the meaning of the sentence: in this revision, the pidgin speakers rather than the children learn the pidgin as their native language. Combining the two sentences through subordination of the second clause is the best choice because it is the most logical and concise revision. The corrected sentence reads: "The leap into a 'true' language is made when the pidgin speakers have children, who learn the pidgin as their native language."

6. **B.** Choice B is the best conclusion because it links to the topic sentence: "The leap into a 'true' language is made when the pidgin speakers have children, who learn the pidgin as their native language." The words *true language* in the conclusion pick up the same words in the topic sentence. Repetition is an effective method of creating unity.

How Do I Get a High Score on Identifying Sentence Error Questions and Improving Sentence Error Questions?

Let's start with reviewing sentences.

Define a Sentence

- Sentence: Leave!

- Sentence: You leave!

- Sentence: You leave early for the airport to make sure you have enough time to check in.

Each of these three word groups is a sentence because each meets the three requirements for a sentence. To be a sentence, a group of words must

1. Have a *subject* (**noun or pronoun**)

2. Have a *predicate* (**verb or verb phrase**)

3. Express a *complete thought*

Recognize Sentence Parts

Every *sentence* must have two parts: a *subject* and a *predicate*. The subject includes the noun or pronoun that tells what the subject is about. The predicate includes the verb that describes what the subject is doing. Here are some examples of complete sentences:

SENTENCE PARTS

[You]	Leave!
Understood subject	*Predicate*
You	leave!
Subject	*Predicate*
You	leave early for the airport to make sure you have enough time to check in.
Subject	*Predicate*

- To find the subject, ask yourself, What word is the sentence describing?

- To find an action verb, ask yourself, What did the subject do?

- If you can't find an action verb, look for a linking verb. The linking verbs include *to be* (*am, are, is, was, were, am being,* etc.), *appear, become, feel, grow, look, remain, seem, smell, sound, stay, taste, turn.*

In most sentences, the subject comes *before* the verb. This is not the case with questions. In a question, the subject often comes *after* the verb. Here are some examples:

Example: Is the ice cream on the counter?

The subject of the sentence is *ice cream.* The verb is *is* (a form of *to be*). The subject comes *after* the verb.

Example: Are you staying home tonight?

The subject of the sentence is *you.* The verb is *are* (a form of *to be*). The subject comes *after* the verb.

To find the subject in a question, rewrite the question as a statement. The question "Is the ice cream on the counter?" becomes "The ice cream is on the counter." Now the subject, *ice cream,* is in the usual position before the verb.

Identify Sentence Types

There are two types of clauses: *independent* and *dependent.*

■ *Independent clauses* are complete sentences because they have a subject and a verb, and they express a complete thought.

■ *Dependent clauses* are not complete sentences because they do not express a complete thought—even though they have a subject and a verb.

Independent and dependent clauses can be used in a number of ways to form the four basic types of sentences: *simple, compound, complex, compound-complex.*

Simple Sentences

A *simple sentence* has one independent clause. That means it has one subject and one verb—although either or both can be compound. In addition, a simple sentence can have adjectives and adverbs. A simple sentence cannot have another independent clause or any subordinate clauses.

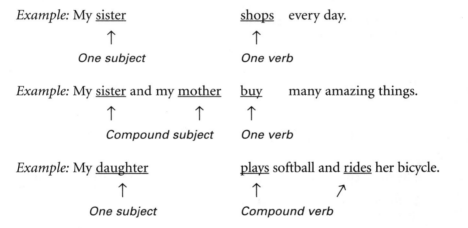

Example: My <u>sister</u>　<u>shops</u>　every day.
　　　　　↑　　　　↑
　　One subject　　One verb

Example: My <u>sister</u> and my <u>mother</u>　<u>buy</u>　many amazing things.
　　　　↑　　　　↑　　↑
　　　Compound subject　One verb

Example: My <u>daughter</u>　<u>plays</u> softball and <u>rides</u> her bicycle.
　　　　　↑　　　↑　　　↗
　　One subject　　Compound verb

Compound Sentences

A *compound sentence* consists of two or more independent clauses. The independent clauses can be joined in one of two ways:

■ With a coordinating conjunction: *for, and, nor, but, or, yet, so*

■ With a semicolon (;)

As with a simple sentence, a compound sentence can't have any subordinate clauses.

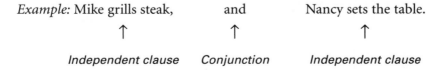

Example: Mike grills steak,　　and　　Nancy sets the table.
　　　　↑　　　↑　　　↑
　Independent clause　Conjunction　Independent clause

You may also add a conjunctive adverb to this construction;

Nancy cooks every day; <u>however,</u> Mike cooks only on weekends.

Complex Sentences
A *complex sentence* contains one independent clause and at least one dependent clause. The independent clause is called the *main clause*. These sentences use *subordinating conjunctions* to link ideas.

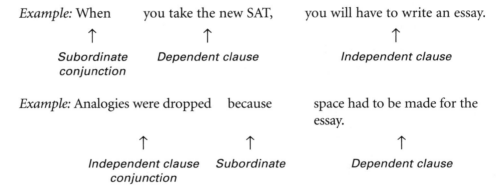

The most common subordinating conjunctions are listed in the following box.

SUBORDINATING CONJUNCTIONS

after	although	as	because	before	even if
even though	if	rather than	since	so	so that
though	unless	until	when	whether	while

Compound-Complex Sentences
A *compound-complex sentence* has at least two independent clauses and at least one dependent clause. The dependent clause can be part of the independent clause.

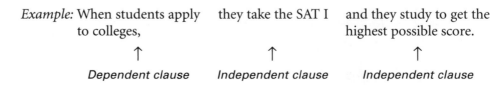

Example: Josh got a new car for graduation,	but he drove badly	so he took driver's education classes over the summer.
↑	↑	↑
Independent clause	*Independent clause*	*Dependent clause*

Identify and Correct Run-on Sentences and Comma Splices

A *run-on sentence* is two incorrectly joined independent clauses.

Example: The Great Seal of the United States was first used by George Washington he glued it onto a document.

A *comma splice* is a run-on sentence with a comma where the two independent clauses run together.

Example: Bob Hope was born in England, his parents came to America when Hope was four years old.

Don't be fooled—run-on sentences are not necessarily long. Some run-on sentences can be very short.

Example: People can be cold they can be cruel.

Example: Roses are red violets are blue.

You can correct a run-on sentence in several different ways.

- Separate the run-on sentence into two sentences with end punctuation such as periods, exclamation marks, and question marks.

  Example: Bob Hope was born in England. His parents came to America when Hope was four years old.

- Add a coordinating conjunction (*and, nor, but, or, for, yet, so*) to create a compound sentence. Be sure to use a comma before the coordinating conjunction in a compound sentence, unless the two independent clauses are very short.

  Example: Bob Hope was born in England, and his parents came to America when Hope was four years old.

- Add a subordinating conjunction to create a complex sentence.

  Example: Bob Hope was born in England, although his parents came to America when Hope was four years old.

- Use a semicolon to create a compound sentence. You may choose to add a conjunctive adverb, such as *however, nevertheless, nonetheless, moreover.*

  Example: Bob Hope was born in England; however, his parents came to America when Hope was four years old.

■ Rewrite the sentence.

Example: Born in England, Bob Hope was four years old when his parents moved to America.

Which revision is best? Choose the way that best suits your purpose, audience, and tone.

Identify and Correct Fragments

As its name suggests, a *sentence fragment* is a group of words that does not express a complete thought. Most times, a fragment is missing a subject, a verb, or both. Other times, a fragment may have a subject and a verb but still not express a complete thought. Fragments can be phrases as well as clauses.

■ Fragment missing a subject

Example: Unanimously voted today to develop a new SAT I.

■ Fragment missing a verb

Example: The Trustees of the College Board to develop a new SAT I.

■ Fragment missing a subject and a verb

Example: While listening to the radio.

■ Fragment with a subject and a verb that does not express a complete thought

Example: Because William Cody killed nearly 5000 buffalo.

You can correct a fragment by adding the missing part to the sentence or by omitting the subordinating conjunction. In some instances, you can also correct a fragment by adding it to another sentence.

Fragment	Sentence
Unanimously voted today to develop a new SAT I.	The Trustees of the College Board unanimously voted today to develop a new SAT I.
The Trustees of the College Board to develop a new SAT I.	The Trustees of the College Board voted to develop a new SAT I.
While listening to the radio.	While listening to the radio, Martha practiced the latest dance steps.
Because William Cody killed nearly 5000 buffalo.	Because William Cody killed nearly 5000 buffalo, he became famous as "Buffalo Bill."
	William Cody killed nearly 5000 buffalo.

Eliminate Unnecessary Words

Some of the questions on the SAT Writing test will ask you to revise sentences to make them simple and direct. For each question, look to cut unnecessary details or ideas that have already been stated. Keep the important detail, but cut any words and ideas that have already been stated in other ways.

Try this sample SAT-style question:

1. <u>At this point in time</u>, the diner was the heart of the neighborhood.

    (A) At this point in time
    (B) Now
    (C) At the present time
    (D) Today it is believed by many that
    (E) As a matter of fact, right now

Answer

1. **B.** This is the most direct, concise choice.

Use Adjectives and Adverbs Correctly

■ Use an adjective to describe a noun or a pronoun.

■ Use an adjective after a linking verb. A *linking verb* connects a subject with a descriptive word. Here are the most common linking verbs: *be* (*is*, *am*, *are*, *was*, *were*, and so on), *seem*, *appear*, *look*, *feel*, *smell*, *sound*, *taste*, *become*, *grow*, *remain*, *stay*, and *turn*.

Example: Tofu cooked this way *tastes* more *delicious* (not *deliciously*).

■ Use an adverb to describe a verb, an adjective, or another adverb.

Use an adverb to	Example
Describe a verb	Experiments using dynamite must be done *carefully.*
Describe an adjective	Rick had an *unbelievably large* appetite for pizza.
Describe an adverb	They sang *so sweetly.*

Follow these rules to make correct comparisons with adjectives and adverbs.

■ Use the comparative degree (*-er* or *more* form) to compare two things.

Example: Your test seems <u>longer</u> than mine. I don't think it is <u>more difficult,</u> however.

■ Use the superlative form (*-est* or *most* form) to compare more than two things.

Example: This is the <u>longest</u> test I have ever taken. It is also the <u>most difficult</u> test I have ever taken.

■ Never use *-er* and *more* or *-est* and *most* together.

Incorrect: This is the <u>more longer</u> of the two tests.

Correct: This is the <u>longer</u> of the two tests.

Review the following box.

Part of Speech	Positive	Comparative	Superlative
Adjective	wide	wider	widest
Adverb	widely	more widely	most widely
Adjective	faithful	more faithful	most faithful
Adverb	faithfully	more faithfully	most faithfully

Good and *bad* do not follow these guidelines. They have irregular forms.

Part of Speech	Positive	Comparative	Superlative
Adjective	good	better	best
Adverb	well	better	best
Adjective	bad	worse	worst
Adverb	badly	worse	worst

Try these sample SAT-style questions:

2. Today's mild weather was <u>more comfortable</u> than yesterday's brisk weather, so the teacher decided to hold class outdoors.

   (A) more comfortable
   (B) most comfortable
   (C) comfortable
   (D) comfortabler
   (E) most comfortablest

3. The dietician thinks that salmon is the <u>better</u> of all fish because it is health-ful and tasty, as well as being easily available.

   (A) better
   (B) good
   (C) goodest
   (D) best
   (E) most good

Answers

2. **A.** This is correct as written, because two things are being compared.
3. **D.** Use the superlative degree, *best,* because more than two things are being compared.

Use the Correct Pronoun Case

Case is the form of a noun or pronoun that shows how it is used in a sentence. English has three cases: *nominative, objective,* and *possessive.* The following box shows the three cases.

Nominative (Pronoun as subject)	Objective (Pronoun as objective)	Possessive (Ownership)
I	me	my, mine
you	you	your, yours
he	him	his
she	her	her, hers
it	it	its
we	us	our, ours
they	them	their, theirs
who	whom	whose
whoever	whomever	whoever

- Use the nominative case to show the subject of a verb.

  Example: We spoke to the teacher about the test.

- Use the objective case to show the noun or pronoun receives the action.

  Example: The teacher was willing to speak to *us.*

- Use the possessive case to show ownership.

  Example: The book is *mine,* not *yours* or *his.*

Try these sample SAT-style questions.

4. The principal knows of no other teacher who is as intelligent as <u>her</u>, and so has recommended her for a raise.

 (A) her
 (B) she
 (C) hers
 (D) them
 (E) they

5. <u>Louise and me</u> have decided to take the SAT this spring, because we have studied all winter.

 (A) Louise and me
 (B) Me and Louise
 (C) Louise and I
 (D) Louise and her
 (E) Her and me

Answers

4. **B.** *She* is the subject of the understood verb *is*. Therefore, the pronoun is in the nominative case. Read the sentence to yourself this way: "The principal knows of no other teacher who is as intelligent as she [is], and so has recommended her for a raise." Choices D and E are wrong because they are plural and the subject (teacher) is singular.

5. **C.** Use the nominative case, since "Louise and I" is the subject of the sentence. They are doing the action. Read the sentence to yourself this way: "[We] have decided to take the SAT this spring, because we have studied all winter." Then read it this way: "Louise and I have decided to take the SAT this spring, because we have studied all winter."

Use Active and Passive Voice Correctly

■ In the *active voice,* the subject performs the action named by the verb.

Example: Ben Franklin first wanted a turkey instead of an eagle as our national symbol.

■ In the *passive voice,* the subject receives the action.

Example: A turkey instead of an eagle was first wanted by Benjamin Franklin as our national symbol.

The active voice is usually preferred to the passive voice because it is less wordy. Try this sample SAT-style question.

6. As he was walking near the boarded-up shopping complex in the center of town, <u>a gold bracelet was found by Herman.</u>

    (A) a gold bracelet was found by Herman.
    (B) Herman found a gold bracelet.
    (C) a bracelet made of gold was found by Herman.
    (D) a gold bracelet Herman found.
    (E) a gold bracelet by Herman was found.

Answer

  6. B. The passive construction has been revised to be active. This makes the sentence less wordy.

Revise Sentences to Create Parallel Structure

Parallel structure means putting ideas of the same rank in the same grammatical structure. Words, phrases, and clauses should be parallel. Match each subsequent element to the first part of the sentence.

■ Parallel words

  Example: A healthful diet contains <u>fruits</u>, <u>vegetables</u>, and <u>protein</u>.

■ Parallel phrases

  Example: The state government can afford <u>to make classes smaller</u>, <u>to repair potholes faster</u>, and <u>to pick up trash earlier</u>, too.

Try these sample SAT-style questions:

7. First it rained, <u>then hail was falling, and finally snow came down.</u>

    (A) then hail was falling, and finally snow came down.
    (B) then hail fell, and we got a lot of snow, too.
    (C) then hail came down, and finally it was snowing.
    (D) then it was hailing, and finally it was snowing.
    (E) then it hailed, and finally it snowed.

8. We moved our sleeping bags closer to the fire, hung blankets over the windows, and <u>more logs were added to the blaze.</u>

    (A) more logs were added to the blaze.
    (B) added more logs to the blaze.
    (C) adding more logs to the blaze.
    (D) adding to the blaze more logs.
    (E) will add more logs to the blaze.

Answers

7. **E.** Each clause should be parallel to "it rained." Start with the clause "it rained." Only "it hailed" and "it snowed" have the same form. The correct sentence reads: "First it rained, then it hailed, and finally it snowed."

8. **B.** The past tense verb *added* parallels *moved* and *hung*. The corrected sentence reads: "We moved our sleeping bags closer to the fire, hung blankets over the windows, and added more logs to the blaze."

Correct Dangling and Misplaced Modifiers

A *dangling modifier* is a word or phrase that describes something that has been left out of the sentence.

Dangling: Making startling new discoveries in science, the Renaissance was a time of rebirth.

Correct: The Renaissance was a time of rebirth when people made startling new discoveries in science.

A *misplaced modifier* is a describing word that is placed too far away from the noun or the pronoun that it is describing. As a result, the sentence does not convey its meaning. It may also produce confusion or amusement. To correct the error, move the modifier as close as possible to the word or phrase it is describing.

Example: The writer read from his new book wearing glasses.

The modifier *wearing glasses* is in the wrong place. The sentence states that the book, not the writer, was wearing glasses. Move the modifier so that the sentence reads: "The writer *wearing glasses* read from his new book."

Try these sample SAT-style questions.

9. Confirming our conversation, <u>the shipment will be ordered</u> on Monday.

   (A) the shipment will be ordered on Monday
   (B) ordering of the shipment will take place
   (C) I have arranged for the shipment to be ordered
   (D) the shipment ordered
   (E) the shipment has been ordered

10. Please take the time to look over <u>the pamphlet that is enclosed with your family.</u>

   (A) the pamphlet that is enclosed with your family.
   (B) the family pamphlet that is enclosed.
   (C) the family that is enclosed with your pamphlet.

(D) the enclosed pamphlet with your family.

(E) the pamphlet that with your family is enclosed.

Answers

9. **C.** Here, the main clause has been rewritten so the subject is modified by the phrase that was dangling. The corrected sentence reads: "Confirming our conversation, I have arranged for the shipment to be ordered on Monday."

10. **D.** As written, the sentence states that the pamphlet is enclosed with the family. The writer means to say that the person should look over the pamphlet with his or her family. Only choice D states the writer's meaning accurately. The corrected sentence reads: "Please take the time to look over the enclosed pamphlet with your family."

How Do I Get a High Score on Improving Paragraph Questions?

Understand the Passage

Always start by making sure you understand the passage. Read it through several times to get the overall meaning. This will help you grasp how ideas are linked.

Look for Relationships among Ideas

Some questions on this part of the test depend on how the sentences fit together. This is especially true when you are asked to clarify unclear pronoun references, correct shifts in tense, and revise run-on sentences and fragments. Therefore, you have to read the sentence(s) under discussion as well as the sentence before and after to answer many of these questions correctly. Study the following model.

---

1   (2) A surprisingly large percentage of the population is burdened by negative feelings they carry through relationships over time. (3) Guilt, bitterness, and cruelty can be emotionally destructive to you and your family (4) You must get rid of them if you wish to lead a happy and productive life. (5) Ridding yourself of these bad feelings can
5   often help you move on with your life.

---

1. In context, which is the best version of the underlined portions of sentences 3 and 4 (reproduced here)?

(A) As it is now.

(B) Guilt, bitterness, and cruelty can be emotionally destructive to you and your family, you must get rid of them

(C) Guilt, bitterness, and cruelty can be emotionally destructive to you and your family, so you must get rid of them

    (D) Because guilt, bitterness, and cruelty can be emotionally destructive to you and your family, you must get rid of them

    (E) Guilt, bitterness, and cruelty can be emotionally destructive to you and your family, so you must get rid of these harmful feelings

Answer

1. **E.** There are two problems here: a run-on sentence and an unclear pronoun reference. Does the pronoun *them* refer to the emotions or the family? Choice A is a run-on sentence, two sentences run together without correct punctuation or conjunctions. Choice B incorrectly joins two complete sentences with a comma, creating a comma splice. Choices C and D correctly join the two sentences but do not correct the unclear pronoun reference. Only choice E correctly joins the two sentences and corrects the unclear pronoun reference.

Predict Appropriate Additions and Conclusions

Another type of question asks you to decide which sentence would follow the previous one or what conclusion would best suit the draft. Thus, you have to consider how the entire passage is developed. Follow these steps:

- Identify the writer's main idea. It may be stated in the topic sentence or you will have to infer it from details in the passage.

- Identify the writer's slant. For example, in a persuasive essay, what is the writer's opinion?

- See which choice best fits with the main idea and the writer's opinion as developed in the draft.

Try these sample SAT-style questions:

---

1   (1) Insect cuisine may not be standard food in the U.S. (2) However, as Miguel Vilar notes in *Science World,* 80 percent of the world's population savors bugs, either as staples of their everyday diet or as rare delicacies. (3) Entomophany (consuming insects intentionally) has yet to catch on in America and Europe in spite of the
5   superior nutritional content of edible insects compared to other food sources. (4) It's time that changed.

---

2. Including a paragraph on which of the following would most strengthen the writer's argument?

    (A) The reasons why people should eat insects.

    (B) The great disadvantages of eating insects.

(C) The different types of insects that people around the world consume.

(D) How to prepare insects so they are palatable or at least edible.

(E) Other odd foods that people around the world consume and reasons why they favor these foods.

---

1   (1) The Earth's atmosphere initially consisted of hydrogen and helium gas. (2) These gasses, being too light for Earth's gravity to hold and subject to high-energy radiation, were "boiled off" into space, and gradually replaced by gasses expelled in volcanic eruptions. (3) Additionally, some water entered the system from icy comets that hit the

5   Earth. (4) Eventually, a new atmosphere was formed, in which carbon dioxide was in much greater concentrations than it is today, and oxygen was probably less than 1% of the atmosphere (Carslaw 2-5).

---

3. Which sentence would be most appropriate to follow sentence 2?

(A) On a similar note, one source of better information about this time period could be biologically mediated isotope distributions in the geological record.

(B) These bacteria then trapped much of the carbon and released oxygen into the atmosphere.

(C) This process is known as "outgassing," and among these gasses were carbon dioxide, chlorine, methane, nitrogen, water vapor, ammonia, and various sulfur compounds.

(D) The oldest fossils of such bacteria are from 3.8 billion years ago, which implies that this buildup of oxygen was a gradual process at first.

(E) High-energy radiation interacted with oxygen molecules in the upper atmosphere and formed ozone.

Answers

2. A. The writer's main idea is stated in the first two sentences: *Insect cuisine may not be standard food in the U.S., but Miguel Vilar notes in* Science World *that 80 percent of the world's population savors bugs, either as staples of their everyday diet or as rare delicacies.* The writer's slant is stated in the last sentence: *It's time that changed.* Clearly, the writer is in favor of people consuming insects. Thus, a paragraph on the advantages of consuming insects would best strengthen the writer's argument.

3. C. Sentence 2 discusses how gasses were "boiled off" into space and gradually replaced by gasses expelled in volcanic eruptions. This is a process. Thus, naming and describing the process in the following sentence makes the most sense.

Practice Multiple-Choice Writing Items

DIRECTIONS: The following sentences require you to identify errors in grammar, usage, style, and mechanics. Not every sentence has an error and no sentence will have more than one error. Each sentence error, if there is one, is underlined and lettered. If there is an error, select the one underlined part that must be changed to make the sentence correct. Elements of the sentence that are not underlined are not to be changed.

1. Facing down <u>hostility and prejudice</u> with <u>unshakable dignity</u> and
A   B

   <u>playing that was superb,</u> Robinson <u>was named</u> Rookie of the Year. <u>No error.</u>
C   D   E

2. The small items sold well, <u>but</u> Strauss found himself <u>stuck with</u> the rolls of
A   B

   <u>canvas it</u> was not heavy <u>enough to</u> be used for tents. <u>No error.</u>
C   D   E

3. The <u>glittering necklaces</u> of Lisa Chin <u>has earned</u> high praise <u>not only</u> from
A   B   C

   the critics <u>but also from</u> jewelry collectors the world over. <u>No error.</u>
D   E

4. <u>Although</u> you use a computer spreadsheet <u>to keep track</u> of your
A   B

   <u>investments, debts, and budget,</u> <u>one</u> must not overspend and rely on credit to
C   D

   make up the shortfall. <u>No error.</u>
E

5. <u>The vacationers saw</u> the Ruyterkade schooner market in <u>Curacao; in addition,</u>
A   B

   they danced <u>at the carnival</u> in Charlotte Amalie, St. Thomas, and
C

   <u>nearly spoke to</u> two dozen real West Indian sailors. <u>No error.</u>
D   E

DIRECTIONS: In each of the following sentences, part or all of the sentence is underlined. Each sentence is followed by five ways of phrasing the underlined part. Choose the best version of the underlined portion of each sentence. Choice A is always the same as the underlined portion of the original sentence. Choose answer A if you think the original sentence needs no revision.

6. Nourishing, low-calorie foods such as fresh fruits, vegetables, lean meats, and seafood <u>is rarely served</u> in homes where people do not have enough money.

   (A) is rarely served
   (B) are rarely served
   (C) is rare served
   (D) is never served
   (E) was rarely served

7. Dr. Seuss, one of the world's most famous children's book <u>authors, he has written</u> books for adults and advertising copy as well.

   (A) authors, he has written
   (B) authors, written by him has been
   (C) authors him has written
   (D) authors written
   (E) authors, has written

8. The story opens in the Dutch West <u>Indies most of the action</u> takes place on a tiny, isolated *cay* (an island composed mainly of coral and sand) in the Caribbean.

   (A) Indies most of the action
   (B) Indies, most of the action
   (C) Indies, the action mostly
   (D) Indies, when most of the action
   (E) Indies, but most of the action

9. The great <u>explorer's astonishing discovery brought him fame</u> around the world and assured him a lucrative book contract.

   (A) explorer's astonishing discovery brought him fame
   (B) explorer's astonishing discovery brought them fame
   (C) explorer's astonishing discovery brought his company fame
   (D) explorer's astonishing discovery brought fame
   (E) fame that was brought to the explorer because of his astonishing discovery

10. After the major argument at the wedding, reconciliation was the <u>most furthest thing</u> from their minds.

(A) most furthest thing
(B) furthest thing
(C) more furthest thing
(D) most further thing
(E) further thing

DIRECTIONS: The following passage is an early draft of an essay. Some parts of the passage need to be rewritten. Read the passage and select the best answers to the questions that follow. Some questions are about particular sentences or parts of sentences and ask you to improve sentence structure and word choice. Other questions refer to parts of the essay or the entire essay and ask you to consider organization and development. In making your decisions, follow the conventions of standard written English. Choose the best answer. Questions 11 to 15 are based on the following draft of an essay.

---

1   (1) The ancient Greeks and Romans dabbled with the idea of building diving bells (2) It wasn't until 1578 that a practical submarine was planned. (3) Cornelius van Drebbel, a Dutch inventor, used many of Bourne's ideas when he created his pre-submarine, "The Turtle," early in the next century. (4) They were made of wood
5   and shaped like a barrel. (5) They were one-person submergibles used during the American revolution against British warships.
   (6) To refuel the U-boats at sea, the Germans created 1,000-to-1,600 ton U-cruisers. (7) It took almost another century for the first true submarines to make their appearance, the German "Unterseeboots." (8) Nicknamed "U-boats," these powerful sub-
10   marines weighed 500-to-700 tons.

---

11. In context, which is the best way to revise and combine the underlined portion of sentences 1 and 2 (reproduced here)?

---

(1) The ancient Greeks and Romans dabbled with the idea of building diving bells (2) It wasn't until 1578 that a practical submarine was planned.

(A) As it is now.
(B) Even though the ancient Greeks and Romans dabbled with the idea of building diving bells, it wasn't
(C) The ancient Greeks and Romans dabbled with the idea of building diving bells it wasn't

(D) The ancient Greeks and Romans dabbled with the idea of building diving bells, it wasn't
(E) The ancient Greeks and Romans dabbled with the idea of building diving bells, for it wasn't

12. Which sentence would be most appropriate to follow sentence 2?

(A) The inventor was the British mathematician William Bourne.
(B) During World War II, the Germans began using submarines against British and American forces.
(C) U-boats were among the most feared weapons of World War II.
(D) Many people refuse to travel in submarines because they fear being in enclosed spaces.
(E) Submarines are rarely used for transporting passengers; rather, their use is largely restricted to military maneuvers.

13. In context, which is the best way to revise and combine the underlined portion of sentences 4 and 5 (reproduced here)?

> *They were made of wood and shaped like a barrel. They were one-person submersibles used* during the American Revolution against British warships.

(A) They were made of wood and shaped like a barrel. They were one-person submersibles used
(B) They were made of wood and shaped like a barrel they were one-person submersibles used
(C) Having been made of wood and shaped like a barrel, they were submersibles used by one person
(D) Made of wood and shaped like a barrel, this one-person submersible was used
(E) Because they are made of wood and shaped like a barrel, they are one-person submersibles used

14. What is the best order of sentences in the last paragraph to create logic and unity?

(A) As it is now.
(B) 7, 8, 6
(C) 7, 6, 8
(D) 6, 8, 7
(E) 6, 7, 8

15. Concluding with a paragraph on which of the following would most strengthen the writer's unity and logic?

   (A) The effectiveness of the U-boats
   (B) How submarines have caused great destruction
   (C) Why people should consider traveling in submarines
   (D) Other forms of transportation, especially cars, trains, and buses
   (E) The history of the world's major conflicts, especially World Wars I and II

Answers

1. **C.** Remember that all elements in a sentence have to be in the same grammatical form. This is called *parallel structure.* "Superb playing"—not "playing that was superb"—parallels "unshakable dignity," since both phrases are composed of a noun modified by an adjective. The correct sentence reads: "Facing down hostility and prejudice with unshakable dignity and superb playing, Robinson was named Rookie of the Year."

2. **C.** This is a run-on sentence, the error occurring between the two independent clauses. Correct the sentence as follows: "The small items sold well, but Strauss found himself stuck with the rolls of canvas *because* it was not heavy enough to be used for tents."

3. **B.** This question tests your knowledge of subject-verb agreement. The subject—*necklaces*—is plural. Thus, it requires a plural verb—*have earned.* All the other choices are correct. The correct sentence reads: "The glittering necklaces of Lisa Chin have earned high praise not only from the critics but also from jewelry collectors the world over."

4. **D.** This question tests consistency of pronoun use: Use the same pronoun throughout. Since the sentence begins with the word *you,* the writer cannot switch to *one* in the middle of the sentence. The corrected sentence reads: "Although you use a computer spreadsheet to keep track of your investments, debts, and budget, you must not overspend and rely on credit to make up the shortfall."

5. **D.** This is a misplaced modifier. The phrase "nearly spoke" means that the tourists *almost* spoke to the sailors. Since this sentence refers to the events the vacationers did indeed complete, the phrase should read "spoke to nearly." The complete sentence should read: "The vacationers saw the Ruyterkade schooner market in Curacao; in addition, they danced at the carnival in Charlotte Amalie, St. Thomas, and spoke to nearly two dozen real West Indian sailors."

6. **B.** This question tests your understanding of subject-verb agreement. The plural subject *foods* takes a plural verb. Here, use *are,* the plural form of the verb *to be:* "Nourishing, low-calorie *foods* such as fresh fruits, vegetables, lean meats, and seafood *are* rarely served in homes where people do

not have enough money." Ignore the intervening prepositional phrase: "such as fresh fruits, vegetables, lean meats, and seafood."

7. E. As written, the sentence is incorrect because there is no reason to include the pronoun *he.* Always start by looking for the easiest and least convoluted way of revising the sentence. The easiest way is deleting the pronoun *he.* The other choices create wordy, awkward, and incorrect sentences. The correct sentence reads: "Dr. Seuss, one of the world's most famous children's book authors, has written books for adults and advertising copy as well."

8. E. As written, this is a run-on sentence, two incorrectly joined sentences. Merely adding a comma (choice B) creates a comma splice. Choice C simply rephrases the sentence but does not correct the run-on sentence. Choice D is illogical, because the subordinating conjunction *when* does not make sense in context. The correct sentence reads: "The story opens in the Dutch West Indies, but most of the action takes place on a tiny, isolated *cay* (an island composed mainly of coral and sand) in the Caribbean."

9. C. Do not use a pronoun to refer to a noun's possessive form (the form that shows ownership). In addition, you cannot use a noun's possessive form as the antecedent to a pronoun, unless the pronoun is also in the possessive case. Thus, since the pronoun *him* is not possessive, it cannot be used to refer to the possessive noun *explorer's.* Choice C puts both the noun and the pronoun in the possessive case (*explorer's, his*)

10. B. Never add both *-er* and *more* (or *less*) or both *-est* and *most* (or *least*) to a modifier. Thus, the corrected sentence should read: "After the major argument at the wedding, reconciliation was the *furthest thing* from their minds."

11. B. You can link related ideas in many ways. When you subordinate ideas, for instance, you make one idea more important than the other. The more important idea is placed in the main clause. Use a subordinating conjunction to link the two sentences and create unity. The subordinating conjunction "even though" shows a cause-and-effect relationship, appropriate to the ideas expressed here. Choice C is a run-on sentence; choice D is a comma splice. The coordinating conjunction *for* in choice E does not make sense in context (although the conjunction *but* would). The correct sentence reads: "Even though the ancient Greeks and Romans dabbled with the idea of building diving bells, it wasn't until 1578 that a practical submarine was planned."

12. A. The sentence "The inventor was the British mathematician William Bourne" directly links with the previous sentence on the planning of a practical submarine and the following sentence on subsequent submarines. The phrase "Bourne's ideas" in sentence 3 is a clue that the previous sentence should refer to Bourne. None of the other sentences fits in context.

13. **D.** Choice D best makes the relationship between ideas clear. Choice B creates a run-on sentence, while choice C is awkward. Choice E changes the meaning of the sentence. It also changes the tense, which violates the consistency of the draft. The correct sentence reads: "Made of wood and shaped like a barrel, this one-person submersible was used during the American Revolution against British warships."

14. **B.** The passage should read: "It took almost another century for the first true submarines to make their appearance, the German 'Unterseeboots.' Nicknamed 'U-boats,' these powerful submarines weighed 500-to-700 tons. To refuel the U-boats at sea, the Germans created 1,000-to-1,600 ton U-cruisers."

15. **A.** Since the entire passage describes submarines from past to present, concluding with a passage on the effectiveness of the U-boats not only follows from the previous paragraph but also shows the progression of submarines from their invention to World War II. Here is a sample paragraph:

---

1 In addition to their size and strength, the U-boats were powerful weapons because they could travel at great speeds underwater. Snorkels, long tubes projecting above the surface of the water, provided U-boats with air while they were submerged. The U-boats launched magnetic torpedoes that zeroed in on the target's hull and acoustical torpe-
5 does that used the noise of the target's propellers to locate the target.

PART 6

Strategies for Success
on the Essay Question

Strategies for Success on the Essay Question

The essay question appears on the new Writing test section of the SAT. You have 25 minutes in which to write the essay.

What Will I Be Required to Write?

Since there are no past exams to analyze, we can predict the types of essays only from the sample questions published by the College Board. Thus far, the essays fall into two main types: *persuasive* and *expository*.

Persuasive Prompts

Persuasive essays argue a point. You must agree or disagree with the writing prompt and give specific reasons to support your opinion. Techniques for writing a successful SAT persuasive essay are discussed at length later in this chapter. Below are two simulated persuasive writing prompts:

Example 1

Philosopher Lewis Mumford argues that the space program is a "futile waste of technology, strictly a military by-product."

Assignment: Does the space program have a practical value? If so, what? If not, what limits should we place on it? Construct an argument explaining your position. Support your views with relevant reasons and examples from your experiences, observations, and reading. To strengthen your position, you might wish to consider alternative or opposing views.

Example 2

The United States should remain an island of plenty in a sea of hunger. The future of humanity is at stake. We are not responsible for the rest of the world.

Assignment: Agree or disagree with this statement. Construct an argument explaining your position. Support your views with relevant reasons and examples from your experiences, observations, and reading. To strengthen your position, you might wish to consider alternative or opposing views.

Expository Prompts

Expository essays explain, show, or tell about a topic. You must analyze a quote or prompt and then give specific information about it. Techniques for writing a successful SAT expository essay are discussed at length later in this chapter. Below are two simulated expository writing prompts:

Example 1

Unquestionably, travel broadens our horizons and teaches us many important things about ourselves and others. However, we can also learn equally valuable lessons by staying home. Explain what you think is one of the most significant lessons we can learn from our own backyard.

Assignment: Complete this statement with an example from your own life, history, literature, or current events. In your essay, explain what you have learned from your own environment. The environment might be your home, school, or town, for example.

Example 2

Life is filled with joy, but also with tragedy. We change as a result of the good and bad things that happen to us. Explain your opinion about what we can learn from our misfortune.

Assignment: Complete this statement with an example from history, literature, current events, or your own experience. In your essay, explain what life lessons can be learned from misfortune.

What Are the Qualities of a Successful Essay?

Regardless of the prompt, all essays must be *clear, consistent, complete,* and *correct.* To make these qualities easier to remember, think of them as the four Cs. They are presented in the following box.

Quality	Explanation
Clear	The essay has an obvious and logical method of organization. The essay has at least three paragraphs: *Introduction:* states the topic and your thesis (opinion) *Body:* provides specific details, examples, and facts *Conclusion:* summarizes your main point and provides resolution Your handwriting can be read easily. You will lose credit for illegibility.
Consistent	The essay answers the question you were asked. The essay stays on topic; it doesn't include irrelevant information. The essay maintains the same tone throughout. The essay maintains the same point of view throughout.
Complete	The essay is finished; you will lose credit if the essay is incomplete. The essay presents an intelligent, insightful way of looking at the topic.
Correct	The writing follows the rules of standard written English. There are few (if any) errors in grammar, punctuation, spelling, usage, capitalization, and so on.

How Are the Essays Scored?

Your essay will be scored by English teachers from around the country who gather in a central location. They spend about a week reading the essays. The scorers use a scale of 1 to 6, with 1 as the lowest score and 6 as the highest score. The scoring guidelines are arranged on a rubric. Here are the general guidelines:

- *Score of 1.* The essay barely touches on the topic or discusses a topic that has nothing to do with the essay question at all.

- *Score of 2.* The essay demonstrates a lack of understanding; either it does not address the topic directly or fails to answer the question. It draws obscure, irrelevant, or bizarre conclusions and is seriously deficient in the conventions of standard written English.

- *Score of 3.* The essay demonstrates an attempt at organization, but the structure is flawed and the supporting detail is weak. There may be serious problems with the mechanics of correct written English.

- *Score of 4.* The essay demonstrates a thorough but not totally convincing discussion of the topic, marked by the sense that the writer has not completely thought out the issue. In addition, there are some writing errors that may distract the reader from the argument and the writer's point.

■ *Score of 5.* The essay demonstrates solid, logical, and persuasive discussion, but it lacks originality or insight. Further, the development lacks grace and style. It may seem a bit predictable and plodding.

■ *Score of 6.* The essay demonstrates originality and imagination. It has a clearly focused discussion made up of coherent arguments of exceptional clarity. This essay leaves the reader convinced of the soundness of the discussion, impressed with the quality of the writing style, and stimulated by the intelligence and insight of the writer.

Here is a sample rubric you can use to assess your own practice essays.

Score of 1

- Very poor organization; ideas scattered and difficult to follow.
- Significant errors in grammar and usage impede meaning.
- Virtually no detail provided.
- Illogical point of view, opinion, or interpretation of the prompt.
- Essay completely off topic.

Score of 2

- Ideas not divided into logical paragraphs.
- Errors in grammar, diction, and sentence structure.
- Insignificant detail provided.
- Essay strays from topic.

Score of 3

- Incomplete organization.
- Paragraphs not developed logically.
- Ideas not linked in a logical manner.
- Inappropriate or insufficient details to support ideas.
- Too many errors in grammar, diction, and sentence structure.

Score of 4

- Answers the question asked in the writing prompt.
- Ideas divided into paragraphs.
- Opinions supported with details, examples, and facts.
- Some errors in style and word use.
- Some errors in grammar or diction; little sentence variety.

Score of 5

- Directly addresses the writing prompt in a logical manner.
- Paragraphs are well-organized.
- Ideas developed with appropriate, interesting examples.
- Uses language skillfully, including appropriate word choice and sentence variety.

Score of 6

- Demonstrates an original and insightful approach to the topic.
- Essay is very well organized.
- Ideas fully developed with appropriate, interesting examples.
- Sophisticated use of language; variety of sentence structures and vocabulary.

Top-Ten Hints for High-Scoring Essays

1. *Analyze the question.* Before you do anything else, make sure that you understand exactly what is required of you. Rephrase the writing prompt and assignment section in your own words to make sure that you comprehend it and grasp any subtle points.

2. *Answer the question.* Follow the directions precisely and do exactly what you're asked to do. Be sure to address every single part of the question. No matter how impressive your writing is, you will not receive any credit if you don't answer the question. If you grasp only one point from this book, make it this point: Directly answer the question you are given and follow the directions exactly.

3. *Use your time wisely.* Since you have 25 minutes for the essay, consider spending your time this way:

   2 minutes planning

   20 minutes writing and revising

   3 minutes editing and proofreading

   If you use an erasable pen, you can revise and edit as you draft. I strongly suggest that you correct your errors as you draft because you may not have time to return to your essay later.

4. *Start writing.* It's natural to start your essay at the beginning with the introduction, but if you're stuck for an opening, don't waste time agonizing. Instead, start where you can, with the body paragraphs. While it's vital that your essay be well-organized and logical, it's equally vital that you get it written in the 25 minutes you have. The best essay in the world won't get you any points if you don't get it down on paper within the time limit.

5. *Keep writing.* If you get stuck, skip some lines and keep on going. If you can't keep on writing, take a few deep breaths and gather your wits. If you really go blank and can't write, move on to another part of the essay. Staring at the paper only wastes time.

Use a clock as you practice writing the essays in this book. This will teach you how to pace yourself so you can make sure that you finish the essay on the day of the test.

6. *Write neatly.* If your writing is illegible, the scorer won't be able to read your paper. If it's merely messy, your scorer might misread a crucial point. And much as we don't like to admit it, neat papers do predispose scorers to grade more kindly. If you suspect that your handwriting is hard to read, print neatly and carefully.

7. *Be focused, serious, and mature.* Some students take the SAT for themselves and their future; others take it for their parents or to be part of the crowd. Other unfortunate students are forced into it, kicking and screaming. If you didn't want to take the test in the first place, this isn't the time to throw the test to prove a point. As an SAT scorer, I've read too many essays that reveal the students' determination to go down in flames to prove they never should have been forced into the test. If you are in this dreadful position, prove the other point: You can do it.

8. *Proofread.* This can be one of the most important steps in any paper, for no matter how valid your points, how precise your examples, if you have made a great many careless writing errors, you will lose credit. While your essay will be evaluated holistically (on the total impression it makes), errors can distract your readers and reduce the effectiveness of your arguments. Always make sure that you have time to proofread, and be as careful as you can to read what is there, not what You think is there.

9. *Deal with panic.* You can psyche yourself up or down—it's all in your head. Convince yourself that you can succeed by working carefully and resolutely. If you start to panic, pause for a second to calm yourself and then soldier on.

10. *Keep perspective.* Always remember that scorers reward you for what you do well. They're not looking for perfection. After all, you have only 25 minutes in which to write your essay. Do the very best you can, but don't obsess about making your essay flawless.

How to Write a High-Scoring *Persuasive* SAT Essay

Persuasive writing moves readers to action or belief. The essay portion of the new SAT will require you to write a persuasive or an expository essay. To determine whether you are dealing with a *persuasive* SAT essay question, look for these key words and phrases:

1. **What is your position on this issue?**

2. **Construct an argument . . .**

3. **As you develop your argument, . . .**

4. **Support your position . . .**

5. **Support your views . . .**

6. **To strengthen your position . . .**

7. **The writer argues . . .**

8. **Discuss the extent to which you agree or disagree . . .**

9. **Present the reasons for your opinion . . .**

10. **Consider opposing views . . .**

Persuasive writing that uses an appeal to reason is often called *argumentation*.

Format of Persuasive Questions

A persuasive prompt will take one of three forms:

1. **A question**

2. **A statement**

3. **A quotation**

Here are three sample persuasive writing prompts with the key words and phrases underlined. Each one takes a different form.

A Question

Should state college tuition be free for all students who graduate college with a B average? After all, state colleges are funded by tax revenues. On the other hand, education taxes are already very high. Further, why should taxpayers without college-aged children be encumbered by this additional tax burden?

Assignment: What is your position on this issue? Construct an argument explaining your position. As you develop your argument, support your views with relevant reasons and examples from your experiences, observations, and reading. To strengthen your position, you might wish to consider alternative or opposing views.

A Statement

You should never tell children their dreams are unlikely or outlandish. Few things are more humiliating, and what a tragedy it would be if they believed it.

Assignment: This statement suggests that children should be allowed to follow their dreams. <u>To what extent do you agree or disagree</u> with this statement? Write an essay in which you explain your point of view. <u>Support your views</u> with specific examples and details drawn from your own experiences, literature, and the arts. <u>As you develop your argument, consider opposing views:</u> for example, it would be cruel as well as wasteful to allow children to chase after outlandish goals.

A Quotation

> And one example, whether love or fear doth work more in a child for virtue and learning, I will gladly report; which may be heard with some pleasure and followed with more profit. Before I went into Germany, I took my leave of that noble Lady Jane Grey . . . "And how came you, madam," I said, "to this deep knowledge of pleasure, and what did chiefly allure you unto it, seeing not many women, but very few men, have attained thereunto?" "I will tell you," quoth she, "and tell you a truth which perchance ye will marvel at. One of the great benefits I had was sharp and severe parents and so gentle a schoolmaster. For when I am in presence either of father or mother, whether I speak, keep silence, sit, stand, or go, eat, drink, be merry or sad, be sewing, playing, dancing, or doing anything else, I must do it, as it were, in such weight, measure, and number, even so perfectly or else I am so sharply taunted, so cruelly threatened, yea, presently sometimes, with pinches, nips, and bobs, that I think myself in hell till time come that I must go to Master Aylmer, who teacheth me so gently, so pleasantly, with such fair allurements to learning, that I think all the time nothing whilst I am with him.

Assignment: In this excerpt from Roger Ascham's *The Schoolmaster,* Lady Jane Grey argues that both love and fear are necessary to educate children. Explain <u>the extent to which you agree or disagree</u> with Lady Jane Grey's position. <u>Support your position</u> with examples from your experiences, observations, and reading.

Current samples released by the ETS indicate that 75 percent of the essay questions are persuasive. If study time is short, concentrate on mastering persuasive rather than expository essays.

Acknowledging the Opposition

All the persuasive writing prompts on the SAT will have two sides. Otherwise, they would be expository rather than persuasive! Choose the side that you can support most strongly. This may or may not be the side you truly believe in, but that's not the point here: Rather, the point is to write the most logical and persuasive essay that you can. By choosing the side you can support the most strongly, you increase your chances of earning a high score. That's because your essay will have stronger proof: examples, details, statistics, and facts.

In *Rhetoric,* Aristotle said: "Whether our argument concerns public affairs or some other subject, we must know some, if not all, of the facts about the subject on which we are to argue. Otherwise, we can have no materials out of which to construct arguments." *Remember:* Effective persuasive writing uses specific support, not vague references to unidentified studies and sources. You can't evaluate "many important experiments" or "recent clinical studies" unless you know how they were undertaken, by whom, and where the results were published.

You do not have to acknowledge the opposition, but your essay will usually be stronger if you do. Don't give the same space to the opposition as you do to your points. Devote more space to *your* argument or place it last in your essay, so readers will understand that it's crucial.

You can deal with the opposition by

- Identifying the main arguments against your side

- Acknowledging the arguments in your writing

- Countering the opposition

When you are addressing an audience that does not agree with your argument, search for *common ground,* or areas of agreement. If you can get readers to agree with you on one point, they are more likely to be persuaded by your other points.

There are three main ways that you can deal with the opposition to decrease its force. These methods are as follows:

1. **Show the opposition is wrong.**

2. **Show the opposition has some merit, but give a point of your own that is just as convincing.**

3. **Show the opposition has merit, but your point is stronger.**

Let's look at each strategy in turn.

Method 1: Show the Opposition is Wrong
Read the practice SAT writing question. Then read the portion of the sample answer that follows. Note how the answer acknowledges the opposition straight away and then sets about disproving it.

Public television, such as PBS, is commercial-free. Should all television be commercial-free? After all, commercials not only encourage rampant consumerism but also set up unrealistic expectations and waste our time.

Assignment: To what extent do you agree or disagree with this statement? Write an essay in which you explain your point of view. Support your views with specific examples and details drawn from your own experiences. As you develop your argument, consider opposing views: For example, television commercials have merit.

Very few people claim to like television commercials. Most people say that television commercials are annoying and insulting. The best that people can say about television commercials is that they give us time to get something to eat. But this view is unfair, since TV commercials have many advantages.

opposition   First of all, many people claim that television commercials are more misleading than informative. They say that television ads manipulate the truth in order to get people to buy products.

rebuttal   While it is true that television advertisers use strategies that encourage viewers to buy things, there are strong laws and regulations that ensure truth in advertising.

Method 2: Show the Opposition Has Some Merit, but Your Point Is Just as Good
Here's another paragraph from the same essay. See how the clever writer dealt with the opposition by presenting a point that is equally convincing. Use this technique if you can't come up with a point that is stronger.

opposition   Some people complain that television commercials are annoying and even in bad taste. People who complain about the ads do have a valid point.

rebuttal   But if the public demanded television commercials that were in good taste, ones that did not manipulate or insult the viewer, we would get better commercials. If enough people wrote to the companies to protest offensive ads, there would be enough pressure to make the commercials better.

Method 3: Show the Opposition Has Merit, but Your Point Is Stronger
For an especially strong essay, acknowledge the other side, but rebut with your own point—and make it very convincing. Here's how one writer did it:

Second, television commercials inform viewers of new products such as no-fat snack foods. They also show us new uses for old products. For example, baking soda ads on TV show us how to use the product to take odors out of the refrigerator and carpets, not just for baking.

opposition   There are some people who say that people can learn about products and services in other ways—through magazine and newspaper ads, for example.

rebuttal   To some extent this is true. However, a person would have to buy and read many, many newspapers and magazines to get as much information from print as we do from television. Who has time to read all these newspapers and magazines? It is clear that television commercials are a much more efficient way to get information about products.

Your Turn
Now, write the essay on TV commercials yourself. As you write, consider how you want to deal with the opposition. Write your answer on a separate piece of paper.

How Do I Arrange My Information?

There are several ways to arrange the information in a persuasive essay. Below are two ways that are especially well suited for answering a persuasive essay question on the new SAT, the chunk method and the slice method.

The Chunk Method

I call this the chunk method because you deal with the main points in chunks, as follows:

- All of *their* side (the opposition)

- All of *your* side

Study this outline:

Persuasive Essay Structure 1: Chunk Method

I.   Introduction
  A. Thesis sentence
  B. Summary of opposition
  C. Summary of your side
  D. Transition or lead-in sentence to the next paragraph

II. Background (if necessary)

III. Opposition (one to two points)
  A. Topic sentence
  B. Point 1
  C. Point 2

IV. Your side of the argument (2 to 4 points)
  A. Topic sentence
  B. Point 1
  C. Point 2
  D. Point 3

V.   Conclusion
  A. Topic sentence
  B. Summarize the opposition
  C. Summarize your side
  D. Make your point

Model Essay

Here's a model persuasive essay organized according to the chunk method. Follow the sidebars as you read to help you analyze the essay's structure.

> Should students be forced to wear uniforms to school? After all, uniforms help parents save money. School uniforms also reduce clothing competition and help safeguard the schools. However, they do impinge on individuality.

Assignment: What is your position on this issue? Construct an argument explaining your position. As you develop your argument, support your views with relevant reasons and examples from your experiences, observations, and reading. To strengthen your position, you might wish to consider alternative or opposing views.

1 Thesis sentence 2 Summary of opposition 3 Summary of your side 4 Transition to the next paragraph 5 Topic sentence 6 Point 1: Opposition 7 Point 2: Opposition	[1] There has been much controversy over whether or not students should be required to wear uniforms to school. [2] School uniforms help parents to save money and help to prevent many conflicts among students. [3] However, forcing students to wear uniforms may cause students to lose their sense of individuality and halt any creativity that they otherwise may express through their wardrobe. [4] Let's examine the advantages of wearing school uniforms. [5] There are several reasons that having school uniforms are beneficial. [6] For example, parents will save money on buying their children clothing and therefore will have more money to spend on extra things. A uniform costs under $100 and the average child needs only two per year. A complete school wardrobe, in contrast, can cost hundreds, even thousands, of dollars. The money saved on uniforms could be put into a savings account for college or even a car. [7] Having uniforms may also eliminate cliques. When I walked through my high school, I could always tell which students were friends with each other because they would be dressed similarly. The "jocks" wore jerseys with team names emblazoned across the back, while the "burn-outs" wore chains, baggy pants, and black T-shirts. If everyone wore uniforms and looked the same, then students from different groups might interact with each other more.
8 Topic sentence 9 Point 1: Your side 10 Point 2: Your side 11 Point 3: Your side	[8] The disadvantages of wearing uniforms outweigh the advantages. [9] First, the peace and uniformity that school uniforms bring comes at a very high price: loss of individuality. I can't imagine how stultifying it would be to wear the same thing every day. I have a close friend who attends a school that requires uniforms. "Because of my uniform, I'm forced to pretend to be someone I'm not," she says. She looks forward to school "dress-down days," when she can choose her own clothing. [10] Further, many people express their emotions and interests through their clothing. For instance, when the Rangers win a big game, I wear my Rangers jersey to school to show my support for the team. If I'm going to a wrestling show after school, I wear my wrestling T-shirt to school. If your school required uniforms, you would not be able to wear the new sweater you got for your birthday or the hat you got at the Yankees' game. [11] Finally, uniforms aren't comfortable. Since they are made to be sturdy and easy to clean, they are often stiff, rough, and scratchy. I tried on my friend's uniform skirt and had difficulty getting comfortable. It certainly wasn't as soft as my fleece pants.
12 Topic sentence 13 Summarize the opposition 14 Summarize your side 15 Make your point	[12] In conclusion, there are both advantages and disadvantages to wearing uniforms. [13] There's no doubt that uniforms help parents save money and reduce conflicts among students. [14] However, uniforms take away individuality and creative expression that often comes from our choice of clothing. [14] Uniforms also restrict our freedom of expression. [14] Last, they are not comfortable and so may actually make it more difficult for kids to concentrate in school. [15] For these reasons and others, students should not be forced to wear uniforms to school.

Your Turn

Now, write this essay yourself. As you write, follow the chunk organizational method you just learned. Write your answer on a separate piece of paper.

The Slice Method

I call this the *slice* method because you deal with the main points in slices, as follows:

■ Point one

Their side (the opposition)

Your side

■ Point two

Their side (the opposition)

Your side

■ Point three

Their side (the opposition)

Your side

Study this outline:

Persuasive Essay Structure 2: Slice Method

I. Introduction
    A. Thesis sentence
    B. Summary of points to follow
    C. Transition or lead-in sentence to the next paragraph

II. Background (if necessary)

III. Your first main point
    A. Topic sentence
    B. Opposition
    C. Your side

IV. Your second main point
    A. Topic sentence
    B. Opposition
    C. Your side

V. Your third main point
    A. Topic sentence
    B. Opposition
    C. Your side

VI. Conclusion
    A. Topic sentence
    B. Summary of the opposition
    C. Summary of your side
    D. Summary of your point

> If you're having a hard time finding the most suitable organizational plan for your ideas, try jotting each main topic on scraps of paper. Arrange the scraps in various ways to see which arrangement makes the most sense, given your purpose and readers.

Model Essay

Here's an essay answering the same question organized by the slice method. Follow the sidebars as you read to help you analyze the essay's structure.

1 Thesis sentence

2 Summary of points to follow

3 Transition to the next paragraph
4 Topic sentence
5 First main point: Opposition

6 First main point: Your side

[1] Should students be forced to wear uniforms to school? [2] Supporters of school uniforms argue that they save money, reduce clothing competition, and help safeguard our schools. [2] The opposition argues that these claims are fraudulent; in fact, school uniforms are little more than a Band-Aid that covers far more serious problems. [3] Let's examine the advantages of wearing school uniforms.

[4] Those who champion school uniforms claim they will help keep clothing budgets reasonable, but will parents really save money? [5] A uniform costs under $100 and the average student needs only two to three per year. A complete school wardrobe, in contrast, can cost hundreds or even thousands of dollars. The money saved on uniforms could be put into a savings account for college or even a car. [6] However, students who have to have all the latest fashions will want these clothes regardless of practicality. They'll find time to wear designer jeans, name-brand shirts, and trendy shoes on weekends, evenings, and holidays. Further, many students who are constrained by uniforms will want expensive accessories. For girls, these "must-have" accessories include extravagant hair ribbons and clips, designer handbags, and high-priced watches. Students of both sexes will still want costly backpacks and pricey gold and silver jewelry. Thus, parents will end up buying uniforms as well as complete school/dress wardrobes.

7 Topic sentence
8 Second main point: Opposition

9 Second main point: Your side

[7] Supporters of school uniforms also argue that uniforms reduce clothing competition. [8] Well, uniforms would certainly diminish informal classroom contests for "best-dressed." How can you try to "one-up" someone if you're both wearing nearly the same thing? [9] However, this conformity comes at a high price: loss of individuality. I can't imagine how stultifying it would be to wear the same thing every day. I have a close friend who attends a school that requires uniforms. "Because I wear a uniform, I'm forced to pretend to be someone I'm not," she says. She looks forward to school "dress-down days," when she can choose her own clothing. Further, many people express their emotions and interests through their clothing. For instance, when the Rangers win a big game, I wear my Rangers jersey to school to show my support for the team. If I'm going to a wrestling show after school, I wear my wrestling T-shirt to school. If your school required uniforms, you would not be able to wear the new sweater you got for your birthday or the hat you got at the Yankees' game.

10 Topic sentence
11 Third main point: Opposition
12 Third main point: Your side

[10] Advocates of school uniforms argue that uniforms can indeed help prevent crime in schools. [11] Yes, they might prevent thugs from smuggling in weapons hidden in baggy pants and jackets. [12] However, if an intruder wants to enter the school and create trouble, he or she will find a way. Uniforms are useless in stopping an adult intruder (such as a noncustodial parent out to snatch his or her child), unless the administration issues identification badges to all adults.

13 Topic sentence

14 Summary of the opposition

15 Summary of your side

16 Summary of your point

[13] In conclusion, school uniforms are a highly controversial topic. [14] Those in favor of school uniforms argue that they cost far less money than a full school wardrobe, decrease obsessions with faddish and costly clothing, and help safeguard our schools. [15] Unfortunately, school uniforms are not the panacea their backers claim. They don't save parents significant amounts on clothing budgets, do little to erase class awareness, and cannot protect our children from intruders. [16] For these reasons and others, students should not be forced to wear uniforms to school.

Notice how smoothly the writer deals with the opposition within each paragraph. Notice that your side is always more fully developed with details and examples than the opposing side. Always save your strongest point for your side to persuade your readers that your point is deserving of more serious consideration.

Your Turn
Now, write this essay yourself. As you write, follow the slice organizational method you just learned. Write your answer on a separate piece of paper.

Chunk or Slice?
When should you use the chunk method, and when should you use the slice method?

Use the chunk method when

- You have more points on your side than the opposition has.
- The opposition is rather weak.
- Your audience is neutral or receptive to your ideas.

Use the slice method when

- You have the same number of points on your side and on the opposition's side.
- The opposition is rather strong.
- Your audience is likely to be hostile to your ideas.

Variations on a Theme
Now that you know the basic format, you can vary it to suit your topic. For example, you may choose to play down the opposition or add examples in story form to make your point. There are numerous variations. Always choose the one that suits your purpose and audience.

Point-by-Point Method

Here's one possible variation, adapted from the persuasive format:

Persuasive Essay Structure 3: Point by Point

I. Introduction
   A. Thesis sentence
   B. Summary of your side
   C. Transition or lead-in sentence to the next paragraph

II. Your first point
   A. Topic sentence
   B. Details and examples
   C. Details and examples
   D. Conclusion

III. Your second point
   A. Topic sentence
   B. Details and examples
   C. Details and examples
   D. Conclusion

IV. Your third point
   A. Topic sentence
   B. Details and examples
   C. Details and examples
   D. Conclusion

V. Conclusion
   A. Topic sentence
   B. Summary of first point
   C. Summary of second point
   D. Summary of third point
   E. Conclusion

Model Essay

Below is a sample SAT question organized by the point-by-point method. Follow the sidebars as you read to help you analyze the essay's structure.

"Television is chewing gum for the mind," a critic once claimed. Is television merely a time-waster, or does it have valuable lessons to teach us?

Assignment: What is your position on this issue? Construct an argument explaining your position. As you develop your argument, support your views with relevant reasons and examples from your experiences, observations, and reading. To strengthen your position, you might wish to consider alternative or opposing views.

Let's Hear It for TV!

1 Thesis statement
2 Summary of your side

3 Transition

4 Topic sentence
5 Details and examples

6 Details and examples

7 Conclusion
8 Topic sentence
9 Details and examples

10 Details and examples
11 Conclusion

12 Topic sentence
13 Details and examples

14 Conclusion

15 Topic sentence
16 Summary of first point
17 Summary of second point
18 Summary of third point

[1] Most people are quick to condemn television as a despoiler of America's youth, but I think TV has a lot going for it. [2] In fact, television has helped me in three very important ways. [2] First, watching television helped me learn English. [2] Second, it taught me a lot about American culture. [2] Finally, television helped me stay out of trouble when I was younger. [3] Television was especially important to me when I first came to America. [3] Most important, watching television helped me learn English.

[4] When I came to the United States, I spoke only a few words of English, but television came to my rescue. [5] Since I was 12 years old, I was placed in the seventh grade. [5] I was the same age as every other student in the classroom, but I could not communicate with a single person. [5] When I got home from school every day, I did not have anything to do since I did not have any friends. [6] To pass the time, I watched cartoons and the local news. [6] As I gradually learned more English, I started watching sitcoms and soap operas. My English improved rapidly. [6] As a result, I was able to communicate more easily with my classmates and teacher and so did much better in school. I made some good friends, too, and felt more at home in my new country. [7] By helping me learn English, television helped me acculturate to American life.

[8] Television also helped me learn about American culture. [9] I found out from watching television that life in America is very different in some regards from life in my birthplace, Korea. [9] In Korea, for example, most of the television commercials are about education. [10] In America, however, most of the commercials are about cars, food, and clothing. [11] This suggested to me that Americans are encouraged to be materialistic. [11] I probably would have learned this eventually without television, but watching TV helped me realize what American life is like much more quickly.

[12] Finally, watching television helped me stay out of trouble. As you have read, I watched a great deal of television when I was a child. [13] Some of the commercials were public service announcements about drug and alcohol abuse. [13] These commercials were very slick and persuasive. [14] As a result, they helped me realize the importance of staying straight. [14] In addition, I rarely hung out at night because I preferred to be inside watching my favorite shows, especially movies.

[15] As an immigrant, I found television an invaluable way of learning English. [16] Thanks to TV, I quickly mastered the rudiments of the language and learned a great deal about American culture. [17] Television also helped me avoid drug and alcohol abuse and even gangs. [18] So don't be so quick to criticize TV; for many of us, it's a lifeline.

Your Turn

Now, write this essay yourself. As you write, follow the point-by-point organizational method you just learned. Write your answer on a separate piece of paper.

Appeal to Reason, Emotion, and Ethics

Aristotle, the Father of Persuasion, believed that argument meant discovering all the available ways of persuasion in a situation that had two equally feasible sides. Aristotle settled on three ways that people could convince others to adopt a certain point of view or approve a course of action. Broadly stated, he identified these three elements as

■ *Logos.* The appeal to the audience's reason

■ *Pathos.* The appeal to the audience's emotions

■ *Ethos.* The degree of confidence that the writer's character or personality inspires in readers

The goal of these three appeals is the same, although each one takes a different approach. Each appeal can be used separately, or they can be combined to increase the effectiveness of your argument. In general, high-scoring SAT essays will appeal to reason and ethics rather than emotion.

Model Essays

Read the following two SAT essays. Decide how much reason, emotion, and ethics the author uses in each one.

> You ask me why I do not write something. . . . I think one's feelings waste themselves in words, they ought all to be distilled into actions and into actions which bring results.

Assignment: Here, Florence Nightingale argues that action is far more important than words. On the other hand, the right words have the power to change the world by moving people to action. Discuss the extent to which you agree or disagree with Nightingale's statement. Support your position by providing examples from your own experience, observations, or reading.

Model 1

Florence Nightingale believed that "one's feelings waste themselves in words," because only "actions . . . bring results." She must have heard enough words in her time to justify her feelings that doing things is far more important than merely talking about them. However, with all due respect to Ms. Nightingale, she is incorrect. Words have torn down mountains that actions could not have budged.

Words stir up the masses and get them to move on an issue. Thomas Paine showed this in his famous series of pamphlets, "Common Sense." Paine wrote his incendiary pamphlets on the eve of the American Revolution to stir up support for the Patriot cause. At that time, only a third of all colonists supported the Revolution: another third were staunch Loyalists, while the last third were indifferent. It was the last camp that Paine convinced with his stirring rhetoric. The "summer soldier and the sunshine patriot" were convinced by his words and took up arms against oppression. On his own, Paine could not have won America's independence, but his pamphlets convinced many colonists that they must seek their freedom from England.

"The Declaration of Independence" is another example of the power of words. This document declared that Americans would no longer allow themselves to be ruled by Great Britain. Thomas Jefferson, the primary author, detailed the reasons for the rebellion. The Declaration created a sense of unity by putting into words what many people thought about King George's outrageous actions against us. The Declaration gave the colonists concrete reasons for fighting and announced to the world that we were no longer a British colony.

Upton Sinclair's novel *The Jungle* didn't have anything to do with revolution, but it served to spark one nonetheless. His book described the atrocities of the Chicago meat-packing industry. He detailed the filthy packing houses, with rats and even human limbs folded into sausage. He told about the workers' terrible lives, oppressed by an unfair system that cheated them out of their youth and strength. The national outcry that resulted from this novel forced the federal government to establish the Pure Food and Drug Act. This not only regulated the industry but also improved the standards of American food to this day. By himself, Sinclair could not have forced the federal government to clean up the food industry, but his words did.

It is sad that Florence Nightingale does not appreciate the power of words to change and shape reality. Perhaps she doesn't realize that without words, she could not have expressed her own feelings in the quote.

Model 2

Florence Nightingale believed that "one's feelings waste themselves in words," because only "actions . . . bring results." She must have heard enough words in her time to justify her feelings that doing things is far more important than merely talking about them. I agree with Ms. Nightingale, for I believe that in the majority of occasions, acting on something outweighs talking it to death.

Granted there are times when the spoken or written word is necessary to arouse the masses and get them to move on an issue. Thomas Paine showed this in his famous series of pamphlets, "Common Sense." Paine wrote his incendiary pamphlets on the eve of the American Revolution to stir up support for the Patriot cause. At that time, only a third of all colonists supported the Revolution: another third were staunch Patriots, while the last third were indifferent. It was the last camp that Paine convinced with his stirring rhetoric. The "summer soldier and the sunshine patriot" were convinced by his words and took up arms against oppression. On his own, Paine could not have won America's independence, but his pamphlets convinced many colonists that they must seek their freedom from England.

But in many more instances, acting on issues accomplishes far more than talking or writing about them. For example, former President Bill Clinton talked tough against terrorism but did not take action. He claimed he would fight against America's enemies, but when the Sudan offered him Osama bin Laden, he refused. Perhaps, if Clinton had taken bin Laden prisoner and sent troops into his lair, America would not have been attacked on September 11. Now that President Bush is taking firm action against terrorism, we stand a chance of making our country safe once again. In most instances, actions do more good than words alone. Although there are times when words are necessary to motivate people to act, words must be supported by action itself.

Your Turn

Now, write this essay yourself. As you write, appeal to reason, emotion, ethics, or any combination that will most effectively persuade your audience. Write your answer on a separate piece of paper.

How to Write a High-Scoring *Expository* SAT Essay

Expository essays explain. You can remember that exposition is writing that explains by using this memory trick: *Exposition = explains.* Further, both words start with the same three letters: *exp.*

Exposition can be organized in the following ways:

- Cause-and-effect analysis
- Chronological order
- Classify-and-divide analysis
- Compare and contrast essays
- Definition essays
- Order of importance (news story)
- Problem and solution essays
- Process analysis (how-to) essays

Exposition shows and tells by giving information about a specific topic. On the SAT essay, the topic will be given to you. How you choose to organize your essay always depends on the following two considerations:

Topic. The subject; what you are writing about

Audience. Who will read your writing

How Do I Arrange My Information?

It's likely that you will arrange the details of your analysis in chronological order or the order of importance. Therefore, let's look at these methods of arranging details. For both methods, use the point-by-point outline as your framework. You learned this method of arranging details earlier in this chapter on page 136.

Using Chronological Order

With this organizational plan, you arrange your ideas in the order in which they happened, from first to last. This is a handy method of organization to use with expository essays if all the ideas are of equal rank. By arranging them in time order, you sidestep the issue of which ones are most important.

You may wish to construct a brief timeline to help you order events.

Chronological essays often include *transitions* that help readers track the order of events. These words include actual dates, with days of the week, months, and years. In addition, you can use the following time-order clue words:

Time-order Transitions			
after	at that time	finally	first, second, etc.
last	later	next	now
subsequently	succeeding	soon after	then

Model Essay

Study this model expository essay.

Great achievements involve . . .

Assignment: Complete this statement with an example from history, literature, current events, or your own experience. Using the completed statement, write a well-organized essay in which you explain what you believe great achievements require.

1 First sentence grabs reader's attention and shows command of language.

When you look back at your life at its end, what will stand out from the daily rhetoric between breakfast and bed? [1] One of the most important parts of your legacy will be your achievements. And if you are able to smile at the great thief as he takes you into the night, your achievements must be of the highest standards. Unfortunately, these goals can prove elusive. Often, they can be achieved only through great risk. [2] We can see this through American history. [3] America is a great country in large part because of the Americans who took risks.

2 Narrows focus to topic.
3 Topic sentence placed last to serve as a lead-in.
4 Main ideas arranged in time order.

[4] The patriots of the American Revolution risked their lives by fighting against the Mother Country, Great Britain. For example, Thomas Paine, an ordinary man who worked at a variety of ordinary jobs, wrote a stirring call to arms in [5] 1776, when most colonists still hoped the quarrel with England could be resolved without bloodshed. Paine's most famous pamphlet, "The American Crisis," convinced many colonists that they would have to fight for freedom. Paine's risk was great indeed: King George put a price on his head. If caught, Paine would have been executed. [6] Paine's brave writings helped achieve freedom for the colonists and independence for America.

5 Date shows time order of events.

6 Writer makes the point.

7 Main ideas arranged in time order.
8 Date shows time order of events.

[7] Centuries later, Dr. Martin Luther King, Jr., took great risks for freedom as well. [8] In the mid-1950s, Dr. King first organized a bus boycott in Montgomery, Alabama, to protest racial segregation in public transportation. King was arrested and jailed; his home was bombed and many threats were made against his life. [9] Finally, King's risk paid off when the Supreme Court outlawed segregation in public transportation in the city. [10] Dr. King showed that nonviolent protest could bring about great achievements.

9 Transition ("finally") shows time order.

10 Writer makes the point.

11 Writer makes the point.

[11] Great achievements often involve great risk. Thomas Paine helped the colonists wrest freedom from Great Britain. His risk? His life. Dr. Martin Luther King, Jr., helped bring racial equality to all Americans. His risk? His life and the lives of his family and friends. [12] Not all achievements require such tremendous peril, but nothing great was ever accomplished without blood, sweat, and tears.

12 Parallel structure shows sophisticated command of language.

Your Turn

Now, write this essay yourself. As you write, use chronological order. Write your answer on a separate piece of paper.

Using Order of Importance
With this organizational plan, you draw attention to your key ideas by placing them first in your essay. By leading with your strongest points, you impress the scorers with your grasp of the issues. You can also arrange ideas from most to least important, or save the second most important point for last. The following diagrams show these variations visually:

Most important point		Most important point
↓		↓
Less important points	or	Least important points
↓		↓
Least important point		Second most important point

You can also use transitions such as *most important, first of all, second,* and so on to show order of importance.

Model Essay

Study this model expository essay:

Students fail in school because of . . .

Assignment: Complete this statement with an example from history, literature, current events, or your own experience. Using the completed statement, write a well-organized essay in which you explain why students fail in school.

1 Topic sentence is on target.

2 Ideas are arranged in order of importance

3 Most important idea
4 Specific details

5 Writer makes the point.

Some people argue that students fail in school because of dull subject matter, poor teaching, or inadequate families. I don't agree. [1] I think that students do poorly in school due to a lack of effort on their own part. Everyone has the opportunity to do well in school. [2] Success depends on individual students, whether they are willing to put in the effort and time required to do their best.

[3] Most importantly, too many students refuse to take responsibility for their actions. [4] They often say, "It's not my fault; the teacher doesn't know how to teach," or "The class is so boring that you can't expect me to pay attention." Instead, students should say, "It's my fault because I didn't study enough" or "I should have turned off the hockey game and opened up the textbook." Sometimes you will get a teacher who isn't that good or a subject that is boring to you. [5] But that's no excuse; you have to deal with it and take charge of your own future.

6 Second most important idea

7 Specific details

8 Specific details

9 Nice touch of humor

10 Writer makes the point.

11 Most important point

12 Second most important point

[6] Secondly, you have to be willing to put in the time to succeed. [7] My friends often say, "I just don't have the time to do all the work they assign in high school." The time is there; it's up to the student to use it wisely. [8] Students have to learn to shut off the Playstation, sign off from AOL, and hang up the telephone. They may have to cut back the number of hours they are working, too, and watch less television. Instead of hanging out with friends every night, they should consider hanging out with them every other night, or just on weekends. [9] Once you finish your school work, you can stand in front of the convenience store as long as you like. Setting clear priorities will make it easier for you to write that term paper and study for that midterm exam.

[10] Achievement in high school is important. It is often a crucial factor in your future. So when students fail in high school, we can place the blame where it belongs: on their shoulders. [11] Most important, students must take charge of their work. [12] Second, they must spend the time they need to do their best. You can't win it if you're not in it.

Your Turn

Now, write this essay yourself. As you write, use order of importance. Write your answer on a separate piece of paper.

Practice Writing Prompts

Complete each of the following writing assignments under test conditions. Be sure to allow yourself no more than 25 minutes for each essay. Pace yourself to make sure you finish the essay in the time required. If you finish with more than a few minutes to spare, you are not spending enough time on details, examples, editing, and proofreading.

1. **"Characters on television can best be described as . . ."**

Assignment: Are they brash and rude? Are they interesting and knowledgeable? Are they somewhere in between? Complete this statement with an example from your own experience. Using the completed statement, write a well-organized essay in which you explain how you describe the characters you watch on television shows.

2. **"Learn the rules; then break some."**

Assignment: Discuss the extent to which you agree or disagree with this assertion. Support your position by providing reasons and examples from your own experience, observations, or reading. Be sure to cite at least two examples.

3. **"What, then, is the American, this new man? He is neither a European nor the descendent of a European; hence that strange mixture of blood, which you will find in no other country. I could point out to you a family whose grandfather was an Englishman, whose wife was Dutch, whose son married a French woman, and whose present four sons now have four wives of**

different nations. *He* is an American who, leaving behind all his ancient prejudices and manners, received new ones from the new mode of life he has embraced, the new government he obeys, and the new ranks he holds. He becomes an American by being received in the broad lap of our great Alma Mater. Here individuals of all nations are melted into a new race of men, whose labors and posterity will one day cause great changes in the world."

Assignment: In this statement, Hector St. Jean de Crevecoeur argues that America is a "melting pot" because we set aside our heritage to embrace a new one. Discuss the extent to which you agree or disagree with his assertion. Support your position by providing reasons and examples from your own experience, observations, or reading. Be sure to cite at least two examples.

4. **"Even if you're on the right track, you'll get run over if you just sit there."**

Assignment: In this statement, American humorist Will Rogers argues for individual action. However, the nail that sticks out gets hammered down, as the Japanese say. Discuss the extent to which you agree or disagree with Rogers's assertion. Support your position by providing reasons and examples from your own experience, observations, or reading.

5. **"A man may die, nations may rise and fall, but an idea lives on."**

Assignment: In this statement, President John F. Kennedy argues that a valuable idea outlives its creator. Discuss the extent to which you agree or disagree with his assertion. Be sure to cite at least two ideas that have outlived their creators. Support your position by providing reasons and examples from your own experience, observations, or reading.

6. **"A successful individual is one who has achieved meaningful work and meaningful love."**

Assignment: Sigmund Freud argues that we need both purposeful work and meaningful love to be considered a "success." Agree or disagree with Freud's position, discussing what you think makes someone a "success." Support your position by providing at least two examples of successful people you know. Be sure to explain what makes them successful in your eyes or society's eyes.

7. **"Without friends no one would choose to live, though he had all other goods."**

Assignment: Aristotle argues that we need friends more than anything else. However, friends can often hurt you as much as they help you. Discuss the extent to which you agree or disagree with Aristotle's assertion. Support your position by providing reasons and examples from your own experience, observations, or reading.

8. **"It has been my experience that one cannot, in any shape or form, depend on human relations for lasting reward. It is only work that truly satisfies."**

Assignment: Bette Davis's statement appears to be the direct opposite of Aristotle's belief in that Davis claims that only work brings lasting pleasure, not friendships, love, or other human bondings. However, some friends and lovers do stick with you for the long haul, while jobs and careers can vanish in the blink of an eye (especially now, with layoffs and a sinking economy). Discuss the extent to which you agree or disagree with Davis's assertion. Support your position by providing reasons and examples from your own experience, observations, or reading.

9. **"Opportunities are usually disguised as hard work, so most people don't recognize them."**

Assignment: Ann Landers (the late author of a newspaper advice column) argues that we make our own opportunities, our own "good luck," by working hard. She suggests that hard work = success, so if you want to get ahead, you have to work hard. On the other hand, some people appear to get by without much effort. They seem to have all the luck. Discuss the extent to which you agree or disagree with Landers's statement. Support your position by providing examples from your own experience, observations, or reading.

10. **"Lawyers are expected to provide free legal services at some time in their careers. Doctors should or should not have the same obligation to provide free medical care at some time in their careers to people who cannot afford care."**

Assignment: What is your position on this issue? Construct an argument explaining your position. Support your views with examples from your experiences, observations, and reading. To strengthen your position, you might wish to consider alternative or opposing views.

11. **"Learning is not attained by chance; it must be sought for with ardor and attended to with diligence."**

Assignment: Here, Abigail Adams, in 1780, argues that learning is a conscious, active process. Successful students work hard at their studies, she suggests. However, learning seems to come naturally and easily to some people—or does it? Discuss the extent to which you agree or disagree with Adams's statement. Support your position by providing examples from your own experience, observations, or reading. To strengthen your position, you might wish to consider alternative or opposing views.

12. **In Meditation 17, English poet John Donne said, "No man is an island, entire of itself; every man is a piece of the continent, a part of the main**

[land] . . . Any man's death diminishes me, because I am involved in mankind; and therefore never send to know for whom the bell tolls; it tolls for thee."

Assignment: In this famous passage, Donne argues that we are all connected to one another. Discuss the extent to which you agree or disagree with his assertion. Support your views with reasons and examples from your experiences, observations, and reading. To strengthen your position, you might wish to consider alternative or opposing views.

13. **"We must believe in luck. For how else can we explain the success of those we don't like?"**

Assignment: Jean Cocteau suggests that we claim people we dislike must be lucky if they are successful. Otherwise, we must face the fact that they work harder than we do, are more intelligent, or are more determined and focused. Discuss the extent to which you agree or disagree with the quote. Support your views with reasons and examples from your experiences, observations, and reading.

14. **"Animals are such agreeable friends—they ask no questions, they pass no criticisms."**

Assignment: George Eliot argues that many pets make great companions. Other people, however, find pets to be dirty, stupid, and even dangerous. What is your position on this issue? Support your views with relevant reasons and examples from your experiences. To strengthen your position, consider opposing views.

15. **"Same-sex schools provide a better education than co-ed schools."**

Assignment: What is your position on this issue? Construct an argument explaining your position. Support your views with relevant reasons and examples from your experiences. To strengthen your position, consider opposing views.

P A R T 7

Two Sample Verbal SAT Tests for Practice

Two Sample Verbal SAT Tests for Practice

The two tests that follow were constructed to represent what you will encounter on the Verbal part of the SAT. Since the new SAT has yet to be given, these tests are based on the press releases issued by the College Board. There is always the chance the College Board will adjust the format as it develops the test.

Answer Sheet—Practice Test 1

Section 1

1 Ⓐ Ⓑ Ⓒ Ⓓ Ⓔ   8 Ⓐ Ⓑ Ⓒ Ⓓ Ⓔ   15 Ⓐ Ⓑ Ⓒ Ⓓ Ⓔ   22 Ⓐ Ⓑ Ⓒ Ⓓ Ⓔ
2 Ⓐ Ⓑ Ⓒ Ⓓ Ⓔ   9 Ⓐ Ⓑ Ⓒ Ⓓ Ⓔ   16 Ⓐ Ⓑ Ⓒ Ⓓ Ⓔ   23 Ⓐ Ⓑ Ⓒ Ⓓ Ⓔ
3 Ⓐ Ⓑ Ⓒ Ⓓ Ⓔ   10 Ⓐ Ⓑ Ⓒ Ⓓ Ⓔ   17 Ⓐ Ⓑ Ⓒ Ⓓ Ⓔ   24 Ⓐ Ⓑ Ⓒ Ⓓ Ⓔ
4 Ⓐ Ⓑ Ⓒ Ⓓ Ⓔ   11 Ⓐ Ⓑ Ⓒ Ⓓ Ⓔ   18 Ⓐ Ⓑ Ⓒ Ⓓ Ⓔ
5 Ⓐ Ⓑ Ⓒ Ⓓ Ⓔ   12 Ⓐ Ⓑ Ⓒ Ⓓ Ⓔ   19 Ⓐ Ⓑ Ⓒ Ⓓ Ⓔ
6 Ⓐ Ⓑ Ⓒ Ⓓ Ⓔ   13 Ⓐ Ⓑ Ⓒ Ⓓ Ⓔ   20 Ⓐ Ⓑ Ⓒ Ⓓ Ⓔ
7 Ⓐ Ⓑ Ⓒ Ⓓ Ⓔ   14 Ⓐ Ⓑ Ⓒ Ⓓ Ⓔ   21 Ⓐ Ⓑ Ⓒ Ⓓ Ⓔ

Section 2

1 Ⓐ Ⓑ Ⓒ Ⓓ Ⓔ   8 Ⓐ Ⓑ Ⓒ Ⓓ Ⓔ   15 Ⓐ Ⓑ Ⓒ Ⓓ Ⓔ   22 Ⓐ Ⓑ Ⓒ Ⓓ Ⓔ
2 Ⓐ Ⓑ Ⓒ Ⓓ Ⓔ   9 Ⓐ Ⓑ Ⓒ Ⓓ Ⓔ   16 Ⓐ Ⓑ Ⓒ Ⓓ Ⓔ   23 Ⓐ Ⓑ Ⓒ Ⓓ Ⓔ
3 Ⓐ Ⓑ Ⓒ Ⓓ Ⓔ   10 Ⓐ Ⓑ Ⓒ Ⓓ Ⓔ   17 Ⓐ Ⓑ Ⓒ Ⓓ Ⓔ   24 Ⓐ Ⓑ Ⓒ Ⓓ Ⓔ
4 Ⓐ Ⓑ Ⓒ Ⓓ Ⓔ   11 Ⓐ Ⓑ Ⓒ Ⓓ Ⓔ   18 Ⓐ Ⓑ Ⓒ Ⓓ Ⓔ   25 Ⓐ Ⓑ Ⓒ Ⓓ Ⓔ
5 Ⓐ Ⓑ Ⓒ Ⓓ Ⓔ   12 Ⓐ Ⓑ Ⓒ Ⓓ Ⓔ   19 Ⓐ Ⓑ Ⓒ Ⓓ Ⓔ   26 Ⓐ Ⓑ Ⓒ Ⓓ Ⓔ
6 Ⓐ Ⓑ Ⓒ Ⓓ Ⓔ   13 Ⓐ Ⓑ Ⓒ Ⓓ Ⓔ   20 Ⓐ Ⓑ Ⓒ Ⓓ Ⓔ   27 Ⓐ Ⓑ Ⓒ Ⓓ Ⓔ
7 Ⓐ Ⓑ Ⓒ Ⓓ Ⓔ   14 Ⓐ Ⓑ Ⓒ Ⓓ Ⓔ   21 Ⓐ Ⓑ Ⓒ Ⓓ Ⓔ   28 Ⓐ Ⓑ Ⓒ Ⓓ Ⓔ

Section 3

1 Ⓐ Ⓑ Ⓒ Ⓓ Ⓔ   4 Ⓐ Ⓑ Ⓒ Ⓓ Ⓔ   7 Ⓐ Ⓑ Ⓒ Ⓓ Ⓔ   10 Ⓐ Ⓑ Ⓒ Ⓓ Ⓔ
2 Ⓐ Ⓑ Ⓒ Ⓓ Ⓔ   5 Ⓐ Ⓑ Ⓒ Ⓓ Ⓔ   8 Ⓐ Ⓑ Ⓒ Ⓓ Ⓔ   11 Ⓐ Ⓑ Ⓒ Ⓓ Ⓔ
3 Ⓐ Ⓑ Ⓒ Ⓓ Ⓔ   6 Ⓐ Ⓑ Ⓒ Ⓓ Ⓔ   9 Ⓐ Ⓑ Ⓒ Ⓓ Ⓔ   12 Ⓐ Ⓑ Ⓒ Ⓓ Ⓔ

Section 5

1 Ⓐ Ⓑ Ⓒ Ⓓ Ⓔ	**8** Ⓐ Ⓑ Ⓒ Ⓓ Ⓔ	**15** Ⓐ Ⓑ Ⓒ Ⓓ Ⓔ	**22** Ⓐ Ⓑ Ⓒ Ⓓ Ⓔ
2 Ⓐ Ⓑ Ⓒ Ⓓ Ⓔ	**9** Ⓐ Ⓑ Ⓒ Ⓓ Ⓔ	**16** Ⓐ Ⓑ Ⓒ Ⓓ Ⓔ	**23** Ⓐ Ⓑ Ⓒ Ⓓ Ⓔ
3 Ⓐ Ⓑ Ⓒ Ⓓ Ⓔ	**10** Ⓐ Ⓑ Ⓒ Ⓓ Ⓔ	**17** Ⓐ Ⓑ Ⓒ Ⓓ Ⓔ	**24** Ⓐ Ⓑ Ⓒ Ⓓ Ⓔ
4 Ⓐ Ⓑ Ⓒ Ⓓ Ⓔ	**11** Ⓐ Ⓑ Ⓒ Ⓓ Ⓔ	**18** Ⓐ Ⓑ Ⓒ Ⓓ Ⓔ	**25** Ⓐ Ⓑ Ⓒ Ⓓ Ⓔ
5 Ⓐ Ⓑ Ⓒ Ⓓ Ⓔ	**12** Ⓐ Ⓑ Ⓒ Ⓓ Ⓔ	**19** Ⓐ Ⓑ Ⓒ Ⓓ Ⓔ	
6 Ⓐ Ⓑ Ⓒ Ⓓ Ⓔ	**13** Ⓐ Ⓑ Ⓒ Ⓓ Ⓔ	**20** Ⓐ Ⓑ Ⓒ Ⓓ Ⓔ	
7 Ⓐ Ⓑ Ⓒ Ⓓ Ⓔ	**14** Ⓐ Ⓑ Ⓒ Ⓓ Ⓔ	**21** Ⓐ Ⓑ Ⓒ Ⓓ Ⓔ	

Practice Test 1

SECTION 1 TIME—25 MINUTES; 24 Questions

> **DIRECTIONS:** The following sentences have one or two blanks, each of which indicates a missing word. Beneath each sentence are five words or pairs of words. Choose the word or pair of words which, when inserted in the sentence, best fits the meaning of the sentence as a whole. Indicate your answer by filling in the corresponding circle on your answer sheet.

1. She delivered her speech with great _____, gesturing flamboyantly with her hands and smiling broadly from her opening remarks to her conclusion.

   (A) inertia
   (B) indolence
   (C) sluggishness
   (D) passivity
   (E) verve

2. They were capable and literate young women trained for the variety of _____ and demanding tasks of farm life.

   (A) facile
   (B) erudite
   (C) effortless
   (D) impossible
   (E) arduous

3. Their reading was _____ for they shared books with one another, often smuggling copies into the factory, to their overseers' _____.

   (A) narrow, consternation
   (B) comprehensive, pleasure
   (C) labored, disregard
   (D) extensive, dismay
   (E) pleasurable, satisfaction

4. Having once got hold, the determined wrestlers never let go, but struggled and wrestled and rolled on the chips _____.

   (A) fastidiously
   (B) sluggishly
   (C) incessantly
   (D) sporadically
   (E) gingerly

5. There were moments, indeed, when warm gushes of pity swept away her instinctive _____ of his condition, when she still found his old self in his eyes as they groped for each other through the dense medium of his weakness.

   (A) delight
   (B) ecstasy
   (C) disregard
   (D) resentment
   (E) liability

6. Although the insurance salesperson appeared to be a(n) _____ business professional, she was really a(n) _____.

   (A) respectable, miscreant
   (B) mediocre, incompetent
   (C) honorable, leader

    (D) ignoble, reprobate
    (E) base, scoundrel

7. If every one of us, in returning to our constituents, were to report the objections he or she has, and endeavor to gain _____ in support of these objections, we might thereby lose all the _____ effects and great advantages resulting naturally in our favor among foreign nations from any real or apparent unanimity.

    (A) partisans, salutary
    (B) fanatics, wretched
    (C) benefactors, dubious
    (D) capitalists, depraved
    (E) despots, careless

8. Despite the flawless _____, I was _____ to read the letter since it was written in Hungarian.

    (A) penmanship, empowered
    (B) stationery, unqualified

    (C) calligraphy, unable
    (D) evidence, ineligible
    (E) tribute, competent

9. Leeza was not consistent in her approach to the situation, at once _____ and _____.

    (A) ethical, devoted
    (B) indiscreet, neglectful
    (C) conscientious, frivolous
    (D) acerbic, bitter
    (E) evasive, indirect

10. Even though the legislation's _____ purpose was to curtail false advertising, its tangible outcome was to _____ free speech.

    (A) realistic, bolster
    (B) apparent, advance
    (C) improbable, laud
    (D) unexpected, sustain
    (E) ostensible, abridge

DIRECTIONS: Each passage is followed by one or more questions. Answer the questions based on what is directly stated or suggested in each passage. Indicate your answer by filling in the corresponding circle on your answer sheet.

Questions 9 and 10 are based on the following passage.

Voting is a privilege some people may take for granted, but it is one of our most precious rights.

1   In 1997, Vermont State representative Sydney Nixon was seated as an apparent one vote winner, 570 to 569. Mr. Nixon resigned when the State House determined, after a recount, that he had actually lost to his opponent Robert Emond 572 to 571. In 1989, a Lansing, Michigan School District millage proposition failed when the final recount produced a tie vote 5,147 to 5,147. On the original
5   vote count, votes against the proposition were ten more than those in favor. The result meant that the school district had to reduce its budget by $2.5 million.

11. Which sentence best summarizes the content of this passage?

    (A) It's not as important to vote as you might think.
    (B) Even minor elections can have very important outcomes.
    (C) As Americans, we are very fortunate to have the right to vote.
    (D) The voting process is laborious and time-consuming, but in the end it is worth the time and trouble.
    (E) Just one vote can and often does make a difference in the outcome of an election.

12. The numbers "572 to 571" mentioned in line 3 serve to emphasize

    (A) how close the outcome was
    (B) how few people exercise their right to vote
    (C) the insignificance of this particular election
    (D) why we need Internet voting rather than paper ballots
    (E) how the voters decided that Nixon was a better candidate than Emond

Questions 13 to 15 are based on the following passage.

The following diary entry was written on April 13, 1645.

1   Mr. Hopkins, the governor of Hartford upon Connecticut, came to Boston, and brought his wife with him, (a godly young woman, and of special parts,) who was fallen into a sad infirmity, the loss of her understanding and reason, which had been growing on her diverse years, by occasion of her giving herself wholly to reading and writing, and had written many books. Her husband, being very
5   loving and tender of her, was loath to grieve her; but he saw his error, when it was too late. For if she had attended to her household affairs, and such things as belong to women, and not gone out of her way and calling to meddle in such things as are proper for men, whose minds are stronger, etc., she had kept her wits, and might have improved them usefully and honorably. He brought her to Boston, and left her with her brother, one Mr. Yale, a merchant, to try what means might be had
10   here for her. But no help could be had.

13. The author of this passage is most likely

    (A) strongly in favor of education for women
    (B) advocating universal health care
    (C) vehemently opposed to educating women
    (D) against people marrying too young
    (E) proposing arranged marriages instead of love matches

14. In line 3, *diverse* most nearly means

    (A) different
    (B) many
    (C) difficult
    (D) divided
    (E) incomparable

15. Which of the following best states the main idea of this passage?

    (A) Education can be very demanding for all young people and can even cause them to suffer a nervous breakdown.

(B) Wealthier people have strong advantages when it comes to educational and medical opportunities.

(C) There is so much household work to be done that it can only be accomplished if spouses share responsibilities equally.

(D) It takes a village to raise a child.

(E) In the seventeenth century, some people believed that women were too delicate to take much learning; rather, they were fit only for household duties.

Questions 16 to 24 are based on the following passage.

In the following essay, the writer discusses work and its relationship to the whole individual.

1   It is one of those fables which out of an unknown antiquity convey an unlooked-for wisdom, that the gods, in the beginning, divided Man into men, that he might be more helpful to himself; just as the hand was divided into fingers, the better to answer its end.

The old fable covers a doctrine ever new and sublime; that there is One Man,—present to all
5   particular men only partially, or through one faculty; and that you must take the whole society to find the whole man. Man is not a farmer, or a professor, or an engineer, but he is all. Man is priest, and scholar, and statesman, and producer, and soldier. In the divided or social state these functions are parceled out to individuals, each of whom aims to do his stint of the joint work, whilst each other performs his. But, unfortunately, this original unit, this fountain of power, has been so dis-
10   tributed to multitudes, has been so minutely subdivided and peddled out, that it is spilled into drops, and cannot be gathered. The state of society is one in which the members have suffered amputation from the trunk, and strut about like so many walking monsters,—a good finger, a neck, a stomach, an elbow, but never a man.

Man is thus metamorphosed into a thing, into many things. The planter, who is Man sent out
15   into the field to gather food, is seldom cheered by any idea of the true dignity of his ministry. He sees his bushel and his cart, and nothing beyond, and sinks into the farmer, instead of Man on the farm. The tradesman scarcely ever gives an ideal worth to his work, but is ridden by the routine of his craft, and the soul is subject to dollars. The priest becomes a form; the attorney a statute-book; the mechanic a machine; the sailor a rope of the ship.

20   In this distribution of functions the scholar is the delegated intellect. In the right state he is Man Thinking. In the degenerate state, when the victim of society, he tends to become a mere thinker, or still worse, the parrot of other men's thinking.

---

16. The phrase "the better to answer its end" in line 3 can best be interpreted to mean

   (A) signal the specific type of division
   (B) show defeat
   (C) better to serve its purpose
   (D) destroy the strength of the whole
   (E) signal the conclusion of the fable

17. The "old fable" in line 4 refers to

   (A) a legend about the naming of parts
   (B) a myth about the beginning of the world
   (C) an allegory about regeneration
   (D) the belief that individuals possess only certain talents
   (E) a parable concerning change and metamorphosis

18. As used in line 5, the word *faculty* most nearly means

(A) a department of learning
(B) aptitude
(C) power
(D) authority
(E) staff

19. The phrase "But, unfortunately" (line 9) does which of the following things?

(A) It signals a transition to a new idea.
(B) It shifts the focus from generalities to individual cases.
(C) It emphasizes the abstract in place of the concrete.
(D) It signals a continuation of a previous line of reasoning.
(E) It shows the distribution of power among individual members of society.

20. Which of the following statements best expresses the writer's attitude toward society?

(A) Society is necessary to ensure that all labor is accomplished.
(B) That government is best which governs least.
(C) Society has destroyed humanity's wholeness.
(D) Society alone can distribute tasks equably among its members.
(E) Lack of social controls has resulted in a sharp rise in industrial accidents.

21. The writer uses the word *ministry* (line 15) in relation to the planter to suggest

(A) the inherent holiness of farming
(B) the farmer would rather be a minister
(C) the farmer worships the soil and its abundance
(D) farming's dependence on the whims of nature
(E) the importance of having jobs we like and can excel in

22. The author's thesis in the third paragraph is developed through

(A) repetition of key words
(B) comparison and contrast
(C) a series of examples
(D) alliteration
(E) aphorisms

23. The tone of this essay is best described as

(A) despairing
(B) fiery
(C) soothing
(D) angry
(E) neutral

24. The language of this essay is best described as

(A) colloquial
(B) scholarly and elevated
(C) florid
(D) biased
(E) vague and colorless

If you finish before time is up, go over your work in this section only.

SECTION 2 TIME—25 MINUTES; 28 Questions

> **DIRECTIONS:** The following sentences have one or two blanks, each of which indicates a missing word. Beneath each sentence are five words or pairs of words. Choose the word or pair of words which, when inserted in the sentence, best fits the meaning of the sentence as a whole. Indicate your answer by filling in the corresponding circle on your answer sheet.

1. It was at this moment, as I stood there with the rifle in my hand, that I first grasped the hollowness, the _____ of the imperialistic dominion of the East.

   (A) success
   (B) triumph
   (C) neutrality
   (D) future
   (E) futility

2. Her unexpected demise, at first mistakenly diagnosed as due to a _____ fever, was later _____ poison.

   (A) mild, attributed to
   (B) moderate, blamed on
   (C) raging, ascribed to
   (D) savage, caused by
   (E) simple, occasioned by

3. She looked bloated, like a body long _____ in motionless water, and of that _____ hue.

   (A) aloft, robust
   (B) immersed, ruddy
   (C) atop, pellucid
   (D) baptized, rosy
   (E) submerged, pallid

4. The pawnbroker's widow was a(n) _____ old woman who loved to gossip and hear herself talk.

   (A) taciturn
   (B) garrulous
   (C) withdrawn
   (D) vicious
   (E) uncommunicative

5. The caretaker did not know she was due in London today (her call there had been planned as a surprise), so his _____ in the manner of leaving this letter, leaving it to wait in the dusk and dust, annoyed her.

   (A) alertness
   (B) attentiveness
   (C) delicateness
   (D) negligence
   (E) frugality

6. That is, some books are to be read only in parts; others to be read but _____, and some few to be read wholly and with _____ and attention.

   (A) cursorily, diligence
   (B) quickly, lethargy
   (C) gingerly, neglect
   (D) thoughtfully, laxity
   (E) discreetly, disregard

7. Through one of the broken panes I heard rain impinge upon the earth again and again, the fine _____ needles of water playing in the already _____ flower beds.

   (A) ceaseless, groomed
   (B) eternal, prim
   (C) incessant, sodden
   (D) gentle, straight
   (E) pungent, saturated

8. The _____ student _____ at the idea that he had to give a speech in class.

   (A) timid, recoiled
   (B) frail, rejoiced
   (C) fragile, reveled
   (D) insolent, relapsed
   (E) bold, repined

9. Now and then we would see her standing motionless in one of the downstairs windows like the carven torso of a(n) _____ in a(n) _____, looking or not looking at us, we could never tell which.

   (A) statue, mistrial
   (B) idle, nook
   (C) idol, niche
   (D) ruffian, courtroom
   (E) reprobate, window

10. A thin _____ pall as of the tomb seemed to lie everywhere upon this room decked and furnished as for a wedding, with a silver hairbrush so tarnished that the monogrammed initials were _____.

    (A) luscious, shrouded
    (B) pure, sheltered
    (C) caustic, apparent
    (D) agreeable, camouflaged
    (E) acrid, obscured

DIRECTIONS: Each of the following passages is followed by questions. Answer each question based on what is directly stated or suggested in the related passage. Indicate your answer by filling in the corresponding circle on your answer sheet.

Questions 11 to 16 are based on the following passage.

Florence Nightingale (1820–1910) was a nurse, hospital reformer, and humanitarian. When the Crimean War broke out in 1854, she was put in charge of all hospital and nursing efforts on the war front, in Turkey.

1   Eventually the whole business of purveying to the hospitals was, in effect, carried out by Miss Nightingale. She, alone, it seemed, whatever the contingency, knew where to lay her hands on what was wanted; she alone possessed the art of circumventing the pernicious influences of official etiquette. On one occasion 27,000 shirts arrived, sent out at her insistence by the Home Government,
5   and were only waiting to be unpacked. But the official "Purveyor" intervened; "He could only unpack them" he said, "with an official order from the Government." Miss Nightingale pleaded in vain; the sick and the wounded lay half-naked, shivering for want of clothing; and three weeks elapsed before the Government released the shipment. A little later, on a similar occasion, Miss Nightingale ordered a Government consignment to be forcibly opened, while the "Purveyor" stood
10   by, wringing his hands in departmental agony.

11. The use of the phrase "she alone" (line 2) gives the reader an idea of Miss Nightingale's

    (A) loneliness
    (B) conceit
    (C) femininity
    (D) uniqueness
    (E) inefficiency

12. Describing the influence of official etiquette as "pernicious" (line 3) reveals the author's awareness of the

    (A) dangers of red tape
    (B) efficiency of command procedure
    (C) lack of blood plasma
    (D) women's liberation movement
    (E) horrors of war

13. The description of the sick and wounded as "half-naked" and "shivering" in line 7 serves as

    (A) an introduction of physical detail
    (B) weather information
    (C) historic documentation
    (D) a contrast to bureaucratic lack of concern
    (E) a metaphor or comparison

14. As used in line 7, the word *vain* most nearly means

    (A) with her ego held in check
    (B) in a conceited manner
    (C) in an arrogant way
    (D) without help from anyone else
    (E) without any success

15. The Purveyor seems concerned only with

    (A) humanity
    (B) the ill men
    (C) the men's needs
    (D) departmental procedure
    (E) Miss Nightingale's requests

16. The tone of the phrase "departmental agony" is

    (A) ironic
    (B) despairing
    (C) serious
    (D) tragic
    (E) funny

Questions 17 to 20 are based on the following passage.

Government agencies fulfill many different functions. Find out how one government agency relates to wildlife and nature.

1   Three Pintail ducks from North America were shot in widely separated places in far distant parts of the world: one duck was taken near Cali, Colombia, South America; one on an island in the Pacific; and the last along the Dart River in England. The South American hunter learned that his duck had come from North Dakota. The weatherman in the Pacific discovered that his bird had been in
5   northern California, more than 4,600 miles away, just 3 months before. The English sportsman found that his Pintail duck just 21 days before had been in Labrador, some 2,200 miles across the Atlantic. How did these hunters know their ducks had come from North America?
    It really isn't such a mystery as it might seem. On the leg of each duck the hunter had found a small aluminum band, which carried a number and a request that the finder of the band report to
10 the Fish and Wildlife Service in Washington, DC, USA. Each hunter did exactly that. When their letters reached the Service in Washington, they were sent to the Bird Banding Office where the band number, species, date of banding, place of banding, and name of the bander are recorded. When people send in bands they have found, the record can be located quickly.

17. According to the details in the first paragraph, how many ducks were shot?

    (A) 3
    (B) 21
    (C) 2200
    (D) 4600
    (E) 21

18. The main purpose of the first paragraph is to

    (A) suggest that hunters are responsible people deeply involved with conserving wildlife
    (B) imply that many people do not believe that hunting is humane
    (C) show that pintail ducks can travel to far points of the globe
    (D) explain how one duck was shot in South America
    (E) advise people to be very careful when they hunt all wildlife, but most especially endangered species

19. According to the information in the second paragraph, the hunters were able to trace the origin of their birds because

    (A) the hunters knew about the Fish and Wildlife Service in Washington, DC
    (B) the ducks carried bands on their legs that provided a way to get information about them
    (C) the hunters wrote letters to Washington, DC
    (D) the band number, species, date of banding, place of banding, and name of the bander are all a matter of public record
    (E) the birds' origins were not a mystery at all

20. Which of the following conclusions can be drawn from the second paragraph?

    (A) Bird banding is expensive and time-consuming.
    (B) It takes a long time to get a reply from the Fish and Wildlife Service in Washington, DC.
    (C) Some ducks have a small aluminum band on their leg.
    (D) Bird banding is an easy way to trace the paths of different kinds of birds.
    (E) All birds should be banded to ensure their survival.

Questions 21 to 28 are based on the following passage.

Millions of years ago, dinosaurs roamed the earth freely. About 65 million years ago, they all died out. Few mysteries have been as baffling—and as compelling—as the disappearance of the dinosaurs. Here are some of the latest theories.

1   Dinosaurs roamed the earth for nearly 150 million years; then they suddenly died out and became extinct. No one knows exactly why. Paleontologists once thought that dinosaurs had such small, inefficient brains that they were somehow responsible for their own dying out. Because dinosaur remains have been found in so many different parts of the world, scientists have had a hard time
5   coming up with a single strong explanation for their sudden demise.

   There are a lot of theories, however, and some of them are fantastic. Some observers, for example, have suggested that the dinosaurs vanished because of raids by extraterrestrial beings. Other theories are more logical but still guesses. The dinosaurs could have died because of some mass disease. That seems unlikely, though, because of the way they were dispersed all over the world. Some
10   speculate that an exploding star bathed the earth in radiation, killing all the dinosaurs. This does not explain why all the other creatures on earth survived. There is also a theory that dinosaurs disappeared because of overcrowding. One well-regarded theory concerns food sources. According to this theory, the dinosaurs ate too many flowering plants and absorbed poisonous chemicals. Since they did not have a well-developed sense of taste, the dinosaurs did not realize that they were eating
15   something that would harm them. These theories remain just that however—theories—because no one to date has been able to prove any of them.

21. Who or what are *paleontologists* (line 2)?

   (A) A type of dinosaur
   (B) Extinct life forms
   (C) Dinosaur bones
   (D) A scientific theory that does not have much credence
   (E) Scientists who study extinct forms of animal life

22. As used in line 4, the word *remains* most nearly means

   (A) leavings
   (B) skeletons
   (C) stay behind
   (D) cadavers
   (E) remnants

23. According to the information in the first paragraph, what is one possible cause for the dinosaurs' disappearance?

   (A) The paleontologists killed them.
   (B) They were inefficient creatures who did not use their food sources wisely.
   (C) They were unable to survive because of their small brains.
   (D) They were attacked by other, more fierce, creatures.
   (E) They lived in many different parts of the world.

24. Which sentence best states the main idea of the first paragraph?

   (A) No one really knows why the dinosaurs vanished.
   (B) It is a real shame that we no longer have dinosaurs to study.
   (C) It is relatively easy to study dinosaurs because so much is already known about them and they are found in so many places around the world.

(D) Paleontologists learn about vanished forms of animal life.

(E) Dinosaurs had such small brains that they could not meet the demands of a changing world.

25. By calling the theories "fantastic" (line 6), the writer is suggesting that on the whole these theories are

(A) well deserving of merit
(B) creative but unrealistic
(C) totally unreasonable
(D) wild and unproved
(E) scholarly and authoritative

26. Which information in the second paragraph can be verified by an outside source?

(A) Visitors from outside our solar system killed off the dinosaurs.
(B) There are many theories that attempt to explain the dinosaurs' disappearance.
(C) The dinosaurs vanished because of a plague.
(D) A star blew up and sent off radiation that killed all the dinosaurs.
(E) The dinosaurs died off when they ate the wrong food.

27. The description in the second paragraph moves from

(A) least logical to most logical
(B) most logical to least logical
(C) causes to effects
(D) chronological order: most distant past to more recent events
(E) inductive to deductive reasoning

28. Which of the following choices can be inferred from the information in the second paragraph?

(A) Very soon, scientists will be able to prove one or more of the theories about the dinosaurs' disappearance.
(B) Most of the theories of the dinosaurs' disappearance are not backed up by sufficient facts to be convincing.
(C) The same exploding star that killed off the dinosaurs also killed off many early cave people.
(D) The disappearance of the dinosaurs is one of the most important problems facing scientists today and has great impact on other research.
(E) The reason for the dinosaurs' disappearance has puzzled many scientists.

If you finish before time is up, go over your work in this section only.

SECTION 3 TIME—15 MINUTES; 12 Questions

> **DIRECTIONS:** The two passages presented here are followed by questions about their content. Answer the questions based on what is directly stated or suggested in the passage. Indicate your answer by filling in the corresponding circle on your answer sheet.

Questions 1 to 12 are based on the following passages.

Both of the following passages concern World War II, 1939–1945. The first passage is excerpted from an article on the events leading up to World War II. The second passage is a comment by Anne Frank. She was the teenager whose diary of her experiences hidden in a secret annex during World War II became famous after her death.

Passage 1

1   World War I (1914–1918) ended for Germany in total defeat. The German people were dissatisfied: the peace treaty was a great humiliation, there was no money, no work and no hope of a better future. In the chaotic 1920s, an unknown Austrian worked his way up to the position of "Fuhrer" (leader) of an insignificant political party in Munich. His name was Adolf Hitler; the party called

5   itself the NSDAP and its followers were called "Nazis." After an unsuccessful coup d'etat, Hitler was put in a comfortable prison, where he wrote his plans for world domination in a book called *Mein Kampf* (*My Struggle*). Hitler said that the German people were "Aryans," the strongest and best race. All other races were inferior, especially the Jews, whom he blamed for everything that was wrong and for all Germany's defeats.

10   Hitler's ideas appealed to many Germans and the NSDAP soon became powerful. In 1933, Hitler was appointed Chancellor of Germany and, within a year, consolidated all power within his grasp. The concentration camps filled up—first with political opponents, particularly Communists and trade union leaders, but soon with Jews, Gypsies, homosexuals; in brief, everyone who disagreed with him or whom he regarded as inferior. The Nazi oppression of the Jews was marked by two sig-

15   nificant events: The Nuremberg Laws and the Wannsee Conference.

The Nuremberg laws, passed in 1935, deprived Jews of citizenship. Jews were forbidden from marrying non-Jews, working in the professions (including law, medicine, journalism, and teaching), and using public transportation. Jews could not drive cars (even their own) or go to the movies or theaters. At the Wannsee Conference, a top-level Nazi meeting in 1942, the "Final Solution of the

20   Jewish Question" was set into motion—the extermination of all Jews in Europe.

All of life in Germany from 1933 on was oriented towards preparation for war. Few people, however, realized this. In September of 1939, World War II began with the invasion of Poland. Between then and 1945, this war was to cost nearly 55 million people their lives. Between the German invasion of the Soviet Union in 1941 and the end of the war in Europe in May 1945,

25   Nazi Germany and its accomplices strove to murder every Jew under their domination. The Jews were not the only victims of Hitler's regime, but they were the only group that the Nazis sought to destroy entirely.

Passage 2

I don't believe that the big men, the politicians and the capitalists alone, are guilty of the war. Oh no, the little man is just as guilty, otherwise the peoples of the world would have risen in revolt long
30   ago! There's in people simply an urge to destroy, an urge to kill, to murder and rage, until all mankind, without exception, undergoes a great change, wars will be waged, everything that has been built up, cultivated, and grown will be destroyed and disfigured, after which mankind will have to begin all over again.

—May 1944

1. The writer of passage 1 uses the redundant phrase "total defeat" (line 1) to

   (A) imply that the Germans were not at fault for losing World War I

   (B) infer that the Germans were overpowered from the start

   (C) emphasize the German feeling of complete and utter disgrace after their defeat

   (D) hint that not all Germans felt the same way about the debacle

   (E) suggest the Germans deserved their defeat in both World War I and World War II

2. Why does the writer place the word *Fuhrer* (line 3) in quotation marks?

   (A) to draw attention to it

   (B) to show it is a foreign word

   (C) to comment ironically that Hitler was no leader

   (D) to make sure that people pronounce it correctly

   (E) because it is deliberately misspelled for emphasis

3. From the details in the passage, what can you infer was Hitler's reason for writing *Mein Kampf*, his plans for world domination?

   (A) He did not have enough to do in jail.

   (B) He always had literary aspirations and considered himself a fine writer.

   (C) He needed the money that the publication would bring to finance his political aspirations.

   (D) He wanted to justify and legitimatize his strategy to the widest possible audience.

   (E) He had been asked to create the plan by his political party.

4. According to passage 1, the Nazis oppression of the Jews was marked by all the following events *except*

   (A) forbidding Jews from marrying non-Jews

   (B) depriving Jews of citizenship

   (C) forbidding Jews from working as teachers and from using public transportation

(D) blaming Jews for Germany's defeat in World War I

(E) forcing Jews to leave the country

5. Based on the details in passage 1, why do you think Hitler's ideas appealed to many Germans?

(A) Hitler came from a well-educated, cultured family so he attracted people looking for a strong leader.

(B) The Germans were looking for someone who could both find a scapegoat for their humiliation and improve economic conditions.

(C) Hitler was an outsider so he could bring fresh, new ideas into the country.

(D) The Germans were swayed by the high quality of Hitler's writing in *Mein Kampf*.

(E) Unlike other leaders of the time, Hitler could carry through on his promises.

6. Passage 1 is organized according to

(A) chronological order

(B) least-to-most important events

(C) most-to-least important events

(D) cause and effect

(E) reasons and causes

7. In passage 2, the phrase "big men" (line 28) is used to connote

(A) powerful people

(B) non-Jews

(C) physically strong people

(D) rulers removed from the action

(E) expatriates living safely abroad

8. In passage 2, Anne Frank sees people as

(A) very different, depending on their economic status

(B) essentially kind, but misruled by tyrants

(C) responsible for their own fate

(D) welcoming change as a way to start anew

(E) helpless pawns on the world stage

9. As used in line 32, the word *disfigured* most nearly means

(A) misshapen

(B) assassinated

(C) handicapped

(D) wounded

(E) marred

10. These passages are similar in that both

(A) were written by the same author

(B) describe the same event in world history

(C) approach the topic from the same point of view

(D) were written for the same audience and purpose

(E) have a marked bias

11. In what way is the tone of passage 2 different from the tone of passage 1?

(A) The tone of passage 2 is lighter and less serious than the tone of passage 1.

(B) The tone of passage 2 more serious than the tone of passage 1.

(C) The tone of passage 2 is less factual than the tone of passage 1.

(D) The tone of passage 2 is more sardonic and sarcastic than the tone of passage 1.

(E) The tone of passage 2 is darker and more pessimistic than the neutral tone of passage 1.

12. What does the second passage add to your understanding of the events leading up to and culminating in World War II in Europe?

(A) How all people reacted to these events

(B) How these events affected one individual

(C) Why these events mattered on the world stage

(D) How these events affected the oppressed Jews of Germany

(E) Ways to prevent future wars

If you finish before time is up, go over your work in this section only.

SECTION 4   TIME—25 MINUTES; Essay

DIRECTIONS: Read the passage presented here and the assignment that follows it. Then plan and write an essay that explains your ideas about the topic. Remember to support your position with both reasons and examples to make your ideas convincing to the reader.

Should fast-food franchises be allowed in schools? After all, many soda companies already pay a great deal of money to be allowed to install soda machines in school. This money pays for much-needed textbooks, school supplies, and repairs. On the other hand, fast food is greatly contributing to the epidemic of obesity among America's youth.

Assignment: Construct an argument explaining your position on this issue. As you develop your argument, support your views with relevant reasons and examples from your experiences, observations, and reading. To strengthen your position, you might wish to consider alternative or opposing views.

SECTION 5   TIME—25 MINUTES; 25 Questions

DIRECTIONS: The following sentences require you to identify errors in grammar, usage, style, and mechanics. Not every sentence has an error, and no sentence will have more than one error. Each sentence error, if there is one, is underlined and lettered. If there is an error, select the one underlined part that must be changed to make the sentence correct and blacken the corresponding circle on your answer sheet. If there is no error, blacken circle E. Elements of the sentence that are not underlined are not to be changed.

1. Some people claim this is the decade of fitness, but, in fact, at least
     A   B   C

    one-third of the American population are classified as obese.   No error.
                                     D   E

2. During the graduation ceremonies, the superintendent of schools told the
     A

    story of the desks and cites their cleaning as evidence of a new spirit of
                      B   C

    responsibility among students. No error.
              D   E

3. The twins are fond of peanuts and eating ice cream, but their parents are
                         A   B

    loath to give the children snacks between meals. No error.
            C   D   E

4. The real estate broker promised to notify my partner and I as soon as the
               A   B

    house was put up for sale so we could make any necessary repairs to the
         C   D

    structure. No error.
        E

5. Either the witness or the defendant were lying, but the judge was unable to
                    A   B

determine <u>which</u> of the two men was <u>committing perjury.</u>   <u>No error.</u>
     C   D   E

6. <u>A close friend of the family,</u> the patient <u>was referred</u> to a psychologist
      A   B

  <u>with several emotional problems</u> to <u>receive counseling.</u>   <u>No error.</u>
      C   D   E

7. The speaker <u>didn't say nothing</u> that the audience had not already
      A

  <u>heard; as a result,</u> the <u>audience quickly</u> lost interest in his speech and
    B   C

  <u>began to talk</u> among themselves.   <u>No error.</u>
    D   E

8. <u>The Word workshop trains employees</u> about maximizing skills <u>to improve</u>
        A   B

  employees' <u>productivity, the Internet</u> training teaches employees
         C

  <u>how to use the Internet</u> for product searches and e-mail to worldwide
      D

  subscribers.   <u>No error.</u>
      E

9. <u>The recipe was complex</u> but is <u>worth it</u> because chicken and biscuits
     A   B

  <u>made this way</u> <u>tastes more deliciously.</u>   <u>No error.</u>
    C   D   E

10. The prominent lawyer won more awards than <u>anyone at</u> the ceremony,
                  A

  <u>which surprised her</u> because <u>she had long taken on</u> unpopular cases
     B   C

  <u>and defendants.</u>   <u>No error.</u>
    D   E

DIRECTIONS: In each of the following sentences, part or all of the sentence is underlined. Each sentence is followed by five ways of phrasing the underlined part. Choose the best version of the underlined portion of each sentence and blacken the corresponding circle on your answer sheet. Choice A is always the same as the underlined portion of the original sentence. Choose answer A if you think the original sentence needs no revision.

11. There have been many controversial World Series, but the <u>most unique one</u> was certainly the thrown World Series of 1919.

    (A) most unique one
    (B) most one-of-a-kind
    (C) unique one
    (D) uniquest one
    (E) one that was the most unique

12. Derek Bickerton, a noted linguist, described some of the best examples of the innate formation of a grammar <u>system he</u> noted that indentured workers on plantations in the South Pacific needed to communicate with each other in order to carry out practical tasks.

    (A) system he
    (B) system when he
    (C) system, he
    (D) system yet he
    (E) system; he

13. It was not until 1966 that an African-American <u>become the coach</u> of a major United States professional sports team.

    (A) become the coach
    (B) became the coach
    (C) coaching
    (D) were coaching
    (E) becoming the coach

14. According to the new personnel policy instituted this year, <u>it is necessary for</u> all employees to select a health plan.

    (A) it is necessary for
    (B) it is required that
    (C) because it is necessary
    (D) since it is necessary
    (E) all employees must select a health plan

15. Each morning when the guards checked my shoulder bag and clanked shut the iron door behind me, the old convict in me <u>rose up</u> full of hatred and rage for the guards, the walls, the terrible indecency of the place.

    (A) rose up
    (B) rosed up
    (C) rised up
    (D) risen up
    (E) rise up

16. <u>A tornado</u> can pick up a house and drop it hundreds of feet away, these are extremely dangerous storms.

    (A) A tornado
    (B) When a tornado
    (C) If a tornado
    (D) Since a tornado
    (E) An tornado

17. The masters of the time were wary of their laborers being able to communicate with each <u>other formed</u> mixed groups of laborers who spoke different languages.

   (A) other formed
   (B) other, formed
   (C) other they formed
   (D) other, so they formed
   (E) other so they have been forming

18. The candidate went to political rallies, spoke at meetings, and <u>she shook many hands.</u>

   (A) she shook many hands
   (B) was shaking many hands
   (C) had been shaking many hands
   (D) realized the importance of shaking hands
   (E) shook many hands

19. The conference will provide training to ensure that our employees are kept abreast of the latest technology advancements <u>and is able to</u> function in the information age.

   (A) and is able to
   (B) and was able to
   (C) is able to
   (D) and being able to
   (E) and are able to

20. Just before the trial was <u>scheduled to start,</u> every one of the confessions mysteriously vanished from the office of the Illinois State Attorney.

   (A) scheduled to start, the
   (B) scheduled to start the
   (C) scheduled to start—the
   (D) scheduled to start: the
   (E) scheduled to start; the

DIRECTIONS: The following passage is an early draft of an essay. Some parts of the passage need to be rewritten. Read the passage and select the best answers to the questions that follow. Some questions are about particular sentences or parts of sentences and ask you to improve sentence structure and word choice. Other questions refer to parts of the essay or the entire essay and ask you to consider organization and development. In making your decisions, follow the conventions of standard written English. After you have chosen your answer, fill in the corresponding circle on your answer sheet.

---

   (1) A difficult time is had by many young people today finding careers that are both pleasurable and profitable. (2) Since many large companies have reduced their staffs—a process called "downsizing"—there are fewer management and support jobs available. (3) When all the discipline of sticking it out in school yields an occupation they do not enjoy, they hold themselves to blame for not feeling more self-confidence. (4) Consequently, they change careers after a few years. (5) They may return to school for retraining or to learn new skills on their own. (6) Others stay with unsatisfactory jobs for much longer. (7) They look to community service, family, and hobbies for the satisfaction they don't find in their jobs.

21. In context, which is the best way to revise and combine the underlined portion of sentence 1 (reproduced here)?

> *(1) A difficult time is had by many young people today finding careers that are both pleasurable and profitable.*

   (A) As it is now.
   (B) Today, a difficult time is had by many young people
   (C) A difficult time is being had by many young people today
   (D) By many young people today, a difficult time is being had
   (E) Many young people today are having a difficult time

22. Which sentence would be most appropriate to follow sentence 2?

   (A) They see their parents' work as more interesting and worthwhile.
   (B) As a result, many young people feel unhappy and dissatisfied with the jobs they get.
   (C) They suffer from a feeling of not having made use of their opportunities.
   (D) "If only I had what it takes," says a young shoe salesman, son of a factory laborer, "then things would have been different."
   (E) Few young people have a strong work ethic, and this is evident by their lack of effort in seeking traditional jobs.

23. Which of the following best replaces the word *they* in sentence 4?

   (A) confident workers
   (B) downsized workers
   (C) some workers
   (D) students
   (E) well-paid workers

24. In context, which is the best version of the underlined portions of sentences 4 and 5? (reproduced here)?

> *Consequently, they change careers after a few years. They may return to school for retraining or learn new skills on their own.*

   (A) As it is now.
   (B) a few years, returning to school for retraining or learning
   (C) a few years they may return to school for retraining or to learn
   (D) a few years, they may return to school for retraining or to learn
   (E) a few years, yet they may return to school for retraining or learn

25. Including a paragraph on which of the following would most strengthen the writer's argument?

   (A) Examples of young people who cannot find profitable and enjoyable careers
   (B) A thorough discussion of budgeting, including examples of budgets for young people
   (C) A complete explanation of the phenomenon of "downsizing"
   (D) The importance of having discipline and earning good grades in school
   (E) A list of schools that offer retraining

Practice Test 1 Answer Key

Section 1

1. **E.** The correct sentence reads: "She delivered her speech with great verve, gesturing flamboyantly with her hands and smiling broadly from her opening remarks to her conclusion." Since the speaker gestures flamboyantly with her hands and smiles broadly from her opening remarks to her conclusion, she is very animated and energized. Only choice E has this meaning.

2. **E.** The correct sentence reads: "They were capable and literate young women trained for the variety of arduous and demanding tasks of farm life." The word *demanding* is your clue: *arduous* means "strenuous or difficult."

3. **D.** The correct sentence reads: "Their reading was extensive for they shared books with one another, often smuggling copies into the factory, to their overseers' dismay." Their reading could be *extensive* (wide-ranging) because they shared books. Their overseers would feel *dismay* (anxiety, fear) because time spent reading would not be time spent working. Overseers are not likely to experience pleasure or satisfaction over an employee's time spent reading, so choices B and C cannot be correct.

4. **C.** The correct sentence reads: "Having once got hold, the determined wrestlers never let go, but struggled and wrestled and rolled on the chips incessantly." If they never let go, they struggled without pause, which matches *incessantly*.

5. **D.** The correct sentence reads: "There were moments, indeed, when warm gushes of pity swept away her instinctive resentment of his condition, when she still found his old self in his eyes as they groped for each other through the dense medium of his weakness." Pity erases her anger and bitterness—her *resentment*.

6. **A.** The correct sentence reads: "Although the insurance salesperson appeared to be a respectable business professional, she was really a miscreant." The word *although* is a contrast clue. The second half of the sentence will be the opposite of the first half. Thus, even though the insurance salesperson appeared to be a *respectable* business professional (something good), she was really a *miscreant* (a criminal or an evil person, something bad).

7. **A.** The correct sentence reads: "If every one of us, in returning to our constituents, were to report the objections he or she has, and endeavor to gain partisans in

support of these objections, we might thereby lose all the salutary effects and great advantages resulting naturally in our favor among foreign nations from any real or apparent unanimity." Focus on the word *support* in the first clause. Every person is trying to gain support for something. People who support you are *partisans.* Now look at the second part of this sentence beginning with "we might thereby lose." What we are losing is good effects. This is shown by the phrase "great advantages." *Salutary* means "beneficial."

8. **C.** The correct sentence reads: "Despite the flawless calligraphy, I was unable to read the letter since it was written in Hungarian." The transition *despite* means "in spite of." Thus, in spite of the flawless calligraphy (handwriting), the speaker could not read the letter since it was written in Hungarian. The word that means "could not" is *unable.*

9. **C.** The correct sentence reads: "Leeza was not consistent in her approach to the situation, at once conscientious and frivolous." Since Leeza is not consistent, the two words must be antonyms (opposites). Of the word pairs given, only *conscientious* (scrupulous, paying attention to details) and *frivolous* (lighthearted, careless) are opposites.

10. **E.** The correct sentence reads: "Even though the legislation's ostensible purpose was to curtail false advertising, its tangible outcome was to abridge free speech." The subordinating conjunction *even though* tells you that the first clause will be the opposite of the second clause. You can infer from context that the first half will be positive and the second half negative. Therefore, even though the legislation's *ostensible* (apparent) purpose was to *curtail* (stop) false advertising, the opposite took place—false advertising was not stopped. We see this in the conclusion: "its tangible outcome was to *abridge* (diminish) free speech."

11. **E.** The entire passage demonstrates how just one vote can and often does make a difference in the outcome of an election.

12. **A.** The numbers "572 to 571" in line 3 serve to emphasize how close the outcome was. Since we don't know how many people live in the town, we cannot conclude that few people exercise their right to vote (choice B). In fact, if the town has only 1500 eligible voters, the turnout was quite robust. The number of votes does not indicate that this particular election was significant or insignificant (choice C). The numbers have nothing to do with the issue of Internet voting rather than the use of paper ballots (choice D). Finally, the vote actually shows that the voters decided that Emond was a better candidate than Nixon since Emond won the election, so choice E cannot be valid.

13. **C.** Here's the key sentence: "For if she had attended to her household affairs, and such things as belong to women, and not gone out of her way and calling to meddle in such things as are proper for men, whose minds are stronger, etc., she

had kept her wits, and might have improved them usefully and honorably." From this sentence, you can infer that the writer is vehemently opposed to educating women. He believes that their minds are too weak to withstand the rigors of education.

14. **B.** If the young wife had spent much time studying and had written many books, *diverse* must mean "many."

15. **E.** The young woman lost her wits ("her understanding and reason") because she spent too much time on education ("giving herself wholly to reading and writing, and had written many books") and too little time on her household duties. Her breakdown could have been prevented, the author believes, "if she had attended to her household affairs, and such things as belong to women." You can figure out when this was written by the date given in the headnote of the passage.

16. **C.** The phrase "the better to answer its end" in line 3 can best be interpreted to mean better to serve its purpose. The word *end* is used here to mean "purpose" or "means." None of the other answer choices conveys this meaning.

17. **D.** The phrase "old fable" in line 4 refers to the belief that individuals possess only certain talents. You can infer this from the first sentence in the second paragraph, especially the last clause: "The old fable covers a doctrine ever new and sublime; that there is One Man,—present to all particular men only partially, or through one faculty; and that you must take the whole society to find the whole man." If you must consider everyone together to find the "whole man," each individual must have only certain abilities. Choice A (a legend about the naming of parts), choice B (a myth about the beginning of the world), choice C (an allegory about regeneration), and choice E (a parable concerning change and metamorphosis) sound sufficiently mythlike to mislead casual readers, but none of these choices expresses the correct meaning.

18. **B.** As used in context, the word *faculty* most nearly means "aptitude." Look back at the sentence: "The old fable covers a doctrine ever new and sublime; that there is One Man,—present to all particular men only partially, or through one faculty . . ." Substitute the word *aptitude* for *faculty* to verify meaning in context. While faculty does mean a "department of learning" (choice A) and "staff" (choice E), those meanings are not required by the context. As you read, be careful to define multiple-meaning words correctly.

19. **A.** The phrase "But, unfortunately" in the second paragraph signals a transition to a new idea. The conjunction *but* is always used to show contrast, as is the case here. None of the other choices conveys this meaning.

20. **C.** The author suggests that society has destroyed humanity's wholeness. This can seen most clearly in the following excerpt: "The state of society is one in which

the members have suffered amputation from the trunk, and strut about so many walking monsters,—a good finger, a neck, a stomach, an elbow, but never a man." None of the other choices shows the correct interpretation.

21. **A.** The writer uses the word *ministry* in relation to the planter to suggest the inherent holiness of farming. The writer suggests that all occupations have their own divinity, but few of us are able to appreciate the dignity and holiness of our work.

22. **C.** The author's thesis in the third paragraph is developed through a series of examples. These include the planter, tradesman, priest, attorney, mechanic, and sailor. While the author does repeat key words (especially *man* and *thinking*), this is not the way he develops his ideas. *Comparison and contrast* (choice B) is also a technique the author uses, but it is not the key method of development in this paragraph. *Alliteration* (choice D) is the repetition of initial consonants. It is not the means of paragraph development in this instance. *Aphorisms* (choice E) are pithy statements. Again, they are not the chief means of paragraph development here.

23. **E.** The tone of this essay is best described as *neutral.* This is another instance of selecting the *best* choice. *Despairing* (choice A), *fiery* (choice B), *soothing* (choice C), and *angry* (choice D) do not accurately reflect the tone.

24. **B.** The language of this essay is best described as "scholarly and elevated." Note the long, complex sentences and the sophisticated use of punctuation (especially semicolons and dashes to show emphasis). This is the opposite of choice A. The language is too straightforward to be accurately described as *florid,* (choice C). *Florid* means "excessively ornate," which is not the case here. The same is true of choice D, *biased.* Since the author provides specific examples, the language cannot be described as *vague and colorless* (choice E).

Section 2

1. **E.** The correct sentence reads: "It was at this moment, as I stood there with the rifle in my hand, that I first grasped the hollowness, the futility of the imperialistic dominion of the East." Something that is *hollow* is "futile." *Futile* means "useless."

2. **C.** The correct sentence reads: "Her unexpected demise, at first mistakenly diagnosed as due to a raging fever, was later ascribed to poison." At first, people mistakenly thought the woman died from a fever. For a fever to kill someone, it must be very strong or *raging*. The second half of the sentence shows a contrast: The later diagnosis attributes her death to poison. *Ascribed* means the same as "assigned or due to."

3. **E.** The correct sentence reads: "She looked bloated, like a body long submerged in motionless water, and of that pallid hue." She would have to be in the water—submerged—to become bloated. *Submerged* is an easy word to figure out because

the prefix *sub* means "under." Something held for a long time underwater would be *pallid* or pale.

4. **B.** The correct sentence reads: "The pawnbroker's widow was a garrulous old woman who loved to gossip and hear herself talk." Someone who "loved to gossip and hear herself talk" is *garrulous,* or talkative. Choice D does not fit the context. Someone who loved to talk can be kind or mean, so we cannot conclude that she was vicious.

5. **D.** The correct sentence reads: "The caretaker did not know she was due in London today (her call there had been planned as a surprise), so his negligence in the manner of leaving this letter, leaving it to wait in the dusk and dust, annoyed her." Since the caretaker has left the letter "to wait in the dusk and dust," he is sloppy or not fulfilling his duties properly. People who act in this manner are *negligent* or careless. *Negligence* is the proper form of the word to fit the context.

6. **A.** The correct sentence reads: "That is, some books are to be read only in parts; others to be read but cursorily, and some few to be read wholly and with diligence and attention." The clue word *but* shows that the books in the second phrase cannot be read the same way as the books in the first phrase. Since the books mentioned first are read "only in parts," the second books must be read differently. The word *cursorily* means that these books are read "superficially." Books read cursorily are skimmed. The last books must be read in a way different from the first two types of books described. Since the first books are read in parts and the second books are skimmed, the third type of books must be read in depth. The word *diligence* describes this, as it means "with patience and close attention."

7. **C.** The correct sentence reads: "Through one of the broken panes I heard rain impinge upon the earth again and again, the fine incessant needles of water playing in the already sodden flower beds." The phrase "again and again" is a synonym for *incessant,* which means "continual." If the water has been coming down in a steady stream, the flower beds must be waterlogged. The closest synonym for waterlogged is *sodden.*

8. **A.** The correct sentence reads: "The timid student recoiled at the idea that he had to give a speech in class." A *timid* (shy) person would *recoil* (draw back, retreat) from the idea of speaking in public.

9. **C.** The correct sentence reads: "Now and then we would see her standing motionless in one of the downstairs windows like the carven torso of an idol in a niche, looking or not looking at us, we could never tell which." An *idol* is a figure that is worshipped. Idols and similar statues are often placed in *niches,* corner or nooks. Do not confuse *idol* (an icon) with *idle* (lazy). Choices D and E are incorrect because people are not likely to make and display statues of *ruffians* (hoodlums) and *reprobates* (scoundrels).

10. **E.** The correct sentence reads: "A thin acrid pall as of the tomb seemed to lie every-where upon this room decked and furnished as for a wedding, with a silver hair-brush so tarnished that the monogrammed initials were obscured." The air in a tomb would be *acrid* or bitter from being confined for so long.

11. **D.** The use of the phrase "she alone" gives the reader an idea of Miss Nightingale's uniqueness. The first sentence reveals that she alone is responsible for the welfare of the suffering.

12. **A.** *Pernicious* means "fatal or deadly." Describing the influence of official etiquette as pernicious reveals the author's awareness of the dangers of red tape. The incident concerning the delay in unpacking shirts already in the hospital shows the author's feelings about "red tape," the official tendency to make things more diffi-cult than they need be.

13. **D.** The description of the sick and wounded as "half-naked" and "shivering" serves as contrast to bureaucratic lack of concern. The author underscores the same point with the example of the shirts unreleased.

14. **E.** As used in this context, *vain* means "without any success." This is shown by the fact that "three weeks elapsed before the Government released the shipment" of clothing for half-naked, shivering, sick, and wounded men.

15. **D.** The Purveyor seems concerned only with departmental procedure. That he could stand by and watch people suffer shows this. The final incident is another exam-ple of his disregard for people's suffering.

16. **A.** The tone of the phrase "departmental agony" is ironic. The department has no agony, but the suffering men do. The author creates irony by contrasting the clerk's "agony" over having to forcibly open a government consignment to the very real suffering of the men.

17. **A.** The answer is directly stated in the first sentence: "Three Pintail ducks from North America were shot in widely separated places in far distant parts of the world."

18. **C.** By describing the far-flung places the pintail ducks were shot, the writer shows that pintail ducks can travel to far points of the globe. Although the other choices may indeed be true, there is no support for them in the paragraph. Be careful not to be lead astray by your own ideology.

19. **B.** The answer is in this sentence: "On the leg of each duck the hunter had found a small aluminum band, which carried a number and a request that the finder of the band report to the Fish and Wildlife Service in Washington, DC, USA." The other choices are not possible without this first step. For example, the hunters could not write letters to Washington, DC, unless the birds were banded. Thus, choice C is incorrect.

20. **D.** There is no support for choice A (Bird banding is expensive and time-consuming) even though it may indeed be the case. The same is true for choice B (It takes a long time to get a reply from the Fish and Wildlife Service in Washington, DC.) Neither is there any textual support for choice E (All birds should be banded to ensure their survival). Choice C (Some ducks have a small aluminum band on their leg) is stated outright, so it's not a conclusion you have to reach.

21. **E.** You can infer from the context that *paleontologists* are scientists who study extinct forms of animal life.

22. **B.** As used in this passage, the word *remains* most nearly means "skeletons." A creature that has become extinct, as stated in the passage, is gone too long to be considered *leavings* (choice A), meaning "leftovers or refuse," or *cadavers* (choice D), meaning "a dead body or corpse." *Remnants* (choice E) are "remainders or residue." The best choice is *skeletons,* the hard bony framework of an animal that may be preserved for millions of years.

23. **C.** The answer is directly stated in the passage: "Paleontologists once thought that dinosaurs had such small, inefficient brains that they were somehow responsible for their own dying out."

24. **A.** The main idea of the first paragraph is: No one really knows why the dinosaurs vanished. You can infer this from the last sentence in the first paragraph: ". . . scientists have had a hard time coming up with a single strong explanation for their sudden demise."

25. **D.** When the writer remarks that the theories are "fantastic," the writer is suggesting that the theories are wild and unproven. You can infer this from the different details. They range from completely crackpot—the dinosaurs having vanished because of raids by extraterrestrials—to plausible—food sources. Taking all these theories together, they suggest a wide and wild range of theoretical ideas.

26. **B.** The only information in the second paragraph that can be verified by an outside source is choice B. All the other choices are theories that cannot be proven.

27. **A.** The writer presents the theories from least logical to most logical, moving from outlandish theories about extraterrestrial beings to more believable theories about food sources.

28. **B.** You can infer that choice B is correct from the last sentence in the passage.

Section 3

1. **C.** The writer of passage 1 uses the redundant phrase "total defeat" to emphasize the German feeling of complete and utter disgrace after Germany was defeated. The adjective *total* shows how completely the German war machine was destroyed.

2. **B.** The writer places the word *Fuhrer* in quotation marks to show it is a foreign word. This is a common rhetorical strategy to set off unfamiliar terms or to emphasize important words and phrases.

3. **D.** Readers can infer that Hitler wrote *Mein Kampf* to justify and legitimatize his strategy. The context clues are evident: as "an unknown Austrian" who "worked his way up to the position of leader of an insignificant political party in Munich," he would want to defend and explain his plans. This would also attract more followers, vital if he was to succeed.

4. **E.** The Nazis oppression of the Jews was marked by all the following events *except* forcing Jews to leave the country. There is no support for this detail in the passage. Remember, use the information in the passage—not what you may already know about the subject—to answer the questions.

5. **B.** You can conclude that Hitler's ideas appealed to many Germans because they were looking for someone to use as a scapegoat for their humiliation and they needed to improve economic conditions. You can draw this conclusion from the sentence: "The German people were dissatisfied: the peace treaty was a great humiliation, there was no money, no work and no hope of a better future." There is no support for any of the other choices.

6. **A.** The first passage is organized according to chronological order, the order of time. The author tracks events from World War I (1914–1918) to the end of World War II (1945). These events are presented in the order in which they occurred, as the dates in the passage show.

7. **A.** The "big men" are those in power, the leaders of governments and industries. You can infer this from the way Anne Frank contrasts the *big men*—the politicians and the capitalists—to the *little men*—the everyday men and women who toil at ordinary jobs.

8. **C.** In passage 2, Anne Frank sees people as responsible for their own fate. You can infer this from her statements about people having an inherent "urge to destroy, an urge to kill, to murder and rage." People have this urge and also have the power to fight it. Thus, they control their own actions.

9. **E.** As used in passage 2, the word *disfigured* most nearly means "marred" (spoiled or damaged). You can immediately eliminate choice B because the word *assassinated* is reserved for the death of high-born or important people. None of the other choices fits the context.

10. **B.** These passages are similar in that both describe the same event in world history—World War II. You can eliminate choice A—were written by the same author—because the headnote explains that this is not the case. You can eliminate choice C—approach the topic from the same point of view—because pas-

sage 1 is from the third-person point of view and passage 2 is from the first-person point of view. You can eliminate choice D—were written for the same audience and purpose—because the headnote explains that passage 1 is part of an article, while passage 2 is part of a diary. Choice E is not true because passage 1 is relatively neutral.

11. **E.** The tone of passage 2 is darker and more pessimistic than the neutral tone of passage 1. You can infer this from the following phrase in passage 2: "an urge to destroy, an urge to kill, to murder and rage." Choice C (The tone of passage 2 is less factual than the tone of passage 1) is wrong because a tone cannot be factual.

12. **B.** The second passage shows how the events leading up to and culminating in World War II in Europe affected one individual. Choice A is wrong because the passage shows only the reaction of one person, Anne Frank. There is no support for any other choices.

Section 4

> Should fast-food franchises be allowed in schools? After all, many soda companies already pay a great deal of money to be allowed to install soda machines in school. This money pays for much-needed textbooks, school supplies, and repairs. On the other hand, fast food is greatly contributing to the epidemic of obesity among America's youth.

> **Assignment:** Construct an argument explaining your position on this issue. As you develop your argument, support your views with relevant reasons and examples from your experiences, observations, and reading. To strengthen your position, you might wish to consider alternative or opposing views.

> *The following model essay would receive a 6, the highest score, for its specific details, organization, and style (appropriate word choice, sentence structure, and consistent facility in use of language). It is an especially intelligent and insightful response.*

> Every student has heard of "mystery meat," that puzzling gray staple of school cafeteria lunches. Students fear and shun mystery meat—with good cause—so it usually gets dumped in the trash. Unfortunately, vegetables, fruits, and juices follow suit, as kids crave burgers, fries, and shakes. Since so much food is wasted, why not give kids what they want to eat in the first place?

> Soda companies have already insinuated themselves into school cafeterias, successfully marketing sugar-rich carbonated drinks to students. In many schools, students can't buy soda during the school day, but as soon as classes end, students flock to the soda machines like lemmings to the sea. School districts don't complain about this arrangement because part of the profits from soda sales goes to pay for such "extras" as athletic equipment, lighting, scoreboards, and field trips. But even if the district does not need the money generated from soda machines to fund "extras," soda companies and other

fast-food franchises should be able to sell their products in schools to fund essential items such as textbooks, field trips, and school repairs. Further, students should have the right to get the foods and carbonated drinks they want, rather than being forced to eat vile "mystery meat."

On the other hand, U.S. Surgeon General David Satcher claims that some 300,000 children a year die from illnesses related to obesity. To help kids eat healthful food, Satcher has called for the removal of fast food from schools. Of course, fast foods aren't the only cause of obesity, but these foods are one of the main reasons why Americans are the fattest people on earth. We are fast becoming the least healthy people, too, succumbing to diseases linked to being overweight, such as heart disease and diabetes. Schools should be teaching students the advantages of eating fruits, vegetables, and broiled rather than fried meats.

Fast-food franchises should be allowed in schools only if they sell healthful food. Some possibilities include juices (currently sold at nearly all fast-food chains), BK Broilers, and McDonald's salads. A change in menu would help schools raise much-needed funds as well as teach students healthy eating habits.

Section 5

1. **D.** The error here is in agreement of subject and verb. Remember that a singular subject requires a singular verb. The singular subject *one-third* requires the singular form of *to be, is.*

2. **B.** The error occurs in verb tense. Tenses must be consistent and logical throughout a sentence and a passage. Here, the sentence begins in the past tense (*told*) and so must continue in the same tense. The word *cites* switches to the present tense. Choice D is correct because we use *among* when three or more people share something and *between* when two people share something.

3. **A.** This is a parallel structure question: The phrase "eating ice cream" does not parallel the phrase "are fond of peanuts." The corrected sentence reads: "The twins are fond of peanuts and ice cream, but their parents are loath to give the children snacks between meals."

4. **B.** This is a question on pronoun case. Pronouns in English have three cases: *nominative, objective,* and *possessive.*

   - Use the nominative case to show the subject of a verb.

     Example: We spoke to the agent about the deal.

   - Use the objective case to show the noun or pronoun receiving the action.

     Example: The agent was willing to speak to *us.*

   - Use the possessive case to show ownership.

     Example: The agent gave *us* his advice.

The following box shows the three cases.

Nominative (Pronoun as subject)	Objective (Pronoun as objective)	Possessive (Ownership)
I	me	my, mine
you	you	your, yours
he	him	his
she	her	her, hers
it	it	its
we	us	our, ours
they	them	their, theirs
who	whom	whose
whoever	whomever	whoever

In this sentence, *me* (together with my partner) is the object of the infinitive *to notify*. Therefore, the pronoun must be in the objective case. The corrected sentence reads: "The real estate broker promised to notify my partner and me as soon as the house was put up for sale so we could make any necessary repairs to the structure."

5. **A.** This is a question on subject-verb agreement. Singular subjects connected by *either . . . or (neither . . . nor, not only . . . but also)* require a singular verb. The singular subject *witness* and the singular subject *defendant* require the singular verb *was,* not the plural verb *were.*

6. **C.** As written, this sentence contains a misplaced modifier, a phrase, clause, or word placed too far from the word or words it modifies (describes.) The misplaced modifier "with several emotional problems" implies that the psychologist has emotional problems, not the patient. The correct sentence reads: "A close friend of the family, the patient with several emotional problems was referred to a psychologist to receive counseling."

7. **A.** The error in this sentence is a double negative: *n't* in *didn't* and *nothing*. The correct sentence reads: "The speaker didn't say anything that the audience had not already heard; as a result, the audience quickly lost interest in his speech and began to talk among themselves." or "The speaker said nothing that the audience had not already heard; as a result, the audience quickly lost interest in his speech and began to talk among themselves."

8. **C.** This is a comma splice, two independent clauses (complete sentences) run together with only a comma to separate them. Two complete sentences cannot be joined with only a comma; they require a semicolon or a coordinating conjunction (*for, and, nor, but, or, yet, so*). One possible correct revision of the sentence reads: "The Word workshop trains employees about maximizing skills to improve

employees' productivity, while the Internet training teaches employees how to use the Internet for product searches and e-mail to worldwide subscribers."

9. **D.** Use an adjective (*delicious*) rather than an adverb (*deliciously*) after a linking verb (*tastes*). The correct sentence reads: "The recipe was complex but is worth it because chicken and biscuits made this way tastes more delicious."

10. **A.** The error here is an illogical comparison. Since the thing you are comparing is part of a group, you have to differentiate it from the group first by using the word *other* or *else*. The corrected sentence reads: "The prominent lawyer won more awards than anyone else at the ceremony, which surprised her because she had long taken on unpopular cases and defendants."

11. **C.** Since *unique* is already in superlative degree, it cannot be further modified.

12. **B.** As written, this is a run-on sentence. Choice B corrects the error by creating a subordinate clause with the subordinating conjunction *when*. Choice C is still a run-on sentence. Choice D does not make logical sense, because the conjunction *yet* does not fit into this context. Choice E is technically correct, since you can use a semicolon to join two independent clauses. However, the conjunction in choice B is better because it serves to link ideas logically. The correct sentence reads: "Derek Bickerton, a noted linguist, described some of the best examples of the innate formation of a grammar system when he noted that indentured workers on plantations in the South Pacific needed to communicate with each other in order to carry out practical tasks."

13. **B.** The past tense *became* is required to show that the action has already taken place. Choices C (*coaching*) and D (*were coaching*) introduce new errors.

14. **E.** Choice E is the best answer because it eliminates unnecessary words. Choices C and D create sentence fragments. The correct sentence reads: "According to the new personnel policy instituted this year, all employees must select a health plan."

15. **A.** This is a question on using the correct form of the verb in the past tense, as required by the sentence. *Rose* is the correct past tense of *to rise*. The correct sentence reads: "Each morning when the guards checked my shoulder bag and clanked shut the iron door behind me, the old convict in me rose up full of hatred and rage for the guards, the walls, the terrible indecency of the place."

16. **D.** As written, this sentence is not complete. The first group of words—"A tornado can pick up a house and drop it hundreds of feet away"—must be subordinated to the main clause—"these are extremely dangerous storms." *Since* is the most logical subordinating conjunction in context. The corrected sentence reads: "Since a tornado can pick up a house and drop it hundreds of feet away, these are extremely dangerous storms."

17. **D.** As written, this is a fragment, since it is missing a subject. Choice B creates a comma splice. Choice C adds the subject, but, without the coordinating conjunction (*so*), it is a run-on sentence. Choice D correctly adds the subject (*they*) and the correct form of the verb. Choice E has the wrong form of the verb. The correct sentence reads: "The masters of the time were wary of their laborers being able to communicate with each other, so they formed mixed groups of laborers who spoke different languages."

18. **E.** This is a question on parallel structure. The phrase "shook many hands" parallels "went to political rallies" and "spoke at meetings." The correct sentence reads: "The candidate went to political rallies, spoke at meetings, and shook many hands."

19. **E.** The question tests subject-verb agreement. The word *employees* is plural, so it requires the plural verb *are*. The correct sentence reads: "The conference will provide training to ensure that our employees are kept abreast of the latest technology advancements and are able to function in the information age."

20. **A.** This sentence is correct as written. Use a comma after an introductory subordinate clause, as shown.

21. **E.** Recast the sentence into the active voice so the subject is doing the action. This makes the sentence more direct and less awkward. The revised sentence reads: "Many young people today are having a difficult time finding careers that are both pleasurable and profitable."

22. **B.** The previous sentence reads: "Since many large companies have reduced their staffs—a process called "downsizing"—there are fewer management and support jobs available." The next sentence shows what happens because there are fewer jobs to be had: "As a result, many young people feel unhappy and dissatisfied with the jobs they get." The transition "As a result" helps link ideas and show cause and effect.

23. **C.** The pronoun *they* refers to some dissatisfied workers. The revised sentence reads: "Consequently, some workers change careers after a few years and make a fresh start."

24. **B.** The revised sentence reads: "Consequently, they change careers after a few years, returning to school for retraining or learning new skills on their own." This version maintains parallel structure in the phrases "returning to school" and "learning new skills." It also correctly subordinates the dependent clause ("returning to school for retraining or learning new skills on their own") to the main clause ("they change careers after a few years.") Choice C is a run-on sentence; choice D is a comma splice. Choice E is illogical because the coordinating conjunction (*yet*) does not make sense in context.

25. **A.** To strengthen the thesis that today young people have a difficult time finding lucrative and enjoyable careers, the writer could give specific examples of recent college graduates who did not manage to secure jobs. As this passage stands, it does not contain any specific examples that support the thesis. The passage does not have anything to do with *budgeting,* (so choice B) is weak. *Downsizing* (choice C) is a minor detail that does not require amplification. Since the writer argues that "the discipline of sticking it out in school" does not always lead to an enjoyable occupation, choice D would not strengthen the thesis. Finally, choice E is a minor detail that does not require amplification.

Answer Sheet—Practice Test 2

Section 1

1 Ⓐ Ⓑ Ⓒ Ⓓ Ⓔ   8 Ⓐ Ⓑ Ⓒ Ⓓ Ⓔ   15 Ⓐ Ⓑ Ⓒ Ⓓ Ⓔ   22 Ⓐ Ⓑ Ⓒ Ⓓ Ⓔ
2 Ⓐ Ⓑ Ⓒ Ⓓ Ⓔ   9 Ⓐ Ⓑ Ⓒ Ⓓ Ⓔ   16 Ⓐ Ⓑ Ⓒ Ⓓ Ⓔ   23 Ⓐ Ⓑ Ⓒ Ⓓ Ⓔ
3 Ⓐ Ⓑ Ⓒ Ⓓ Ⓔ   10 Ⓐ Ⓑ Ⓒ Ⓓ Ⓔ   17 Ⓐ Ⓑ Ⓒ Ⓓ Ⓔ   24 Ⓐ Ⓑ Ⓒ Ⓓ Ⓔ
4 Ⓐ Ⓑ Ⓒ Ⓓ Ⓔ   11 Ⓐ Ⓑ Ⓒ Ⓓ Ⓔ   18 Ⓐ Ⓑ Ⓒ Ⓓ Ⓔ
5 Ⓐ Ⓑ Ⓒ Ⓓ Ⓔ   12 Ⓐ Ⓑ Ⓒ Ⓓ Ⓔ   19 Ⓐ Ⓑ Ⓒ Ⓓ Ⓔ
6 Ⓐ Ⓑ Ⓒ Ⓓ Ⓔ   13 Ⓐ Ⓑ Ⓒ Ⓓ Ⓔ   20 Ⓐ Ⓑ Ⓒ Ⓓ Ⓔ
7 Ⓐ Ⓑ Ⓒ Ⓓ Ⓔ   14 Ⓐ Ⓑ Ⓒ Ⓓ Ⓔ   21 Ⓐ Ⓑ Ⓒ Ⓓ Ⓔ

Section 2

1 Ⓐ Ⓑ Ⓒ Ⓓ Ⓔ   8 Ⓐ Ⓑ Ⓒ Ⓓ Ⓔ   15 Ⓐ Ⓑ Ⓒ Ⓓ Ⓔ   22 Ⓐ Ⓑ Ⓒ Ⓓ Ⓔ
2 Ⓐ Ⓑ Ⓒ Ⓓ Ⓔ   9 Ⓐ Ⓑ Ⓒ Ⓓ Ⓔ   16 Ⓐ Ⓑ Ⓒ Ⓓ Ⓔ   23 Ⓐ Ⓑ Ⓒ Ⓓ Ⓔ
3 Ⓐ Ⓑ Ⓒ Ⓓ Ⓔ   10 Ⓐ Ⓑ Ⓒ Ⓓ Ⓔ   17 Ⓐ Ⓑ Ⓒ Ⓓ Ⓔ   24 Ⓐ Ⓑ Ⓒ Ⓓ Ⓔ
4 Ⓐ Ⓑ Ⓒ Ⓓ Ⓔ   11 Ⓐ Ⓑ Ⓒ Ⓓ Ⓔ   18 Ⓐ Ⓑ Ⓒ Ⓓ Ⓔ   25 Ⓐ Ⓑ Ⓒ Ⓓ Ⓔ
5 Ⓐ Ⓑ Ⓒ Ⓓ Ⓔ   12 Ⓐ Ⓑ Ⓒ Ⓓ Ⓔ   19 Ⓐ Ⓑ Ⓒ Ⓓ Ⓔ   26 Ⓐ Ⓑ Ⓒ Ⓓ Ⓔ
6 Ⓐ Ⓑ Ⓒ Ⓓ Ⓔ   13 Ⓐ Ⓑ Ⓒ Ⓓ Ⓔ   20 Ⓐ Ⓑ Ⓒ Ⓓ Ⓔ   27 Ⓐ Ⓑ Ⓒ Ⓓ Ⓔ
7 Ⓐ Ⓑ Ⓒ Ⓓ Ⓔ   14 Ⓐ Ⓑ Ⓒ Ⓓ Ⓔ   21 Ⓐ Ⓑ Ⓒ Ⓓ Ⓔ

Section 3

1 Ⓐ Ⓑ Ⓒ Ⓓ Ⓔ   5 Ⓐ Ⓑ Ⓒ Ⓓ Ⓔ   9 Ⓐ Ⓑ Ⓒ Ⓓ Ⓔ   13 Ⓐ Ⓑ Ⓒ Ⓓ Ⓔ
2 Ⓐ Ⓑ Ⓒ Ⓓ Ⓔ   6 Ⓐ Ⓑ Ⓒ Ⓓ Ⓔ   10 Ⓐ Ⓑ Ⓒ Ⓓ Ⓔ   14 Ⓐ Ⓑ Ⓒ Ⓓ Ⓔ
3 Ⓐ Ⓑ Ⓒ Ⓓ Ⓔ   7 Ⓐ Ⓑ Ⓒ Ⓓ Ⓔ   11 Ⓐ Ⓑ Ⓒ Ⓓ Ⓔ
4 Ⓐ Ⓑ Ⓒ Ⓓ Ⓔ   8 Ⓐ Ⓑ Ⓒ Ⓓ Ⓔ   12 Ⓐ Ⓑ Ⓒ Ⓓ Ⓔ

Section 5

1 Ⓐ Ⓑ Ⓒ Ⓓ Ⓔ   8 Ⓐ Ⓑ Ⓒ Ⓓ Ⓔ   15 Ⓐ Ⓑ Ⓒ Ⓓ Ⓔ   22 Ⓐ Ⓑ Ⓒ Ⓓ Ⓔ

2 Ⓐ Ⓑ Ⓒ Ⓓ Ⓔ   9 Ⓐ Ⓑ Ⓒ Ⓓ Ⓔ   16 Ⓐ Ⓑ Ⓒ Ⓓ Ⓔ   23 Ⓐ Ⓑ Ⓒ Ⓓ Ⓔ

3 Ⓐ Ⓑ Ⓒ Ⓓ Ⓔ   10 Ⓐ Ⓑ Ⓒ Ⓓ Ⓔ   17 Ⓐ Ⓑ Ⓒ Ⓓ Ⓔ   24 Ⓐ Ⓑ Ⓒ Ⓓ Ⓔ

4 Ⓐ Ⓑ Ⓒ Ⓓ Ⓔ   11 Ⓐ Ⓑ Ⓒ Ⓓ Ⓔ   18 Ⓐ Ⓑ Ⓒ Ⓓ Ⓔ

5 Ⓐ Ⓑ Ⓒ Ⓓ Ⓔ   12 Ⓐ Ⓑ Ⓒ Ⓓ Ⓔ   19 Ⓐ Ⓑ Ⓒ Ⓓ Ⓔ

6 Ⓐ Ⓑ Ⓒ Ⓓ Ⓔ   13 Ⓐ Ⓑ Ⓒ Ⓓ Ⓔ   20 Ⓐ Ⓑ Ⓒ Ⓓ Ⓔ

7 Ⓐ Ⓑ Ⓒ Ⓓ Ⓔ   14 Ⓐ Ⓑ Ⓒ Ⓓ Ⓔ   21 Ⓐ Ⓑ Ⓒ Ⓓ Ⓔ

Practice Test 2

SECTION 1   TIME 25—MINUTES; 24 Questions

> **DIRECTIONS:** The following sentences have one or two blanks, each of which indicates a missing word. Beneath each sentence are five words or pairs of words. Choose the word or pair of words which, when inserted in the sentence, best fits the meaning of the sentence as a whole. Indicate your answer by filling in the corresponding circle on your answer sheet.

1. After an unsuccessful day spent seeking work, I returned to the cellar of the old building which our poverty compelled us to _____.

    (A) inhabit
    (B) inhibit
    (C) vacate
    (D) desert
    (E) hobbit

2. The _____ boxer withstood the most punishing blows imaginable; the audience thought he would fall, but he did not even _____.

    (A) stalwart stand
    (B) fragile, rise
    (C) impotent, spring up
    (D) strapping, recant
    (E) robust, stumble

3. Even though the acrobat knew he might injure himself performing the unfamiliar stunt, with a show of _____, he tried it anyway.

    (A) timidity
    (B) bravado
    (C) pusillanimity
    (D) intelligence
    (E) affectation

4. The electorate was so _____ that voter turnout was the lowest in the decade.

    (A) apathetic
    (B) neurotic
    (C) indolent
    (D) shiftless
    (E) crafty

5. The mourners set up a chorus of _____, their _____ cries echoing throughout the cathedral.

    (A) merriment, morose
    (B) wailing, buoyant
    (C) lamentations, mournful
    (D) sobbing, cheerful
    (E) jubilation, melancholy

6. The candidate had a blameless record and an _____ home life: in short, there was nothing embarrassing in her past.

    (A) imaginary
    (B) actual
    (C) abundant
    (D) exemplary
    (E) opulent

7. After the new highway was built, traffic no longer passed through the old farmland with its _____ buildings and rusted tractors, the entire scene like a gaping sore.

(A) dilapidated
(B) flourishing
(C) picturesque
(D) thrifty
(E) quaint

8. The guilty robber tried to _____ their suspicions with many sincere accounts of his innocence, but the police were not _____ and arrested him anyway.

(A) alleviate, botched
(B) augment, cozened
(C) assuage, blundered
(D) magnify, mislead
(E) allay, deceived

9. The young girl, _____ and shy, was nonetheless welcomed in the community and made to feel _____.

(A) gregarious, ostracized
(B) demure, comfortable
(C) loquacious, honored
(D) garrulous, revered
(E) awkward, disenfranchised

10. The _____ local businessman was so concerned about maintaining his blameless reputation that he steered clear of any potentially controversial topics, no matter how _____ they really were.

(A) celebrated, contentious
(B) eminent, disputed
(C) conniving, harmless
(D) prominent, innocuous
(E) mendacious, spurious

DIRECTIONS: Each of the following passages is followed by one or more questions. Answer the questions based on what is directly stated or suggested in each passage. Indicate your answer by filling in the corresponding circle on your answer sheet.

Questions 11 to 13 are based on the following passage.

Recently, the U.S. Bureau of Land Management (BLM) reported that two-thirds of its holdings in the West were in poor or unsatisfactory condition. The following passage describes this situation.

1   Damage to rangeland is only one measure of the destructiveness of current grazing patterns. Forests also suffer from livestock production, as branches are cut for fodder or entire stands are leveled to make way for pastures. The roster of impacts from forest clearing includes the loss of watershed protection, loss of plant and animal species, and on a larger scale, substantial contributions of

5   the greenhouse gas carbon dioxide to the atmosphere. Latin America has suffered the most dramatic forest loss due to inappropriate livestock production. Since 1970, farmers and ranchers have converted more than 20 million hectares of the region's moist tropical forests to cattle pasture.

       Although the environmental status of drier rangeland may defy simple quantification, there is little debate that degradation is occurring in environments where rainfall is more plentiful and reg-

10 ular. Ranchers commonly overstock their land with cattle, leading to weed invasion and erosion. In the savannas of northern and central Mexico, livestock are stocked at nearly four times the land's carrying capacity. And wealthy nations are not immune from the effects of overgrazing on range-land. Spain and Portugal still bear the scars of pro-sheep land policies that began hundreds of years ago. The western United States is likewise left with a sad legacy: The great cattle boom of the last

15 century annihilated native mixed-grass ecosystems. And unsustainable practices—including over-stocking and grazing cattle for too long in the same place—continue on much of the 110-million-hectare area of public land the federal government leases to ranchers.

11. Damage to rangeland is caused by all the following *except*

(A) increasing the greenhouse effect
(B) losing plant and animal species
(C) building too many homes and office buildings on land formerly set aside for pasture
(D) mowing down acres of trees to create new pastures and cutting branches to use as cattle fodder
(E) using detrimental pasturing methods

12. The word *immune* (line 12) is used to mean

(A) exempt
(B) responsible
(C) liable
(D) accountable
(E) sickened

13. The writer's purpose is most likely to

(A) convince people to leave the big cities and become ranchers
(B) describe a problem that affects third-world nations far more than it affects developed indus-trial nations
(C) force the government to stop leasing public land to ranchers until the situation with poor grazing practices is resolved
(D) alert people to a serious problem and press for change
(E) show that this problem affects only grazing land in Europe, not the United States

Questions 14 to 24 are based on the following passage.

Do people have to travel around the world—or even leave their hometowns—to become well-educated? What benefits (if any) does travel confer? American Transcendentalist philosopher Ralph Waldo Emerson ponders this question in the following passage.

1   It is for want of self-culture that the superstition of Traveling, whose idols are Italy, England, Egypt,
retains its fascination for all educated Americans. They who made England, Italy, or Greece venerable
in the imagination, did so by sticking fast where they were, like an axis of the earth. In manly hours we
feel that duty is our place. The soul is no traveler; the wise man stays at home, and when his necessi-
5   ties, his duties, on any occasion call him from his house, or into foreign lands, he is at home still and
shall make men sensible by the expression of his countenance that he goes, the missionary of wisdom
and virtue, and visits cities and men like a sovereign and not like an interloper or a valet.
       I have no churlish objection to the circumnavigation of the globe for the purposes of art, of
study, and benevolence, so that the man is first domesticated, or does not go abroad with the hope of
10   finding somewhat greater than he knows. He who travels to be amused, or to get somewhat which he
does not carry, travels away from himself, and grows old even in youth among old things. In Thebes,
in Palmyra, his will and mind have become old and dilapidated as they. He carries ruins to ruins.
       Traveling is a fool's paradise. Our first journeys discover to us the indifference of places. At home
I dream that at Naples, at Rome, I can be intoxicated with beauty and lose my sadness. I pack my
15   trunk, embrace my friends, embark on the sea and at last wake up in Naples, and there beside me is
the same sad self, unrelenting, identical, that I fled from. I seek the Vatican and the palaces. I affect
to be intoxicated with sights and suggestions, but I am not intoxicated. My giant goes with me
wherever I go.

14. What purpose does the following sentence serve: "They who made England, Italy, or Greece venerable in the imagination, did so by sticking fast where they were, like an axis of the earth." (lines 2–3)?

(A) It introduces the essential conflict in the essay.

(B) It underscores the immaturity of Europeans when compared to the sophistication of Americans.

(C) It berates people who choose to visit Europe before they tour America.

(D) It unifies the essay's imagery.

(E) It conveys the impression that the world revolves around Europe rather than America.

15. At the end of the last sentence of the first paragraph (lines 4–7), the writer compares someone who travels for the wrong reasons to a

(A) great ruler

(B) weak monarch

(C) statue

(D) servant

(E) brave and masculine traveler

16. In line 8, *churlish* most nearly means

(A) cantankerous

(B) intelligent

(C) logical

(D) defensible

(E) twisted

17. As used in line 9, *domesticated* means

(A) trained
(B) educated and well-informed
(C) subdued
(D) tame
(E) well-mannered

18. The phrase "He carries ruins to ruins" in line 12 refers to

(A) stealing valuable artifacts from foreign countries and smuggling them to America
(B) elderly people traveling to dangerous old cities
(C) traveling too much, which will result in premature aging
(D) traveling for the wrong reasons, which will deplete your sense of purpose and intelligence
(E) ruining the trip for others by traveling for selfish reasons

19. The writer believes that travel

(A) provides a unique educational opportunity for people of all ages, but especially to the mature and seasoned individual
(B) is too expensive to be undertaken without great thought
(C) can bridge the gap between the "haves" and the "have-nots"
(D) enables people to run away from themselves and their inner lives
(E) enriches our soul by giving us a wider view of people who are different from us

20. The writer's topics and themes include all the following *except*

(A) knowledge and wisdom
(B) cultural appreciation
(C) self-awareness
(D) spiritual growth
(E) nature and the natural world

21. The writer of this essay would be *least* likely to

(A) take a year-long tour of Europe for pleasure and diversion
(B) stay home during his annual vacation to write and study
(C) travel to a foreign land to help the victims of a terrible natural tragedy such as an earthquake or flood
(D) engage in contemplation and introspection
(E) encourage a young person to study abroad

22. Who or what is the "giant" of the last sentence?

(A) people who travel too much
(B) the self that is unable to find beauty at home and cannot be affected by the simple experiences of daily life
(C) our conscience
(D) the guilt we carry as citizens of the richest nation on the Earth
(E) depression

23. The writer uses the word *affect* in line 16 to mean

(A) pretend
(B) effect
(C) impress
(D) confirm
(E) prove to be

24. Which of the following statements best summarizes the writer's theme?

(A) There's no substitute for seeing the world.

(B) Travel is wasted on the young, because they are too callow to appreciate the wonders they see.

(C) No matter where we travel, we can never escape from ourselves.

(D) Travel is a delightful diversion for people of all ages.

(E) Only the young should travel; it is too dangerous for the elderly.

If you finish before time is up, go over your work in this section only.

SECTION 2   TIME—25 MINUTES; 27 Questions

DIRECTIONS: The following sentences have one or two blanks, each of which indicates a missing word. Beneath each sentence are five words or pairs of words. Choose the word or pair of words which, when inserted in the sentence, best fits the meaning of the sentence as a whole. Indicate your answers by filling in the corresponding circle on your answer sheet.

1. Our regiment occupied a position that was _____; a blunder now meant sure destruction.

(A) minor
(B) unrecognized
(C) trivial
(D) vital
(E) petty

2. The foolproof poison was as colorless as water, almost tasteless, quite _____ in coffee, milk, or any other beverage; further it was _____ during an autopsy.

(A) imperceptible, untraceable
(B) indistinct, discernible

(C) vague, manifest
(D) apparent, conspicuous
(E) palpable, obvious

3. She had had one great disappointment in life, but we were never quite sure what it was, since it was _____ to only in _____ and far-off looks, and so we all felt that it was important that she never be let down again.

(A) referred, shouts
(B) pointed, bellows
(C) ascribed, clamor
(D) alluded, whispers
(E) attested, sinecures

4. Not wishing to marry, the girl discouraged the proposals of each young man by _____ that each _____ should present her with his bank statements.

   (A) demanding, connoisseur
   (B) requiring, altruist
   (C) resisting, despot
   (D) refusing, autocrat
   (E) stipulating, suitor

5. Concentrating on the weeds, the elderly lady seemed very intent and _____, as through she were in another world.

   (A) intimate
   (B) remote
   (C) immediate
   (D) venomous
   (E) amiable

6. In spite of our _____, Rita continued down the street and _____ the odd-looking stranger, asking for directions to the restaurant.

   (A) qualms, ignored
   (B) contentment, accosted
   (C) suspicions, disregarded
   (D) misgivings, approached
   (E) mistrust, slighted

7. Although the town councilman had a well-deserved reputation for _____, at the information session that night he was so _____ that everyone received a great deal of information about the proposed tax increase.

   (A) taciturnity, quiet
   (B) reserve, voluble
   (C) verbosity, boorish
   (D) impertinence, churlish
   (E) reticence, mute

8. Someone who loves freedom has an _____ toward oppression and dictatorship.

   (A) empathy
   (B) insight
   (C) understanding
   (D) antipathy
   (E) obstinacy

9. The _____ with which the flight attendant soothed the passengers' muttered concerns and calmed their outright panic at the sudden acceleration showed her _____ and skill.

   (A) expertise, compassion
   (B) aptness, cruelty
   (C) surfeit, insufficiency
   (D) deluge, equanimity
   (E) ability, savageness

10. The _____ of job opportunities in the current job market _____ prospective employees from trying to find a well-paying, secure job.

    (A) profusion, deludes
    (B) excess, dismays
    (C) deficiency, helps
    (D) insufficiency, reassures
    (E) paucity, disheartens

DIRECTIONS: Each passage is followed by questions. Answer the questions based on what is directly stated or suggested in each passage. Indicate your answer by filling in the corresponding circle on your answer sheet.

Questions 11 to 14 are based on the following passage.

What constitutes "good" food? The following passage discusses one overlooked fast food.

1   What could be easier than grabbing a juicy cheeseburger, a creamy thick shake, and a bag of salty fries from a fast-food drive-in? It's quick and it tastes great. These fast foods just seem to satisfy our taste buds in ways that lettuce, tofu, and bean sprouts can't. Unfortunately, in recent years Americans have discovered that many of their favorite fast foods are empty calories with no nutri-

5   tion. Cheeseburgers and fries are loaded with salt and fat; fried chicken can send more cholesterol counts soaring. But what about people who just can't make it through a week without some fast food? Consider pizza. Although it is usually lumped together with all the other "fast foods"— burgers, fried chicken, hot dogs, and fries, pizza is *not* the same as these foods. Pizza contains many of the vitamins and minerals that we need. This is especially true when the pizza is made with fresh

10   ingredients: the crust provides us with carbohydrates, an excellent low-calorie source of energy; the cheese and meat provide our bodies with the building blocks of protein; and the tomatoes, herbs, onions, and garlic supply us with vitamins and minerals.

---

11. What is the topic of this passage?

(A) pizza's relative nutritional value, when compared to other convenience foods

(B) the overall importance of good nutrition

(C) fast foods

(D) the importance of eating well at all times

(E) the importance of avoiding all fast foods in favor of well-balanced, home-cooked meals

12. The writer interrupts the narrative with the short sentence "Consider pizza" (line 7) to

(A) make this sentence (and the idea it represents) blend into the rest of the passage smoothly

(B) underscore the fact that pizza is a fast food, not a real meal

(C) emphasize pizza's popularity among health-conscious Americans

(D) prepare readers for the ideas about pizza that follow

(E) provide emphasis through sentence variety

13. According to this passage, what have many Americans learned recently?

(A) Pizza tastes better than other fast foods.

(B) Fast foods have a lot of salt and fat.

(C) Pizza costs less than other fast foods.

(D) Many fast foods taste great.

(E) Convenience foods are rarely as convenient as people assume.

14. The implied main idea of this passage is that

   (A) people should stay away from all junk food

   (B) many fast foods are not good for you

   (C) pizza is healthier for you than many people think

   (D) pizza gives us carbohydrates for energy

   (E) people should not eat any fast foods at all

Questions 15 to 18 are based on the following passage.

In the following passage, the author describes some different kinds of whales and their characteristics. The passage focuses on smaller whales, called "dolphins" or "porpoises."

1   There is a great deal of confusion over what the forty different species that belong to the family *Delphinidae* are called. For example, is a small cetacean a "dolphin" or a "porpoise"? Some people distinguish a *dolphin* as a cetacean having a snout or beak, while a *porpoise* usually refers to one with a smoothly rounded forehead. The larger members of this porpoise and dolphin family are

5 called "whales," but they nonetheless fit the same characteristics as their smaller relatives. The number of different names for these creatures reflects the confusion of long-ago sailors as they tried to classify them. Unfortunately, identifying them in their home in the sea is not easy, for the main differences between members of the species is in their skeleton structure.

     The size of the bottlenose dolphin varies considerably from place to place. The largest on record

10 are a 12.7 foot male from the Netherlands and a 10.6 foot female from the Bay of Biscay. The heaviest dolphin on record weighed in at 1,430 pounds. A newborn calf, in contrast, is 38.5 to 49.6 inches long and weighs 20 to 25 pounds.

     Bottlenose dolphins are mainly fish-eaters. In the wild, they feed on squid, shrimp, and a wide variety of fishes. In some waters, the bottlenose have gotten in the habit of following shrimp boats,

15 eating what the shrimpers miss or throw away. They often hunt as a team, herding small fish ahead of them and picking off the ones that don't stay with the rest of the group. And they eat a lot! A United Nations report claims that a group of dolphins off the California coast eats 300,000 tons of anchovies each year, whereas commercial fishermen take only 110,000 tons.

---

15. The 40 different species that belong to the family *Delphinidae* have been referred to as all the following designations except

   (A) dolphin
   (B) porpoise
   (C) shrimpers
   (D) cetacean
   (E) whales

16. What is the main idea of the first paragraph?

   (A) People have trouble telling dolphins, porpoises, and whales apart.

   (B) People long ago thought that dolphins were fish.

   (C) Porpoises have smoothly rounded foreheads.

   (D) There are 117 different varieties of cetaceans.

   (E) Whales, which are very large, are not very similar to their smaller cousins, dolphins and porpoises.

17. According to this passage, the largest dolphin ever measured was

(A) a newborn calf
(B) female
(C) remarkably similar to smaller whales
(D) from the Bay of Biscay
(E) from the Netherlands

18. As stated in the passage, some dolphins follow shrimp boats because

(A) dolphins like to eat anchovies
(B) this is a hunting technique they use
(C) shrimpers make the dolphins into pets
(D) dolphins eat a lot
(E) they pick up the shrimp that the shrimp boats leave behind

DIRECTIONS: Each of the passages presented is followed by questions. Answer the questions based on what is directly stated or suggested in the following passage. Indicate your answer by filling in the corresponding circle on your answer sheet.

Questions 19 to 27 are based on the following passage.

The following essay concerns what would be necessary to create a perfect world. The author compares and contrasts the current world to his vision of an ideal world.

1   Now, estimate how few of those who do work are occupied in essential trades. For, in a society where we make money the standard of everything, it is necessary to practice many crafts which are quite vain and superfluous, ministering only to luxury and licentiousness. Suppose the host of those who now toil were distributed only over as few crafts as the few needs and conveniences demanded
5   by nature. In the great abundance of commodities which must then arise, the prices set on them would be too low for the craftsmen to earn their livelihood by their work. But suppose all those fellows who are not busied with unprofitable crafts, as well as all the lazy and idle throng, any one of whom now consumes as much of the fruits of other men's labors as any two of the workingmen, were all set to work and indeed to useful work. You can easily see how small an allowance of time
10 would be enough and to spare for the production of all that is required by necessity or comfort (or even pleasure, provided it be genuine and natural). . . .
    Now is not this an unjust and ungrateful commonwealth? It lavishes great regards on so-called gentlefolk and banking goldsmiths and the rest of that kind, who are either idle or mere parasites and purveyors of empty pleasures. On the contrary, it makes no benevolent provisions for farmers,
15 colliers, common laborers, carters, and carpenters without whom there would be no commonwealth at all. After it has misused the labor of their prime and after they are weighted down with age and disease and are in utter want, it forgets all their sleepless night and all the great benefits received at their hands and most ungratefully requites them with a most miserable death.

Yet when these evil men with insatiable greed have divided up among themselves all the goods
20   which would have been enough for all the people, how far they are from the happiness of the
Utopian commonwealth? In Utopia all greed for money was entirely removed with the use of money.
What a mass of trouble was then cut away! What a crop of crimes was then pulled up by the roots!
Who does not know that fraud, theft, rapine, quarrels, disorders, brawls, seditions, murders, treasons,
poisonings, which are avenged rather than restrained by daily executions, die out with the destruc-
25   tion of money? Who does not know that fear, anxiety, worries, toils, and sleepless nights will also per-
ish at the same time as money? What is more, poverty, which alone money seems to make poor,
forthwith would itself dwindle and disappear if money were entirely done away with everywhere.

19. In the opening lines, the speaker is critical of

(A) workingmen who do not suit their abilities to their jobs
(B) the indolent upper classes
(C) unnatural pleasures and diversions
(D) essential trades
(E) our contempt for trades and elevation of the aristocracy

20. As used in line 3, *licentiousness* most nearly means

(A) a disregard for morals
(B) extravagance
(C) comfort
(D) delicacy
(E) self-denial

21. The phrase "any one of whom now consumes as much of the fruits of other men's labors as any two of the workingmen" (lines 7–8) refers to which of the following?

(A) "the fruits of other men's labors"
(B) "all those fellows"
(C) "unprofitable crafts"
(D) "useful work"
(E) "the lazy and idle throng"

22. The "unjust and ungrateful commonwealth" in line 12 refers to

(A) America
(B) the workingmen
(C) the vain and foolish upper classes
(D) the current system of government
(E) the author's proposed system of government

23. The speaker's bias in the second paragraph (lines 12–18) is

(A) toward the workingman
(B) against the workingman
(C) toward the commonwealth
(D) toward banking goldsmiths
(E) against age and disease

24. The tone of the last paragraph (lines 19–27) is best described as

(A) passionate and critical
(B) relaxed and self-assured
(C) tentative
(D) calm and dispassionate
(E) violent

25. With which of the following statements would the author *most* likely agree?

(A) A penny saved is a penny earned.
(B) Money is the root of all evil.
(C) Money makes the world go 'round.
(D) You can't win it if you're not in it.
(E) Money is essential.

26. The author's style is best described as

(A) highly abstract
(B) objective
(C) highly allusive
(D) informal and relaxed
(E) formal and elevated

27. Which is the best title for this excerpt?

(A) Utopia
(B) The Collapse of the Commonwealth
(C) Economics and the Common Man
(D) The Rich versus the Poor
(E) Work and Play

> If you finish before time is up, go over your work in this section only.

SECTION 3   TIME—15 MINUTES; 14 Questions

DIRECTIONS: The two passages presented are followed by questions about their content. Answer the questions based on what is directly stated or suggested in the passages. Indicate your answer by filling in the corresponding circle on your answer sheet.

Questions 1 to 14 are based on the following passages.

The topic of energy creation and consumption has become increasingly urgent, as utility rates continue to increase exponentially. As consumers continue to demand more energy for their homes, cars, offices, and recreational needs, it has become apparent that we must develop new ways to approach the generation and use of fuels. The following two passages discuss the challenges we face powering our lives in the new century. Each reading also offers some possible solutions.

Passage 1

1   America's electric utilities are finding that helping their customers use energy more efficiently can be a cost-effective and reliable alternative for meeting electricity demand growth. The opportunities for efficiency improvements are myriad and potential savings real, but customers and utilities have been slow to invest in the most cost-effective energy-efficient technologies available.

5   The energy efficiency of today's buildings and electric equipment and appliances falls far short of what is technically available. This efficiency gap has been attributed to a variety of market, institutional, technical, and behavioral constraints. Electric utility energy-efficiency programs have great potential to narrow this gap and achieve significant energy savings.

      Utilities' energy-efficiency programs promise savings for customers and utilities, profits for share-
10   holders, improvements in industrial productivity, enhanced international competitiveness, and reduced environmental impact. But along with opportunities, greater reliance on energy efficiency as a resource to meet future electricity needs also entails risks—that efficient technologies will not perform as well as promised, that anticipated savings will not be truly cost effective in practice, and that costs and benefits of energy-efficiency programs will not be shared equally among utility customers.

15   In 2002, utility power generation accounted for 39 percent of total primary energy use in the United States, and electricity consumption is growing faster than overall use. Current growth forecasts range from 1 to 3.5 percent per year over the next decade. Meeting this new demand could require construction of the equivalent of 50 to 220 new 1,000-megawatt power plants over 10 years. The differences in estimated new capacity needs reflect hundreds of billions of dollars for utility
20   rate payers. Of course, prospective electricity demand growth rates are uncertain, adding to the risks that utilities face in planning and building for the future.

      Energy-efficiency advocates have long maintained that it can be cheaper for rate payers and better for the environment and society to save energy rather than build new power plants. This view is now embraced by many utilities, regulators, shareholders, and customers and is already shaping our
25   future. With more than ten years of experience with utility energy-efficiency programs, initial results are promising, but many uncertainties remain.

      Efforts to harness the utility sector to achieve greater energy efficiency have focused on three strategies. Demand-side management programs—utility-led efforts intended to affect the timing or amount of customer energy use. Examples include rebates, loans, energy audits, utility installation
30   of efficiency equipment, and load-management programs.

      Integrated resource planning—a technique used by utilities and regulators to develop flexible plans for providing reliable and economical electricity supply through a process that explicitly compares supply- and demand-side resource options on a consistent basis and usually has opportunities for public participation.

35   Regulatory incentives for investment in energy-saving technologies adopted to offset the bias against energy-efficiency investments in traditional rate-making methods. Typically, utility profits have been based on the total value of capital invested and the amount of power sold—creating a strong financial disincentive against energy efficiency or other investments that could reduce power sales and utility revenues. Examples include mechanisms decoupling utility revenues from power sales, cost
40   recovery or rate basing of efficiency program expenditures, and performance bonuses and penalties.

      More than thirty states have adopted integrated resource planning and demand-side management programs, and programs are being developed rapidly in most of the remaining states.

Passage 2

1   To the Editor:

      After reading your editorial about the need to add more lights in the local parks, schools, and shopping center parking lots, I'd like to shed a different type of light on this proposal. The majority of people in the world enjoy the night-time environment without artificial lights. Consider nature's illumination,

5   such as the magnificent Hale-Bopp comet. We didn't need artificial light to see it. Remember how
romantic a stroll under the stars can be? It's quite a bit nicer without glaring street lights. Surely our
children deserve to see stars at night from their homes, just as they can see trees and birds in the day-
time. However, our ever-increasing use of outdoor lights in both cities and the countryside is destroy-
ing our ability to savor the natural wonders of the night, an immeasurable loss to our civilization.

10   Now, no one will dispute that outdoor lighting is vital around important street intersections to
make them more readily visible. However, it is a myth that more light reduces crime. Towns across
America that have reduced nighttime light—to increase crime or to save taxpayer money—report
that crime rates remained unchanged or actually decrease. Other studies note that bright security
lights can actually promote crime and be potentially dangerous to police officers, as criminals hide

15   in the shadows. Prison inmates convicted of breaking and entering rank large dogs, music, and the
appearance of having someone home as stronger deterrents than lighting to preventing crimes.
        Then there is the cost. Our town has a population of around 25,000. Our annual street lighting
bill is more than $500,000! Major cities like New York, Miami, and Las Vegas spend tens of millions
of dollars every year on electricity to light their streets.

20   We might be better off with less artificial light at night rather than more. For example, we can
consider mandating that all sign lighting be recessed, shielded, and mounted at the top, pointing
downward and only on the sign; that closed businesses turn off all signage and parking-lot lighting
after a certain hour; that floodlights be banned unless they are shielded to avoid glare; and that
non-security lights around other public buildings be turned off after a certain hour. Further, we

25   should consider using different types of lighting. With the new energy-efficient sodium, metal-
halide, and fluorescent lamps now available, one can generally get the same amount of light on the
ground simply by shielding a lamp that uses half (or even a third) of the electricity of older or exist-
ing unshielded lamps; these new lamps put out several times more light (lumens) per watt than did
older incandescent and mercury-vapor lamps, but power-utility companies are loathe to tell the tax-

30   payer that they are so efficient, and they often replace 200-watt mercury-vapor lamps with 200-watt
metal-halide or HPS lamps, resulting in 2 to 8 times more light on the ground!
        Simply installing more bright lights at night is unlikely to create any significant benefits. We deserve
an aethestically-pleasing night-time environment that includes the ability to see hundreds of stars.

1. According to passage 1, utilities have not helped their customers maximize savings because the utilities

   (A) have not invested in new technology
   (B) are not willing to help customers
   (C) are not aware of the new technologies available
   (D) realize that power sources are already as efficient as they can be
   (E) are too large and cumbersome to meet customers' needs

2. As stated in passage 1, the chief cause of the efficiency gap is

   (A) efficient technologies do not perform well

   (B) potential savings are unrealistic
   (C) disinterest on the part of customers
   (D) a combination of technical, behavioral, market, and institutional constraints
   (E) inept management

3. According to passage 1, energy-efficiency programs can realize savings for

   (A) customers but not utilities
   (B) utilities but not customers
   (C) shareholders only
   (D) no one, which is why they are not worth the economic outlay
   (E) customers, utilities, and shareholders

4. Among the risks the first author cites for relying on greater energy efficiency are

   (A) consumer distrust of new technologies
   (B) concerns about equal distribution of profits
   (C) fears that savings will not be real
   (D) problems with the utility sector itself
   (E) worries that nuclear reactors are not safe

5. What is the relationship of electricity consumption to overall energy use, according to passage 1?

   (A) They are growing at the same rate.
   (B) Electricity consumption is growing more quickly.
   (C) Electricity consumption is growing more slowly.
   (D) No one has successfully determined the relationship between electricity consumption and overall energy use.
   (E) There is no relationship at all.

6. According to passage 1, who will pay for the construction of new power plants to meet increased power needs?

   (A) utility companies, rate payers, and the federal government
   (B) the state and federal governments
   (C) foreign governments
   (D) the state government
   (E) utility users

7. According to passage 1, more and more people are coming to believe that

   (A) we should conserve energy rather than erect new power plants
   (B) the federal government should step in and regulate the energy industry
   (C) wind and solar power are the cheapest and safest way to generate power for the future
   (D) energy efficiency is an unworkable plan
   (E) nuclear power may not be the safest power source, but it is certainly the least expensive

8. Which of the following programs is most popular, as stated in passage 1?

   (A) regulatory incentives
   (B) integrated resource planning and demand-side management programs
   (C) integrated resource planning and regulatory incentives
   (D) demand-side management programs and regulatory incentives
   (E) rebate programs and voluntary cutbacks

9. Passage 1 was most likely written by

   (A) the speaker for a utility company
   (B) a company bidding on a new power plant
   (C) a disgruntled rate payer
   (D) a contented rate payer
   (E) an unbiased observer

10. The word *shed* in line 3 of passage 2 is used to mean

   (A) a small wooden hut
   (B) cast off

(C) shine

(D) hovel

(E) exfoliate

11. Why does the writer of passage 2 note in the beginning of lines 10–11 that "Now, no one will dispute that outdoor lighting is vital around important street intersections to make them more readily visible"?

(A) You can infer that the writer sells outdoor lighting.

(B) By acknowledging valid opposition early on, the writer strengthens his or her argument by gaining credibility.

(C) By presenting the other side, the writer shows that the opposing argument does not have the slightest shred of legitimacy.

(D) The writer was involved in a minor car accident because of insufficient street lighting.

(E) Showing the importance of street lights demonstrates the writer's concern with keeping kids safe.

12. Which of the following can you infer from passage 2?

(A) The writer has studied this issue very carefully and has a firm grasp on the facts.

(B) This issue has made the front pages in the local newspaper.

(C) The writer has gathered an impressive array of experts to support him or her.

(D) The writer detests all forms of artificial illumination.

(E) The issue will likely be resolved shortly, most probably to the writer's satisfaction.

13. Unlike passage 1, passage 2

(A) is written from the third-person point of view

(B) is unbiased and does not argue a point

(C) is unsupported by specific evidence, such as facts and examples

(D) is written from the first-person point of view and has a strong argument to propose

(E) has a malicious, almost spiteful tone

14. The authors of these two passages would most likely agree that

(A) the government must step in and regulate utility prices

(B) taxpayers are clearly paying too much for power

(C) people should rethink the way they use energy

(D) ratepayers, not politicians, can best decide the most effective use of power

(E) since we are going to run out of power sooner than we think, we should use the power we have wisely

---

If you finish before time is up, go over your work in this section only.

SECTION 4   TIME—25 MINUTES; Essay

> **DIRECTIONS:** Read the excerpt below and the assignment that follows it. Then plan and write an essay that explains your ideas about the topic. Remember to support your position with both reasons and examples to make your ideas convincing to the reader.

A classic is a book that . . .

Assignment: Complete this statement with an example from literature, history, or your own experience. Using the completed statement, write a well-organized essay in which you explain what you think makes a book a "classic."

SECTION 5   TIME—25 MINUTES; 25 Questions

> **DIRECTIONS:** The following sentences require you to identify errors in grammar, usage, style, and mechanics. Not every sentence has an error and no sentence will have more than one error. Each sentence error, if there is one, is underlined and lettered. If there is an error, select the one underlined part that must be changed to make the sentence correct and blacken the corresponding circle on your answer sheet. If there is no error, blacken circle E. Elements of the sentence that are not underlined are not to be changed.

1. Just before midnight on <u>April 14, 1912,</u> the <u>more dramatic</u> and famous of
                              A   B

   all maritime disasters <u>occurred, the</u> sinking of <u>the *Titanic*.</u> <u>No error.</u>
                             C   D   E

2. The new hotel is the <u>most luxurious lodge</u> ever built, with its
                              A

    <u>beautifully decorated rooms</u>, <u>glittering crystal chandeliers</u>, and
                    B   C

    <u>food service that was elaborate</u>. <u>No error.</u>
                    D   E

3. The color barrier that <u>had keeped</u> major league sports <u>white-only</u>
                              A   B

    <u>did not fall</u> in baseball until <u>1947</u>. <u>No error</u>
            C   D   E

4. In <u>1850,</u> twenty-one year old peddler Levi Strauss <u>traveled from</u> New York
        A   B

    to San <u>Francisco to</u> sell small items <u>and</u> canvas to the gold prospectors.
                    C   D

    <u>No error.</u>
        E

5. In 1968 and <u>1969, the NBA championship was won by the Celtics</u> with
                    A   B

    Russell <u>as</u> <u>player-coach</u>. <u>No error.</u>
              C   D   E

6. It's true that <u>many</u> overweight <u>people claim</u> to have an <u>unbelievable large</u>
                    A   B   C

    capacity for <u>food, but</u> scientists have yet to locate a gene responsible for
                        D

    appetite regulation. <u>No error.</u>
                                E

7. Today's highly technological society <u>had placed</u> <u>an overwhelming</u> abundance
                                            A   B

    <u>of pleasures</u> <u>at our fingertips</u>. <u>No error.</u>
          C   D   E

8. In the eighteenth and nineteenth <u>centuries, the</u> average Irish citizen planted
                                                A

   potatoes <u>and eats</u> about <u>10 pounds of potatoes</u> a day—<u>and little else</u>.
             B   C   D

   <u>No error.</u>
     E

9. Consider <u>immigrants who</u> come to this country with <u>hardly nothing</u> yet
                  A   B

   succeed in <u>learning English</u>, <u>obtaining jobs, and supporting</u> their families.
                   C   D

   <u>No error.</u>
     E

DIRECTIONS: In each of the following sentences, part or all of the sentence is underlined. Each sentence is followed by five ways of phrasing the underlined part. Choose the best version of the underlined portion of each sentence and blacken the corresponding circle on your answer sheet. Choice A is always the same as the underlined portion of the original sentence. Choose answer A if you think the original sentence needs no revision.

---

10. A temporary worker may be hired for a week, a month, or a few <u>months there</u> is no guarantee of continued employment.

  (A) months there
  (B) months, there
  (C) months; there
  (D) months, but
  (E) months for

11. A new language can come into being as a <u>pidgin, a pidgin is</u> a makeshift jargon containing words of various languages and little in the way of grammar.

  (A) pidgin, a pidgin
  (B) pidgin a pidgin
  (C) pidgin,
  (D) pidgin, because it is
  (E) pidgin and it is a

12. Because I am interested in nutrition, I am glad that Luis gave <u>my sister and I</u> a year's subscription to a health and fitness magazine.

  (A) my sister and I
  (B) me and my sister
  (C) I and my sister
  (D) we
  (E) my sister and me

13. For this reason, very few people suspected the players had been bought; nevertheless, the very next day <u>a suggestion was made by sportswriter Hugh Fullerton</u> that something was not legitimate.

    (A) a suggestion was made by sportswriter Hugh Fullerton
    (B) sportswriter Hugh Fullerton made a suggestion
    (C) a suggestion was made by Hugh Fullerton, a sportswriter
    (D) a suggestion was being made by sportswriter Hugh Fullerton
    (E) a suggestion had been made by sportswriter Hugh Fullerton

14. Our ancestors had to plant and <u>were cultivating</u> their own foods, but since we can just drive to the local supermarket or restaurant and pick what we want, we often eat too much.

    (A) were cultivating
    (B) to cultivate
    (C) cultivating
    (D) cultivated
    (E) had been cultivating

15. <u>Being that</u> the iceberg ruptured 5 of the 16 watertight compartments, the ship sunk into the icy waters of the North Atlantic.

    (A) Being that
    (B) Being
    (C) If
    (D) Because
    (E) Yet

16. <u>Rushing up the stairs of the museum, the tomb of the Egyptian king was seen</u>, in all its awe-inspiring majesty.

    (A) Rushing up the stairs of the museum, the tomb of the Egyptian king was seen
    (B) Rushing up the stairs of the museum, the tomb of the Egyptian king was seen by us
    (C) The tomb of the Egyptian king was seen rushing up the stairs of the museum,
    (D) As we rushed up the stairs of the museum, we saw the tomb of the Egyptian king
    (E) Rushing up the stairs of the museum, the tomb of the Egyptian king had been seen

17. It meant that the pig or cow that would usually have been sold to pay the rent had to be <u>slaughtered</u> there was nothing to fatten it on.

    (A) slaughtered
    (B) slaughtered, because
    (C) slaughtered,
    (D) slaughtered because
    (E) slaughtered, but

18. <u>The captain caught sight of the iceberg passing by through the porthole,</u> but by then it was too late to alter the course.

    (A) The captain caught sight of the iceberg passing by through the porthole,
    (B) As the captain passed through the porthole, he caught sight of the iceberg,
    (C) Looking through the porthole, the captain caught sight of the iceberg passing by,
    (D) The captain, through the porthole, caught sight of the iceberg passing by,

(E) Passing by through the porthole, the captain caught sight of the iceberg,

19. When Europeans first settled in the New World in the seventeenth and eighteenth centuries, <u>they brought their culinary heritage and their recipes with them.</u>

   (A) they brought their culinary heritage and their recipes with them

   (B) they bring their culinary heritage and their recipes with them

   (C) their culinary heritage and their recipes with them were brought

   (D) they having brought their culinary heritage and their recipes with them

   (E) their culinary heritage and their recipes with them they brought with them

---

DIRECTIONS: The following passage is an early draft of an essay. Some parts of the passage need to be rewritten. Read the passage and select the best answers to the questions that follow. Some questions are about particular sentences or parts of sentences and ask you to improve sentence structure and word choice. Other questions refer to parts of the essay or the entire essay and ask you to consider organization and development. In making your decisions, follow the conventions of standard written English. After you have chosen your answer, fill in the corresponding circle on your answer sheet.

---

(1) Everyone is interested in solar energy now. (2) The reason is that the fuels we use are very expensive, and the supply of these fuels is shrinking every day. (3) The cost of home heating oil, for example, has gone up more than 50% in the past decade. (4) The figures are not much better for natural gas and electric. (5) You should learn how the sun can provide heat for buildings. (6) There are a few facts about your home's heating system that you should know.

(7) Most houses and apartment buildings have a furnace that burns fuel and is the heat source for the whole building. (8) A thermostat measures the room temperature and signals it to send more or less heat.

---

20. In context, which is the best way to revise and combine the underlined portion of sentences 1 and 2 (reproduced here)?

Everyone is interested in solar energy now. The reason is that the fuels we use are very expensive, and the supply of these fuels is shrinking every day.

   (A) As it is now.
   (B) Everyone is interested in solar energy now
   (C) Everyone is interested in solar energy now,
   (D) Everyone is interested in solar energy now because
   (E) Everyone is interested in solar energy now, being that

21. Which sentence would be most appropriate to follow sentence 4?

    (A) As our oil and natural gas reserves shrink further, the price can only climb higher.
    (B) Solar energy can also be used to heat water and cook food.
    (C) Most furnaces burn oil or natural gas to produce heat.
    (D) Houses that don't have furnaces are usually heated with electricity.
    (E) Nuclear energy carries risks, but solar energy is safe.

22. In context, which is the best version of the underlined portion of sentences 5 and 6 (reproduced here)?

    > *You should learn how the sun can provide heat for buildings. There are a few facts about your home's heating system that you should know.*

    (A) As it is now.
    (B) Before you learn how the sun can provide heat for buildings, there are
    (C) You should learn how the sun can provide heat for buildings there are

    (D) Learning by you should occur concerning how the sun can provide heat for buildings because there are
    (E) You should learn how the sun can be providing heat for buildings, so there are

23. Which of the following best replaces the word *It* in sentence 8?

    (A) the thermostat
    (B) the furnace
    (C) the house or apartment
    (D) the building
    (E) the temperature

24. Including a paragraph on which of the following would most strengthen the writer's argument?

    (A) the rising prices of fossil fuels
    (B) the inevitable shortage of fossil fuels
    (C) the dangers of nuclear energy
    (D) the advantages of solar energy
    (E) the importance of conserving energy

Practice Test 2 Answer Key

Section 1

1. **A.** The correct sentence reads: "After an unsuccessful day spent seeking work, I returned to the cellar of the old building which our poverty compelled us to inhabit." None of the other words has the meaning required by the sentence: to "occupy" or "live in."

2. **E.** The correct sentence reads: "The robust boxer withstood the most punishing blows imaginable; the audience thought he would fall, but he did not even stumble." The robust boxer is so strong and healthy that he does not stumble even under the strongest punches.

3. **B.** The correct sentence reads: "Even though the acrobat knew he might injure himself performing the unfamiliar stunt, with a show of bravado, he tried it anyway." *Bravado* means "pretense." The acrobat is putting on a brave front, pretending that he can do the stunt.

4. **A.** The correct sentence reads: "The electorate was so apathetic that the voter turnout was the lowest in the decade." When you feel *apathetic* about a person or a situation, you do not care about it. If voters are apathetic or indifferent to candidates or issues, they are not likely to get out and cast their votes. As a result, voter turnout will be low.

5. **C.** The correct sentence reads: "The mourners set up a chorus of lamentations, their mournful cries echoing throughout the cathedral." A *lamentation* is an expression of sorrow, so it would be *mournful,* or sad.

6. **D.** The correct sentence reads: "The candidate had a blameless record and an exemplary home life: in short, there was nothing embarrassing in her past." *Exemplary* means "flawless, unblemished."

7. **A.** The correct sentence reads: "After the new highway was built, traffic no longer passed through the old farmland with its dilapidated buildings and rusted tractors, the entire scene like a gaping sore." *Dilapidated* means "run down." The sentence clue "rusted tractors" reveals that the farmland is in very bad repair. Choices C and E both mean "attractive" rather than "shabby," but "shabby" is the meaning required by the sentence.

8. **E.** The correct sentence reads: "The guilty robber tried to allay their suspicions with many sincere accounts of his innocence, but the police were not deceived and arrested him anyway." To *allay* means "reduce" or "lessen." Even though the robber tried to reassure the police that he was innocent, the police were not fooled (*deceived*).

9. **B.** The correct sentence reads: "The young girl, demure and shy, was nonetheless welcomed in the community and made to feel comfortable." You can eliminate choices A, C, and D based on the first blank. *Gregarious* means "outgoing"; *loquacious* and *garrulous* mean "talkative." None of the other words makes sense with *shy*. *Disenfranchised* (choice E) means "deprived of the right to vote." Only choice B offers words that make sense in both blanks. Even though the girl was modest and shy, people made her feel welcome.

10. **D.** The correct sentence reads: "The prominent local businessman was so concerned about maintaining his blameless reputation that he steered clear of any potentially controversial topics, no matter how innocuous they really were." Someone who is *prominent* is well-known, perhaps even famous. *Innocuous* means "harmless." Thus, the well-known businessperson steers clear of even the most innocent topics to avoid any controversy. You can eliminate choices C and E because someone who is *conniving* (scheming) or *mendacious* (untruthful) would not necessarily be concerned about maintaining a good reputation.

11. **C.** Damage to rangeland is caused by all the following *except* building too many homes and office buildings on land formerly set aside for pasture. Every other choice can be found in the passage. Choice A—increasing the greenhouse effect—is found in the sentence: "The roster of impacts from forest clearing includes . . . substantial contributions of the greenhouse gas carbon dioxide to the atmosphere." Choice B—losing plant and animal species—is found in the same sentence: "The roster of impacts from forest clearing includes . . . loss of plant and animal species." Choice D—mowing down acres of trees to create new pastures and cutting branches to use as cattle fodder—comes from the sentence: "Forests also suffer from livestock production, as branches are cut for fodder or entire stands are leveled to make way for pastures." Choice E—using detrimental pasturing methods—comes from the sentence: "Ranchers commonly overstock their land with cattle, leading to weed invasion and erosion."

12. **A.** The word *immune* (line 12) is used to mean "exempt." This means that wealthy nations are not excused from the effects of overgrazing on rangeland. You can infer this from the sentences that follow: "Spain and Portugal still bear the scars of pro-sheep land policies that began hundreds of years ago. The western United States is likewise left with a sad legacy: The great cattle boom of the last century annihilated native mixed-grass ecosystems."

13. **D.** The writer's purpose is most likely to alert people to a serious problem and press for change. Choice C—force the government to stop leasing public land to ranchers until the situation with poor grazing practices is resolved—is too specific. The writer does not propose any specific solution. Choices B and E cannot be correct because the writer shows that the problem is worldwide and affects wealthy nations as well as disadvantaged ones. There is no support for choice A: convince people to leave the big cities to become ranchers.

14. **E.** The *simile* in this sentence serves to convey the impression that the world revolves around Europe rather than America. This is conveyed through the phrase "like an axis of the earth." The simile does not introduce the essential conflict in the essay (Choice A), because the essay does not have a conflict. A *conflict* in literature is a "struggle" or "fight." There are two kinds of conflict. In an *external conflict*, characters struggle against a force outside themselves. In an *internal conflict*, characters battle a force within themselves. In this excerpt, Ralph Waldo Emerson is expressing his opinion on travel and trying to convince us that his point of view is correct or at least deserves serious consideration. Choice B is wrong because neither the simile nor the essay underscores the immaturity of Europeans when compared to the sophistication of Americans. Indeed, the topic of immaturity never comes up. Choice C is wrong because Emerson does not berate people who choose to visit Europe before they tour America; rather, he believes that we should look into our souls for enlightenment rather than seeking diversion through travel. Choice D is wrong because this simile does not serve to unify the essay's imagery.

15. **D.** At the end of the first paragraph, the writer compares someone who travels for the wrong reasons to a servant. You can figure this out by knowing that a *valet* is a "servant." The information is found in the following line: "and visits cities and men like a sovereign and not like an interloper or a valet." Choice A (great ruler) is a result of misreading "and visits cities and men *like a sovereign* and not like an interloper or a valet."

16. **A.** The word *churlish* in the phrase "I have no churlish objection" (the second paragraph) most nearly means "cantankerous." "I have no churlish objection to the circumnavigation of the globe for the purposes of art," Emerson says, suggesting that he is not being cranky in his objection.

17. **B.** The connotation of the word *domesticated* in the phrase "so that the man is first domesticated" is "educated and well-informed." This is a difficult question because *domesticated* has several different meanings. Choices A and C are synonyms with the most common meaning, but not the one that fits the context. Choice C does not make sense in context. Choice E is wrong because Emerson does not discuss how Americans act when they travel abroad, only that such travel rarely serves its purpose of enlightenment.

18. **D.** The phrase "He carries ruins to ruins" in the second paragraph refers to traveling for the wrong reasons, which will deplete your sense of purpose and intelligence. A close reading of the passage reveals Emerson's belief that someone who "travels to be amused, or to get somewhat which he does not carry, travels away from himself" will find his soul grows weary through the useless search. The misguided traveler becomes a ruin visiting the ancient cities and monuments.

19. **D.** The writer believes that travel enables people to run away from themselves and their inner lives. You can infer this from the passage in the second paragraph cited in the answer to question 18 as well as from sentences such as this one: "Traveling is a fool's paradise." Choice A is wrong because Emerson believes just the opposite of this statement: Travel does *not* provide a unique educational opportunity for people of all ages, but especially the mature and seasoned individual. The same is true for choice E, which is again the opposite of Emerson's thesis: Travel does *not* enrich our soul by giving us a wider view of people who differ from us. Emerson never deals with the issue of cost, so choice B cannot be correct. The same is true for Choice C.

20. **E.** The writer's topics and themes include all the following *except* nature and the natural world. Emerson treats knowledge and wisdom (choice A) at great length, as shown in this quote: ". . . by the expression of his countenance that he goes, the missionary of wisdom and virtue, and visits cities and men like a sovereign and not like an interloper or a valet." He also discusses cultural appreciation (choice B), revealed in this passage: "I have no churlish objection to the circumnavigation of the globe for the purposes of art, of study, and benevolence." The entire passage focuses on self-awareness (choice C) and spiritual growth (choice D) as shown in the passages cited earlier in this explanation.

21. **A.** The writer of this essay would be *least* likely to take a year-long tour of Europe for pleasure and diversion because that is precisely what he condemns. This is evident in the following passage: "He who travels to be amused, or to get somewhat which he does not carry, travels away from himself, and grows old even in youth among old things." He is in favor of looking inward to find knowledge, so choice B (stay home during his annual vacation to write and study) is wrong. He would be in favor of traveling to a foreign land to help the victims of a terrible natural tragedy such as an earthquake or flood, so choice C is wrong. This is shown in the sentence "I have no churlish objection to the circumnavigation of the globe for the purposes of art, of study, and benevolence" (lines 8–9). The word *contemplation* shows that choice D (*engage in contemplation and introspection*) cannot be correct. The same is true for choice E, (encourage a young person to study abroad), thanks to the prepositional phrase "of study" in lines 8–9.

22. **B.** The "giant" of the last sentence is the self that is unable to find beauty at home and cannot be affected by the simple experiences of daily life. We carry this with

us always because it defines who we are. Since Emerson does not travel too much (or at all, if he can avoid it), choice A, people who travel too much, cannot be correct. Choice C, our conscience, is close, but choice B is more precise. Since Emerson does not discuss the unequal distribution of assets, choice D (the guilt we carry as citizens of the richest nation on earth) cannot be correct. Choice E, depression, is too big a leap, for we have no proof at all that he is depressed. On the contrary, he seems quite content with his life of study and introspection at home.

23. **A.** The writer uses the word *affect* (line 16) to mean "pretend." The writer pretends to be overcome (*intoxicated*) with everything that he sees, but he is only making believe. You can tell this from the word *not* in the second clause: "I am *not* intoxicated."

24. **C.** The theme is best stated by choice C: No matter where we travel, we can never escape from ourselves. You can see this especially in the last two lines: "I affect to be intoxicated with sights and suggestions, but I am not intoxicated. My giant goes with me wherever I go." Choice A is wrong because is it the opposite of the writer's theme. The same is true of choice D. There is no support for choices B (Travel is wasted on the young, because they are too callow to appreciate the wonders they see) and E (Only the young should travel; it is too dangerous for the elderly).

Section 2

1. **D.** The completed sentence reads: "Our regiment occupied a position that was vital; a blunder now meant sure destruction." Since a mistake (*blunder*) would be disastrous, the position had to be important or *vital*.

2. **A.** The completed sentence reads: "The foolproof poison was as colorless as water, almost tasteless, quite imperceptible in coffee, milk, or any other beverage; further it was untraceable during an autopsy." What makes the poison foolproof is that it is *imperceptible*—it cannot be perceived or noticed in a drink and it cannot be traced in an autopsy. Remember that the prefixes *im-*, *un-*, and *in-* usually mean "not."

3. **D.** The completed sentence reads: "She had had one great disappointment in life, but we were never quite sure what it was, since it was alluded to only in whispers and far-off looks, and so we all felt that it was important that she never be let down again." Since no one is sure what the disappointment is, it is never stated outright. Instead, it is *alluded* to or hinted at in a soft voice, another word for *whispers.*

4. **E.** The completed sentence reads: "Not wishing to marry, the girl discouraged the proposals of each young man by stipulating that each suitor should present her with his bank statements." When you *stipulate* something, you set conditions. In this case, the girl demands that each young man show her his bank statement. A *suitor* is an admirer, someone who is trying to woo and win a lover.

5. **B.** The completed sentence reads: "Concentrating on the weeds, the elderly lady seemed very intent and remote, as through she were in another world." When used as an adjective, the word *remote* means "isolated or set apart."

6. **D.** The completed sentence reads: "In spite of our misgivings, Rita continued down the street and approached the odd-looking stranger, asking for directions to the restaurant." The clue words are the phrase "in spite of," because it signals a shift in thought. *Even though* Rita's friends had *misgivings* or doubts, she nonetheless *approached* the stranger by walking up to him or her and asking for directions.

7. **B.** The completed sentence reads: "Although the town councilman had a well-deserved reputation for reserve, at the information session that night he was so voluble that everyone received a great deal of information about the proposed tax increase." The town councilman is *reserved* or quiet and close-mouthed. As a result, no one would expect him to speak much. That's why everyone is surprised that the councilman is so voluble—that he talks so much. You can infer that *voluble* means "talkative" from the context clue that everyone felt they had "received a great deal of information about the proposed tax increase." You can receive a lot of information only if someone communicates. In this instance, it's easiest to communicate through words.

8. **D.** The completed sentence reads: "Someone who loves freedom has an antipathy toward oppression and dictatorship." *Antipathy* means "hostility," so someone who loves to be free would naturally be against that which restricts freedom: oppression and dictatorship.

9. **A.** The completed sentence reads: "The expertise with which the flight attendant soothed the passengers' muttered concerns and calmed their outright panic at the sudden acceleration showed her compassion and skill." The flight attendant does her job well; she has *expertise,* training and skill. Her *compassion* (tenderness) is an important part of her expertise. Only choices A, B, and E offer words that make sense in the first blank. When you look at the second blank, only choice A makes sense.

   When you encounter long sentence completion items such as this one, break them into smaller parts. Use the punctuation, especially commas and semicolons, as your guide for logical divisions.

10. **E.** The completed sentence reads: "The paucity of job opportunities in the current job market disheartens prospective employees from trying to find a well-paying, secure job." The lack (*paucity*) of jobs *disheartens* (discourages) applicants.

11. **A.** The topic of this passage is pizza's relative nutritional value, when compared to other convenience foods. The author recognizes that people do not always have the option of preparing home-cooked meals (choice E) as much as they might want to. Thus, the author is suggesting we choose the best alternative—pizza— from the array of available fast foods.

12. **E.** The writer interrupts the narrative with the short sentence "Consider pizza" to provide emphasis through sentence variety. Notice that many of the sentences in this passage are long, especially at the end. By breaking the pattern with a two-word sentence, the writer draws attention to it. This is important because this sentence is the main idea.

13. **B.** Recently, many Americans have learned that fast foods have a lot of salt and fat. You can infer this from lines 3–5: "Unfortunately, in recent years Americans have discovered that many of their favorite fast foods are empty calories with no nutrition. Cheeseburgers and fries are loaded with salt and fat."

14. **C.** The implied main idea of this passage is that pizza is healthier for you than many people think. You can infer this from the facts about pizza in the second half of the passage: "Although it is usually lumped together with all the other 'fast foods'—burgers, fried chicken, hot dogs, and fries, *pizza is not the same as these foods. Pizza contains many of the vitamins and minerals that we need.* This is especially true when the pizza is made with fresh ingredients: *the crust provides us with carbohydrates,* an excellent low-calorie source of energy; *the cheese and meat provide our bodies with the building blocks of protein; and the tomatoes, herbs, onions, and garlic supply us with vitamins and minerals.*"

15. **C.** The 40 different species that belong to the family *Delphinidae* have been referred to as all the following designations *except* shrimpers. The shrimpers are fishermen who catch shrimp; they are not themselves fish.

16. **A.** The main idea of the first paragraph is that people have trouble telling dolphins, porpoises, and whales apart. This is especially clear in the last sentence of the first paragraph: "Unfortunately, identifying them in their home in the sea is not easy, for the main differences between members of the species is in their skeleton structure."

17. **E.** According to the second paragraph, the largest dolphin ever measured was from the Netherlands. This is directly stated in the sentence: "The largest [dolphin is] . . . a 12.7 foot male from the Netherlands . . ."

18. **E.** As stated in the third paragraph, some dolphins follow shrimp boats because they pick up the shrimp that the shrimp boats leave behind. This is stated in the sentence: "In some waters, the bottlenose have gotten in the habit of following shrimp boats, eating what the shrimpers miss or throw away." While some of the other choices describe accurate statements about dolphins, they do not show the cause-and-effect relationship required by the context.

19. **B.** In the opening lines, the speaker is critical of the indolent upper classes. *Indolent* means "lazy." You can infer that the speaker feels this way first from the lines: "For, in a society where we make money the standard of everything, it is necessary to practice many crafts which are quite vain and superfluous, ministering only to luxury and licentiousness." Then you can add what you learn from this

passage: "But suppose all those fellows who are not busied with unprofitable crafts, as well as all the lazy and idle throng, any one of whom now consumes as much of the fruits of other men's labors as any two of the workingmen . . ."

20. **A.** As used in the first paragraph, *licentiousness* most nearly means "a disregard for morals." The writer argues that in his day, the lazy upper classes are concerned with physical pleasure.

21. **E.** The phrase "any one of whom now consumes as much of the fruits of other men's labors as any two of the workingmen" refers to the "lazy and idle throng." The writer is criticizing upper-class people who live off the work of others.

22. **D.** The "unjust and ungrateful commonwealth" in the second paragraph refers to the current system of government. The writer criticizes the government this way because he feels that the political leaders have not corrected the inequity in the distribution of wealth—or even taken any steps in that direction.

23. **A.** In the second paragraph, the speaker is biased toward the workingman. This is evident when he says that common workers ("farmers, colliers, common laborers, carters, and carpenters") keep the country running. Without these workers, the writer says, "there would be no commonwealth at all." He describes how the common workers are discarded after they are no longer useful: "After it has misused the labor of their [the workers'] prime and after they are weighted down with age and disease and are in utter want, it forgets all their sleepless night and all the great benefits received at their hands and most ungratefully requites them with a most miserable death."

24. **A.** The tone of the last paragraph is best described as passionate and critical. You can infer this from the passionate description of "evil men with insatiable greed" who have "divided up among themselves all the goods which would have been enough for all the people." You can also infer the writer's passionate tone from the emotional list of crimes: "fraud, theft, rapine, quarrels, disorders, brawls, seditions, murders, treasons, poisonings." These are all loaded words with strong negative overtones. Finally, you can infer the passionate and critical tone from the "fear, anxiety, worries, toils, and sleepless night" that torment the average worker.

25. **B.** The author would most likely agree with the phrase: "Money is the root of all evil." He blames greed and selfishness for society's inequity and the workers' sad plight.

26. **E.** The author's style is best described as formal and elevated. You can deduce this from the long sentences with multiple clauses, formal diction (word choice), and lack of contractions.

27. **A.** "Utopia" is the best title for this excerpt because the writer describes what he thinks would make a perfect world: a lack of greed for money.

Section 3

1. **A.** According to passage 1, utilities have not helped their customers maximize savings because the utilities have not invested in new technology. You can infer this from the following passage from the first paragraph: "The opportunities for efficiency improvements are myriad and potential savings real, but customers and utilities have been slow to invest in the most cost-effective energy-efficient technologies available."

2. **D.** As stated in passage 1, the efficiency gap is caused not by a single factor but by a combination of factors. You can deduce the answer from the following sentence: "This efficiency gap has been attributed to a variety of market, institutional, technical, and behavioral constraints."

3. **E.** According to passage 1, energy-efficiency programs can realize savings for customers, utilities, and shareholders. To find the answer, return to the following passage: "Utilities' energy-efficiency programs promise savings for *customers* and *utilities*, profits for *shareholders*, improvements in industrial productivity, enhanced international competitiveness, and reduced environmental impact."

4. **C.** Among the risks the first author cites for relying on greater energy efficiency are fears that savings will not be real. The information comes from the following passage: "But along with opportunities, greater reliance on energy efficiency as a resource to meet future electricity needs also entails risks—that efficient technologies will not perform as well as promised, *that anticipated savings will not be truly cost effective in practice* and benefits of energy-efficiency programs will not be shared equally among utility customers."

5. **B.** According to passage 1, electricity consumption is growing more quickly than overall energy use. This comes from the following passage: "In 2002, utility power generation accounted for 39 percent of total primary energy use in the United States, and *electricity consumption is growing faster than overall use.*"

6. **E.** According to passage 1, construction of new power plants will be paid for by utility users. You can infer the answer from this passage: "Energy-efficiency advocates have long maintained that *it can be cheaper for rate payers* and better for the environment and society to save energy rather than build new power plants."

7. **A.** According to passage 1, more and more people are coming to believe that we should conserve energy rather than erect new power plants. The answer can be inferred from this passage: "Energy-efficiency advocates have long maintained that it can be cheaper for rate payers and better for the environment and society *to save energy rather than build new power plants.*"

8. **B.** As stated in passage 1, integrated resource planning and demand-side management programs are the most popular. The information comes from this passage:

"More than thirty states have adopted integrated resource planning and demand-side management programs, and programs are being developed rapidly in most of the remaining states."

9. **D.** Passage 1 was most likely written by an unbiased observer. You can infer this because the writer reports the facts rather than using them to further a specific thesis or argument.

10. **C.** The word *shed* in line 3 of passage 2 is used to mean "shine." The sentence is: "I'd like to shed a different type of light on this proposal." It's a clever pun on the theme of light in this letter.

11. **B.** By acknowledging valid opposition early on, the writer strengthens his or her argument by gaining credibility. This is one of the classic rhetorical strategies for writing effective argumentative essays, as you learned in Part 6. Choice C (By presenting the other side, the writer shows that the opposing argument does not have the slightest shred of legitimacy) doesn't make sense. Choice E (Showing the importance of street lights demonstrates the writer's concern with keeping kids safe) is incorrect because you cannot draw this conclusion from the facts presented. There is no textual proof for choices A and D.

12. **A.** You can infer from passage 2 that the writer has studied this issue very carefully and has a firm grasp on the facts. This is evident from the specific statistics the writer cites in the next-to-last paragraph.

13. **D.** Unlike passage 1, passage 2 is written from the first-person point of view and has a strong argument to propose. Note that the writer uses *I*, the first-person pronoun. This is not the case in passage 1, which is written from the third-person point of view. As noted in the answer to question 9, the first passage was written by an unbiased observer. The other choices are not supported in the passage.

14. **C.** The authors of these two passages would most likely agree that people should rethink the way they use energy. Passage 1 notes that "More than thirty states have adopted integrated resource planning and demand-side management programs, and programs are being developed rapidly in most of the remaining states." Passage 2 argues outright that we should use less outdoor artificial illumination at night.

Section 4

"A classic is a book that. . . ."

Assignment: Complete this statement with an example from literature, history, or your own experience. Using the completed statement, write a well-organized essay in which you explain what you think makes a book a "classic."

The following model essay would receive a 6, the highest score, for its specific details, organization, and style (appropriate word choice, sentence structure, and consistent facility in the use of language).

Nonfiction as well as fiction can become a classic, of course, but for our purposes here, I'm just going to deal with fiction. What makes a novel, short story, or epic a classic is its relevance to reality. Someone who creates a classic novel must deal with the conflict at the heart of a narrative in a realistic way that shows the human spirit at work. In the end of the book, it doesn't matter if the conflict is won or lost; rather, what matters is our ability to identify with the conflict. Classics can improve our lives and help ease us over the rough patches by getting us to relate to the tribulations of the characters they portray. In addition, a classic must leave readers with a strong sense of emotion, whether it's sadness, joy, sorrow, or even regret. *The Catcher in the Rye,* by J. D. Salinger, is a classic because it fits these criteria.

Like the main character, Holden Caufield, almost everyone has felt alienated at one point or another in their lives. Salinger's portrait of a lost youth struggling to find his place in the world is both realistic and wrenching. Readers really get a sense of Holden's feelings, especially his lingering grief at his brother Allie's death and his paralyzing fear of growing up. When Holden is upset, as when he loses the fencing foils during the meet, he adopts a pose of false bravado, attempting to appear "cool" and unconcerned. This is the classic teenage pose. When my friends and I feel lost or embarrassed, we often retreat into the same shell. It's not our fault, we mutter. It's all the fault of a "phony," corrupt world that doesn't understand us. As the conflict builds to its climax, we see Holden start to realize that he can't stay a child forever and thus hide from the adult world. The novel's ending is ambiguous, because readers don't know how much Holden will be able to manage after his breakdown. But this ambiguity doesn't matter because we have sympathized with Holden's pain and cheered his victory over much of it. At the end of the novel we feel hope, because Holden's example has lighted the way for us.

The Odyssey by Homer is also a classic, one that few would dispute has earned its place in the literary hall of fame. This epic shows the strength of the human spirit in overcoming seemingly insurmountable obstacles. Separated from his home and family, Odysseus must struggle through a series of perilous trials to return home. Odysseus draws on his indomitable will, keen intelligence, and heroic nature, whether he's dealing with the bloodthirsty Cyclops or the seductive Sirens. As humans, we identify with Odysseus because we like to think that we, too, would prove to be heroic if placed in danger. When Odysseus returns home after ten long years, regains his kingdom, and banishes his wife Penelope's suitors, we cheer. If Odysseus can overcome these trials, we can overcome the problems that beset us.

We should read classics because they show us things about ourselves that can help us deal with our reality—no matter how different it may seem from the reality of the novel. Of course few of us are wealthy prep school boys and fewer still are epic heroes, but that doesn't stop us from identifying with the problems these characters face and learning from their mistakes and triumphs. Besides, classics are great reads. And what could be more fun than a good read!

Section 5

1. **B.** Use the superlative degree (*most*) to show the comparison is among more than two objects or instances, which is the case here. The corrected sentence reads: "Just before midnight on April 14, 1912, the most dramatic and famous of all maritime disasters occurred, the sinking of the *Titanic*."

2. **D.** The last phrase—"food service that was elaborate"—is not *parallel* (in the same grammatical form) as the other two phrases in the sentence—"beautifully decorated rooms" and "glittering crystal chandeliers." The corrected sentence reads: "The new hotel is the most luxurious lodge ever built, with its beautifully decorated rooms, glittering crystal chandeliers, and elaborate food service."

3. **A.** *Kept* is the correct past participle for *to keep*. The principal part comes after a helping verb, such as *had, is, are, was, were, had been, would have been*. The correct sentence reads: "The color barrier that had kept major league sports white-only did not fall in baseball until 1947."

4. **E.** This sentence is correct as written.

5. **B.** Unless the speaker is not known or you wish to avoid assigning blame (for example, "A mistake was made,") use the active voice rather than the passive voice. In the active voice, the subject is the doer of the action ("the Celtics won the NBA championship"). In the passive voice, in contrast, the action is done to the subject ("The NBA championship was won by the Celtics"). The active voice is considered more vigorous, clear, and succinct than the passive voice. The complete corrected sentence reads: "In 1968 and 1969, the Celtics won the NBA championship, with Russell as player-coach."

6. **C.** The sentence has a mistake in adjective and adverb use. Adverbs modify (describe) verbs, adjectives, and other adverbs. Therefore, use the adverb *unbelievably* rather than the adjective *unbelievable* to modify the adjective *large*. The phrase looks like this:

unbelievably	*large*	*capacity*
↑	↑	↑
adverb	adjective	noun

   The correct sentence reads: "It's true that many overweight people claim to have an unbelievably large capacity for food, but scientists have yet to locate a gene responsible for appetite regulation."

7. **A.** The mistake is in verb use. The sentence requires "has placed" rather than "had placed" because the sentence is in the present tense. The correct sentence reads: "Today's highly technological society has placed an overwhelming abundance of pleasures at our fingertips."

8. **B.** Use verbs consistently. Since the sentence begins in the past tense (*planted*), do not switch to the present (*eats*). The correct sentence reads: "In the eighteenth and nineteenth centuries, the average Irish citizen planted potatoes and ate about 10 pounds of potatoes a day—and little else."

9. **B.** The sentence contains a double negative: "hardly nothing." The correct sentence reads: "Consider immigrants who come to this country with hardly anything yet succeed in learning English, obtaining jobs, and supporting their families."

10. **C.** There are two complete sentences here. The first sentence is: "A temporary worker may be hired for a week, a month, or a few months." The second sentence is: "There is no guarantee of continued employment." When they are incorrectly joined, they become a run-on sentence. Remember that you can correct a run-on sentence in one of three ways:

    • Separate the run-on sentence into two sentences with a period.
    • Add a comma and a coordinating conjunction (*for, and, nor, but, or, yet, so*).
    • Add a semicolon.

    Only choice C correctly joins the two sentences. Choice D requires a comma between the sentence and the coordinating conjunction. Choice E makes no sense with the conjunction *for.* The correct sentence reads: "A temporary worker may be hired for a week, a month, or a few months; there is no guarantee of continued employment."

11. **C.** As written, this is a type of run-on sentence called a "comma splice." Removing the comma (choice B) does not correct the run-on sentence. The revision shown in choice C is best because it eliminates the wordiness and expresses the idea most clearly. The revised sentence reads: "A new language can come into being as a pidgin, a makeshift jargon containing words of various languages and little in the way of grammar."

12. **E.** The error is in the *case* of pronouns. Luis is doing the action (giving a year's subscription), so Luis is the subject. My sister and the speaker are receiving the action, so they are in the objective case: "my sister and me." The correct sentence reads: "Because I am interested in nutrition, I am glad that Luis gave my sister and me a year's subscription to a health and fitness magazine." You may wish to read the sentence with the plural pronoun to help you "hear" the correct version: "Because I am interested in nutrition, I am glad that Luis gave *us* a year's subscription to a health and fitness magazine." Choices B and C are incorrect because the speaker is always named last ("my sister and I, "not" I and my sister").

13. **B.** The phrase is in the passive voice and would be better in the active voice. In general, unless the speaker is not known or you wish to avoid assigning blame ("A mistake was made") use the active voice rather than the passive voice. In the active voice, the subject is the doer of the action ("I hit the ball"). In the passive voice, in contrast, the action is done to the subject ("The ball was hit by me"). The active voice is considered more vigorous, clear, and succinct. Only choice B is in the active voice.

14. **B.** The mistake is in parallel structure, matching sentence parts. The phrase "Our ancestors had to plant and were cultivating their own foods" should read: "Our ancestors had to plant and to cultivate their own foods." This creates parallel infinitive phrases ("to plant" and "to cultivate"). The corrected sentence reads: "Our ancestors had to plant and to cultivate their own foods, but since we can just drive to the local supermarket or restaurant and pick what we want, we often eat too much."

15. **D.** The correct phrase is "since" or "because," never "being that." The corrected sentence reads: "Since the iceberg ruptured 5 of the 16 watertight compartments, the ship sunk into the icy waters of the North Atlantic."

16. **D.** "Rushing up the stairs of the museum, the tomb of the Egyptian king was seen" is a *dangling construction* because it has nothing to modify. Correct a dangling construction by providing a noun or pronoun to which the dangling construction can be attached, as in choice D.

17. **B.** As written, this is a run-on sentence, two sentences incorrectly joined. Adding the subordinating conjunction *because* correctly subordinates the second clause ("there was nothing to fatten it on") to the first clause ("It meant that the pig or cow that would usually have been sold to pay the rent had to be slaughtered"). Add a comma before a coordinating or subordinating conjunction. The correct sentence reads: "It meant that the pig or cow that would usually have been sold to pay the rent had to be slaughtered, because there was nothing to fatten it on."

18. **C.** This part of the sentence is a *misplaced modifier*. Obviously, the iceberg did not pass through the porthole. The phrase "through the porthole" modifies "caught sight of" and should be placed nearer to it, rather than next to *passing*. The correct sentence reads: "Looking through the porthole, the captain caught sight of the iceberg passing by, but by then it was too late to alter the course."

19. **A.** This sentence is correct as written.

20. **D.** Choice D is best because it eliminates the unnecessary words to create a concise and logical sentence. The revised sentence reads: "Everyone is interested in solar energy now because the fuels we use are very expensive, and the supply of these fuels is shrinking every day." Choice B is a run-on sentence; choice C is a comma splice. Choice E creates an awkward sentence.

21. **A.** Choice A follows the previous two sentences by describing the shortage of fossil fuels. None of the other sentences makes sense in context, although each is true.

22. **B.** The best version is choice B. "Before you learn how the sun can provide heat for buildings, there are a few facts about your home's heating system that you

should know." Subordinating the first clause ("You should learn how the sun can provide heat for buildings") to the second clause ("there are a few facts about your home's heating system that you should know") creates logic by showing the relationship between ideas. Choice C is a run-on sentence. Largely because it is in the passive voice, choice D is wordy and awkward. Choice E has an incorrect verb form (*be providing*).

23. **B.** The *thermostat* signals the furnace to send more or less heat. None of the other choices makes sense in context.

24. **D.** A paragraph about the advantages of solar energy fits best with the opening sentence: *Everyone is interested in solar energy now.* Further, the writer has not yet explained why consumers should support solar energy.

Index

Index